Canvas® LMS

by Marcus Painter and Eddie Small

Canvas® LMS For Dummies®

Published by: **John Wiley & Sons, Inc.,** 111 River Street, Hoboken, NJ 07030-5774, www.wiley.com

Copyright © 2022 by John Wiley & Sons, Inc., Hoboken, New Jersey

Published simultaneously in Canada

For general information on our other products and services, please contact our Customer Care Department within the U.S. at 877-762-2974, outside the U.S. at 317-572-3993, or fax 317-572-4002. For technical support, please visit https://hub.wiley.com/community/support/dummies.

Wiley publishes in a variety of print and electronic formats and by print-on-demand. Some material included with standard print versions of this book may not be included in e-books or in print-on-demand. If this book refers to media such as a CD or DVD that is not included in the version you purchased, you may download this material at http://booksupport.wiley.com. For more information about Wiley products, visit www.wiley.com.

Library of Congress Control Number: 2021952520

ISBN 978-1-119-82842-6 (pbk); ISBN 978-1-119-82843-3 (ebk); ISBN 978-1-119-82844-0 (ebk)

SKY10032073_121721

Contents at a Glance

Table of Contents

Introduction

Canvas LMS — or *Learning Management System* — is a web-based course management platform that supports online learning and teaching. Used by educators, administrators, and students across the globe, it is an accessible and intuitive ecosystem that supports student learning and communication whether used in a fully remote-teaching model, a hybrid model, or alongside in-person teaching.

We've heard from many educators and school administrators begging for material that helps Canvas LMS users get "up and running" with the platform quickly, and although we always recommend checking out the Canvas Community website, or even investing in professional development and training from the Center for Leadership and Learning at Instructure, we still hear people say, "I wish there was a *Canvas LMS For Dummies*." So to that end, we've written that book! And you are here because you already know and love Canvas, you are relatively new to Canvas and want to learn more, or you are brand new to Canvas and looking for an efficient way to get started quickly. This book bottles every ounce of what you hope to accomplish and gives it to you in a nice Panda package.

About This Book

We firmly and wholeheartedly believe that you, as an educator, are the most valuable part of the educational community. Educators influence society on a world-wide scope. You inspire thought, you encourage creativity, and you set your students on a road toward future successes.

You are reading this book because you value everything in the previous paragraph. You recognize that teaching is about being a lifelong learner. We believe this book can act as your guide on your Canvas LMS journey. It is a primer for all things Canvas LMS and a resource you can refer back to regularly. And it is our hope that you have a bit of fun while learning.

This book gives you the basics to get up and running with Canvas LMS. You take a spin through the major aspects of the platform, all while we provide you with best practices, thought leadership, and concrete use cases. We both have many years of experience using Canvas as students, as teachers, and as Canvas LMS administrators. We believe we can provide a learning experience in this book that is unmatched by any other platform. We also love that we have been able to write a book that — we feel — balances learning and "click-by-click" instruction with a bit of fun, while also being easy to read. We hope that *Canvas LMS For Dummies* becomes a regularly revisited resource for you in your ongoing Canvas journey.

Foolish Assumptions

Okay, elephant in the room time. In writing this book, clearly a new Canvas LMS user is the prime target audience. However, we speak to all levels of Canvas Pandas throughout these chapters.

You're likely reading this book for one or two of the following reasons:

>> You are brand new to using Canvas LMS and are establishing your foundational knowledge. You're in the right place!

>> You are relatively new to Canvas LMS. Maybe you used it during the pandemic in a sort of emergency, fly-by-the-seat-of-your-pants sort of way, and now you want to improve for your learners. You're in the right place!

>> You've recently switched from one of the *other guys* and you need to start off on the right foot with Canvas LMS. You're in the right place!

>> You are a Canvas LMS user who is a lifelong learner who is always looking for ways to improve at this beautiful craft we call teaching. Again, you're in the right place!

Icons Used in This Book

Throughout this book, icons in the margins highlight certain types of valuable information that call out for your attention. Here are the icons you'll encounter.

TIP

The Tip icon marks tips and shortcuts that you can use to make Canvas LMS easier.

REMEMBER

Remember icons mark the information that's especially important to know. To siphon off the most important information in each chapter, just skim through these icons.

TECHNICAL
STUFF

The Technical Stuff icon marks information of a highly technical nature that you can normally skip over, unless you happen to be an IT geek in your district or institution.

WARNING

The Warning icon tells you to watch out! It marks important information that may save you headaches, frustrations, or unnecessary struggle within Canvas LMS.

Beyond the Book

In addition to the abundance of information and guidance related to Canvas LMS that we provide in this book, you get access to even more help and information online at Dummies.com. Check out this book's online Cheat Sheet. Just go to www.dummies.com and search for "Canvas LMS For Dummies Cheat Sheet."

Where to Go from Here

Before we really get going, please take note that this book is not necessarily designed to be read in a conventional linear way. Though we hope you do that, this book can also be used in a desk reference manner. Maybe you are just curious about a certain element within Canvas LMS. Refer to the Table of Contents and go read about it. Our hearts will be full and our pride overflowing if this book gets beat up, marked up with highlighter and scribbled notes in the margins, and riddled with sticky notes.

So what's next? This may be a good time for you to take a moment and honestly assess your teacher toolbelt. What are you great at in teaching? What are you good at, but there's room for improvement? What can you own as a weakness to improve upon? And here's the tough one that we don't like to consider: What have you blatantly avoided in your teaching that you know is important, but you're too scared to tackle?

These types of questions are important for all of us to consider as we learn more about Canvas LMS. We always say that Canvas is as deep as it is wide. That means that it can be intimidating to tackle without a plan, without some sort of focus, or without any guidance. Don't worry, you've come to the right place, Pandas. We are here to help. We invited a bunch of our Panda Pals to drop knowledge on you and guide you in your learning.

Whatever your reasons are for reading this book, positivity throughout your reading of these chapters is going to be essential in your journey through Canvas LMS. So, right up front, we ask you to give yourself some room to fail. And we don't say that in the wonderfully mystic, edu-celebrity, keynote sort of way. We say, give yourself room to fail because it will absolutely happen as part of actual growth and learning. None of us relish failure. Nobody says, "I just adore failing, it gives me such a rush of happiness." Nope! That is not real life. We are here to share the brutal honesty of learning as adults. Learning throughout this book may be tough, it may be humbling at times, and it may force you to look at your work differently moving forward. We hope all of these things happen. Whether you've been in education for 20 years or 20 days, it's go time!

1

Getting Started with Canvas LMS

Get familiar with the Canvas Learning Management System and discover who uses Canvas from the K-12 setting through higher education.

See how Canvas is used in online and hybrid learning environments as well as in traditional in-person classrooms.

Discover how the COVID-19 pandemic reinvented the educational landscape, bringing the terms *asynchronous* and *synchronous* learning into the mainstream.

Figure out what it means to help learners in the digital space and how best to present your course material online.

See how Canvas can be leveraged for all learning styles, from visual and aural learners to verbal and physical learners, too.

Chapter **1**

The Who, What, When, Where, and Why of Canvas

Regardless of whether you are an aspiring Canvas Panda or you are a proper Panda Professional, we all share the same goal: to do what is best for the learners in our classrooms. You understand that *blended learning* — the mixture of traditional face-to-face instruction with digital media in any teaching modality — is here to stay; you may have struggled through teaching during the COVID-19 pandemic, one of the most arduous times in history (let alone in your educational career); and you now are looking to use one of the most powerful educational technology (edtech) platforms in the world. You are in the right place.

With nearly 30 million paid users worldwide, 1.5 million active users within the Canvas community, 13 U.S. states adopting Canvas LMS and/or Instructure-powered products statewide, and tremendous growth in Europe, Latin America, and the Asia-Pacific, you are among an enormous group of fellow Pandas all working toward the same universally important goal.

This chapter provides you with an overview of the Canvas LMS ecosystem and the reasons why it is such a powerful educational technology tool. You also get a preview of the topics you will explore in more detail throughout this book.

Who Uses Canvas?

The answer to this question is fairly simple: a world of educators, administrators, and learners who are focused on teaching and learning beyond the walls of a conventional classroom.

Educators

Next to students, educators are the biggest users of Canvas LMS in the educational sector. We hope that school administrators, social workers, instructional coaches, and office staff also gain helpful insights into how Canvas LMS can make learning and communication better for all by reading this book as well.

As educators ourselves, we have had very different Canvas experiences. In 2018, Eddie worked as the innovation coach at Central Nine Career Center, an adult and continuing education career center in Indiana. As most of the students who came to Central Nine were familiar with Canvas LMS already, having used it in school prior to coming to the center, Central Nine administration decided that it needed to consider adopting a learning management system (LMS), too. Eddie was well-versed in all things edtech and was extremely excited about the possibility of adopting and implementing Canvas LMS. Within a few months, Central Nine had made the decision to adopt Canvas LMS, and Eddie took on the task of facilitating a year-long implementation plan with a pilot teacher team that he named the "Panda Pilots." It was a great success! While Eddie was in those early stages of adopting and implementing Canvas LMS, he was constantly collaborating with Marcus. Marcus is what we refer to as an "OG" or "original gangsta" of Canvas LMS.

Marcus's background with Canvas started back in 2013. He was teaching high school English at a small rural school district in Indiana. As he recalls, the original reason for adopting Canvas LMS was because in the flatlands of Indiana, two inches of snow could shut down school for the day. Some of you know exactly what we are talking about, but for those who don't, the situation was this: Even a minimal amount of snow could close school due to the hazardous road conditions caused by the blowing and drifting of snow. So, in any given school year, Marcus would see roughly six to ten school days canceled by inclement weather. Those lost instructional days would be added to the end of the school year and every time that happened, end of the year events such as graduation ceremonies, open houses, awards nights, athletic events, and on and on, had to be rescheduled. This rescheduling of events over and over became quite a strain on relations between the school district and the community members.

Believe it or not, the primary reason his district adopted Canvas LMS back then was to attempt to avoid this calendar nightmare. The philosophy was simple. Having Canvas would enable teachers to provide work, mostly busy work in those days, to students even when they were not in school, thereby avoiding a full cancellation of the day. So, Marcus has been using Canvas for a long time. Though the journeys are clearly different, that is precisely what we felt made our collaboration work so well. To this day, we still often see Canvas LMS from completely different viewpoints and are constantly learning from each other's experiences in working with teachers.

The point right now is that many teachers worldwide from all types of teaching backgrounds — K-12, higher education, career and technical education, and beyond — find their way to Canvas LMS. (In Chapter 3 you take a look around the Canvas interface, and in Chapter 4 you discover the steps to setting up your very first Canvas course.)

Administrators

Administrators use Canvas LMS, too. Canvas is one of the few edtech platforms that can and should be used as regularly by administrators as it is by teachers in classrooms. Think about that. How many digital platforms do you use each day? How many of those can be effectively leveraged by an administrator? The answer is that there are very few, but Canvas LMS is one of the most effective platforms for administrators to utilize on a day-to-day basis.

Our primary experience is in the K-12 setting, but when you think about the myriad of ways administrators can use Canvas to lead within their buildings, you can see that an administrator not using Canvas LMS is an administrator who is working hard, but maybe not working intelligently. Whether you are a principal, an assistant principal, a curriculum director, or the superintendent of your district, leveraging Canvas LMS is absolutely critical, worthwhile, and effective.

We have all said this before: *This meeting could've been an email!* Well, as administrators continue to learn Canvas LMS, they can leverage the platform to save everyone time and struggle within the day-to-day grind of teaching. In Chapter 8, we go into the ins and outs of using the Canvas communication tools to not only make learning personal for your learners, but also help you streamline communication between departments and clearly communicate with stakeholders.

TIP

Did you know that there is an entire department at Instructure that solely focuses on educational thought leadership and provides professional development to school and district administrators? The Center for Leadership and Learning (www.instructure.com/product/canvas/leadership-development) works with hundreds of administrators every year to assist them in their implementation of the Canvas LMS, Canvas for Elementary, and MasteryConnect platforms, in order to better lead by example.

School staff

The phrase, *it takes a village* is likely one of the most appropriate phrases to apply to teaching and learning. In the K-12 setting, there are instructional coaches, technology coaches, technology integrationists, innovation coaches, paraprofessionals, councilors, teacher aides, and about a dozen other titles that all fall under this umbrella of "other folks who support learning who need to be fluent in their use of Canvas LMS." In Marcus's experience in some small- to medium-sized school districts, he would often leverage some of the classroom aides and paraprofessionals on campus to ensure that everyone could assist a student with learning via Canvas LMS. In short, adults in the building should be functional, if not fluent, in using Canvas LMS because it is one of the few digital platforms that truly impacts nearly every stakeholder associated with a school district or university.

Students

Last, but certainly not least, millions of student learners use Canvas LMS every single day. Whether the student is a kindergartener in Kansas, a preteen in Oregon, a teenager in England, a college student at the University of Notre Dame, or a student of dental hygiene in Australia, Canvas LMS students are as diverse and as powerful as ever. As with so many other technology platforms, often the adults struggle more with new technology than the kids do. Canvas LMS is quite intuitive, and with some basic knowledge of the platform and a little bit of time to become acclimated, students always find a way to see learning success within Canvas.

TIP

One of the best things you can do as an educator or administrator is to find a way to also be a student within the Canvas LMS platform. This is a point that is paramount when learning Canvas LMS. As an educator, you need to create, design, and build content for your students, but you should also experience that content *as a* student. (You discover how to use the Student View in Canvas to check out how your courses appear on students' screens in Chapter 4.)

REMEMBER

In much the same way you design a lesson backward, starting with the desired outcome, as an educator you always want to consider how your lesson design in Canvas LMS looks, feels, and works from the student perspective. We are all life-long learners. We are all students.

What Is an LMS?

LMS is short for *learning management system*. What is that? We like to put it like this: A learning management system, like Canvas, is an accessible and intuitive ecosystem for teaching and learning. We use the word *ecosystem* because when done properly, student learning, communication, and more can all "live" within this platform.

Your experience with an LMS as a teacher has likely been similar to one of the following stories:

> **Story 1:** You had never heard of an LMS, the pandemic hit in 2020, and your district rushed to buy an LMS (maybe Canvas) so that teachers could continue to teach virtually, remotely, or in any of the other modalities of learning we have seen over the past few years.

> **Story 2:** You had been using other LMS platforms like those that rhyme with "Cruelogy," "Poodle," "Pits Burning," or "Moogle Glassbroom," and your district finally got wise and moved from those platforms to Canvas LMS.

> **Story 3:** You have been using an LMS for years, even before the pandemic. Maybe you were teaching online courses in higher education, maybe you were teaching in a virtual K-12 school setting, or maybe your district simply had a bit more foresight and adopted an LMS years ago.

Regardless of the path through the jungle that brought you to Canvas, you are here now. So, let's embrace the opportunity to learn together, teach better, and improve at our craft.

TIP

If you are reading this book and you are reluctant to use Canvas or you think that its sole purpose was "to get us through the pandemic," then you're definitely going to need to keep reading. We believe, and most blended learning experts would also agree, that use of an LMS should be an integral part of your day-to-day teaching and learning, regardless of circumstances.

When Should You Use Canvas?

What is so powerful about Canvas LMS is that it can and, in our opinions, *should* be the hub of all things in your classroom, regardless of what learning modality you are working within: traditional, hybrid, or remote. We have both taught in fully face-to-face settings where our students used Canvas every single day. We have both taught within a hybrid modality where we saw students on certain days of the week, while other students were completely remote. And, we have both taught in a fully remote-learning modality where we went for months without being face to face with our students. The great equalizer in all of it is Canvas LMS. It is empowering. You are reading this book so that you can gain those Panda Powers. When you've finished this book, you will have the basic skills, strategies, and motivation to do amazing things with your students this school year and beyond.

REMEMBER

A healthy balance between traditional, hybrid, and even remote-learning teaching models can provide opportunities for student success, both inside and outside the classroom. So when should you use Canvas? In our opinions, all the time.

Traditional learning

As we state earlier in this chapter, Marcus was using Canvas LMS years before any pandemic. His district had a need to extend learning outside of the classroom, his administration had a vision of how to accomplish that, and Canvas LMS was the solution. What his district quickly realized was that Canvas LMS was so much more than just a bandage to place on its issues with weather-related school cancellations. It also soon realized that Canvas was more than a depository for digital stuff or a digital locker. Through a bit of early training, extensive effort by the technology department, and additional support from techy teachers in the district, administrators in the school district began to see the full power of utilizing a learning management system within the traditional school environment.

Through ongoing training provided by both technology team members and by teachers who were excited to share what they were learning, Marcus's district began to evolve the use of Canvas over the course of those first few years. Teachers began transitioning conventional classroom activities into Canvas. Things like bell ringers, heat checks, exit tickets, simple quizzes and tests, and the like, all began to find themselves living within Canvas. That didn't happen and won't happen overnight. However, in Marcus's experience, the buy-in happens slowly at first, but when everyone begins to truly understand the Panda Powers of Canvas, the transition and full integration of Canvas into the traditional classroom setting becomes clear.

Hybrid and online learning

Online, distance, remote, virtual, web-based, or cyber learning. Whichever term you may have used or heard over the past decade or so, they all lead to one inevitable fact: True and authentic learning can happen wherever there are learners and educators. We don't need to be in the same building anymore.

While we realize that there are specific differences and rationale for using any of the previous terms to describe a remote-learning situation, to us, these terms all signal a need for a learning management system. Again, none of those learning modalities were invented during the COVID-19 pandemic. They all existed before the pandemic, but the pandemic simply pushed these learning modalities into the mainstream and made them all commonplace for most educational settings.

If you are teaching within a hybrid or fully online environment, you already know that nothing is possible without an LMS like Canvas. Canvas provides the bridge you need between you and your students. Canvas LMS is where the teaching is done, where the collaboration happens, where the communication flows, and where grading, assessment, and feedback find a home. In Part 3 of this book, we dive deep into the bamboo of these very things.

If you were teaching in a hybrid or fully online learning environment due to the pandemic, then you simply had to learn very quickly about what many educators were already doing. We say this all the time: *The pandemic pushed educators off of the ledge of digital learning.* We believe that this was one of the greatest and most unfortunate parts of the pandemic. Education probably needed a "shock to the system" in order to get us moving toward more effective teaching and learning and better implementation of technology. We believe that education, as a whole, may have been getting just a little bit complacent and stale. The last few years have really pushed educators to think differently, reinvigorate our own learning, and ultimately become even better for kids.

Where Is Canvas Used?

Canvas is built for learners. It supports all types of learners and all learning modalities. Here are the most popular ways Canvas is being used today.

K-12: Panda Cubs

Canvas LMS has become the proven, powerhouse learning management system within the K-12 space. It may not have always been that way, however. There was a time years ago when educators would suggest that Canvas was best for high school and higher education students, and that it wasn't user-friendly enough for young learners. Marcus always took issue with that because he was working in districts that were using Canvas in kindergarten through twelfth grade and he knew that the usability was all about proper design within the platform.

TIP

Now, because Canvas LMS is constantly evolving and improving, Instructure, the parent company of Canvas, has designed and implemented a fully functional Canvas for Elementary platform. This platform took all the best elements from Canvas, implemented research about young learners and early literacy, and built a platform that is fully conducive to the fundamental needs of kindergarten through fifth grade students. Schools now have the option of either Canvas LMS or Canvas for Elementary to use with those young learners.

Higher Education: Panda Pupils

Higher education is an amazing place for the use of Canvas LMS. Unfortunately, for us, we are of a certain age where we didn't really use any sort of learning management system in our own college days. Marcus is so old that he recalls spending hours in the university library using a magnifying glass to look up entries in the *Oxford English Dictionary*.

However, these days, colleges and universities are able to leverage Canvas LMS to facilitate better course content within traditional courses, as well as for all the different variants of courses they offer. More opportunities to learn equals more learning, which we believe can only be good for the world.

Career and technical education: Panda Professionals

Yes, Canvas can also be a valuable platform in the career and technical education space. CTE for short, career and technical education has seen a recent boom in interest at both the federal and state levels as skills-based training continues to see an uptick in enrollment.

TIP

Although there is still work to do in finding ways to recreate "hands-on" experiences with our students in CTE classrooms, a robust LMS offers the opportunities to expand virtually, with more focus and attention to details when in person. Often we see CTE programs "flipping" their classrooms using Canvas. For example, CTE teachers may post non-lab and independent work on Canvas, and free up in-class time for those necessary hands-on tasks and projects.

Why Do Folks Use Canvas?

The final question we are left with is *Why use Canvas?*. If you are a teacher in an urban, Title 1 school teaching third grade, or an AP English teacher at a private Catholic school, why Canvas LMS?

The importance of blended learning

We have made this point already and you will see it throughout this book. One of our unifying messages or biggest takeaways we hope you get from this book is that blended learning and strategic implementation of digital tools is the most important part of education in today's world and the educational landscape of the future. We can't and won't go into all the reasons why blended learning and effective technology integration is best for learning. There are entire books dedicated to that exact topic. However, what we want all of you Pandas to truly embrace, understand, and believe is that *blended learning is better learning.* It gives educators the ability to expand learning outside of the walls of your classrooms. It enables you to do things with learning that may have been impossible when you were growing up.

Blended learning and technology create almost endless possibilities to inspire learners. Isn't that why we teach? If so, then why not embrace a tool like Canvas LMS as a vehicle to transport your students toward success? Think of Canvas LMS as the DeLorean for teaching. If you are familiar with the *Back to the Future* movie trilogy, you know that the DeLorean was the vehicle used to help Marty and Doc Brown travel through time. Think of Canvas LMS as your DeLorean, because using it can take learning to places that were impossible without it.

REMEMBER

Blended learning also enables us, as educators, to truly meet students' needs with content and learning experiences in a variety of ways. It enables us to leverage technology to better meet the needs of all types of learners. We dig more into that in Chapter 12 later on in this book.

TIP

Blended learning strategies, implemented through Canvas LMS, also enable more enriching opportunities for student voice and choice. Through elements within Canvas LMS like Discussions, Media Recorder, Media Feedback, Modules, Mastery Paths, and Pages, we have a wealth of opportunity as educators to create opportunities for students to express their understanding of content and to make decisions about *how* they learn and how they *express* that learning.

Finally, blended learning provides a pathway through the educational jungle for improved student engagement. Let's shine a spotlight on the chubby Panda in the room! How many of you have felt as if you are basically competing against technology for the attention of students? Maybe you feel that today's learners don't even have the ability to pay attention in school because they stare at YouTube and social media from the moment they get home until the moment they go to bed. Maybe you feel that education can never compete for students' attention when put up against video games, social media, and virtual reality.

Though all of these are certainly valid feelings that we have heard educators express over the years, our retort to that would be to stop fighting it and lean into it. This may be a bit controversial for some of you. However, if you think about the trends in education over the past decade, what are they? Gamification, virtual reality in the classroom, video production, podcasting, project-based learning, and so on. If you're desperately romanticizing the concept of "back to normal," then you're missing your chance to evolve, to impact, and to inspire learners. So, for all of those reasons, we believe that leaning into blended learning concepts and strategies, through the DeLorean that is Canvas LMS, just makes the most sense.

The flexibility of efficient educators

The number one complaint most adult professionals have, and in our case, educators have, is that we never have enough time. Throughout the chapters in this book, we point out the multitude of ways Canvas LMS provides educators with more time through a more efficient approach to everything you do in the classroom.

TIP

As technology coaches in the K-12 setting, both of us have seen firsthand how saving incremental chunks of time throughout the week, month, quarter, or semester can happen when we implement Canvas LMS effectively. Marcus would always tell teachers that they must invest a bit of time up front in order to save a lot of time later on. That can be a tough "sell" to educators who already feel like they have no time to dedicate to learning Canvas, building modules, redesigning lessons, creating quizzes, and so on. However, educators who have taken this approach and truly dedicated themselves to learning and embracing a blended approach with Canvas LMS as the centerpiece of their classroom attest to the fact that doing the work early pays off later in the school year and even more so year after year. So, when we talk about efficiency, we are ultimately asking you to trust us. We know you're reading this book, dedicating extra time right now, and you are hoping for a big payoff of time later. We will get there.

When you have tools at your fingertips like SpeedGrader, quizzes, modules, discussions, and announcements, you soon see that the more dedicated you are to learning and becoming proficient with these tools, the more time you begin to save yourself. There is a pot of gold full of time at the end of this rainbow.

Another key element we want to stress to you, Pandas, is the immense amount of flexibility available to you within Canvas LMS. For some of you, the thought of flexibility is enticing and exciting because you see that as giving you options to help students succeed. Maybe you're like Marcus, who rarely taught in the same way in two consecutive years because he figured that if he wasn't stoked about what he was teaching or how he was teaching it, his students wouldn't be either. For that reason, Marcus constantly rebuilt and reevaluated how he taught to try new approaches to what he did. If he loved something and it was well received by students, it might stick for a few years; if not, it was time to redesign. The inherent flexibility within Canvas LMS has always been one of the elements we love most about it.

TIP

If you've designed something in Canvas LMS and you didn't like everything about it, chances are good that you can redesign that lesson, assignment, or module differently. That is such a powerful option as you navigate through your early stages of using Canvas LMS. This book provides you with some of those foundational skills and as you continue to grow within Canvas, you continue to discover new ways to design.

You may be saying to yourself, *I don't want options. Just tell me how to do something and I'll do it that way.* We completely understand that perspective and many of the educators we have worked with over the years feel the exact same way. It is a fair perspective. However, we look at the flexibility of Canvas LMS like a baseball player may look at learning a new position, or the way a computer programmer may problem-solve different solutions, or the way a chef may create a dish. We see flexibility providing all of us with the highest possibility for success.

REMEMBER

Educators who know the "ins and outs" of Canvas LMS provide themselves with options to meet the needs of a diverse student body with a variety of learning needs. It enables us to be problem-solvers because we have the knowledge to do so. We say that we want our students to be problem-solvers, and with the built-in flexibility of Canvas LMS, you learn how to leverage the platform to see more success with your students.

As we begin our journey, we simply ask you to be open-minded, keep your students in mind, and understand that this book is designed to provide you with the foundational skill set you need to function efficiently in your classrooms and spark your creative interest in continuing your learning, evolving your skills, and further implementing Canvas LMS into your teaching and learning ecosystem.

» Defining synchronous and asynchronous learning

» Understanding what learners need in the digital space

» Using Canvas for all learning styles

Chapter **2**

Shifting Your Mindset

So it happened. The COVID-19 global pandemic forced a number of us to adapt on the fly, work from home, or even reinvent "school" in the blink of an eye. But what got us through likely the most challenging time in our careers is the inherent flexible mindset of educators across the globe. And we believe that it is this flexibility and adaptability that make educators one of the greatest groups of professionals in the world. Once the spotlight was turned up to 11, we all did what so many in the profession do best. We got to work for the betterment of our students.

Regardless of where you are in your career as an educator, it's go time. The events over the past few years have changed the educational landscape forever. It forced a mindset shift and created a mantra. Yes, things are going to be difficult, and yes, it's all going to be very new at first. This is precisely why being an educator is not only fun, but also sometimes frustrating. Know that these peaks and valleys, these valiant triumphs and epic fails, are all part of why we chose education as our lifelong passion project.

In this chapter, you explore how the the pandemic changed the educational landscape and how learning management systems like Canvas LMS have and will continue to play an important role in education moving forward. You dive into the differences between synchronous and asynchronous learning and look at how educators can help learners in the digital space.

You also look at some of the do's and don'ts of online course design. It is a completely different tree to climb as an aspiring Canvas Panda when you have to learn how to take so much of the lesson building you've already done and rebuild it into Canvas LMS. The great news is that this is not a fad. Blended learning, online learning, and all of the hybrid learning modalities require us, as educators, to continue to sharpen our skills. We must continue to shift not only our mindset, but also our day-to-day classroom practices.

The Pandemic That Reinvented Education

TIP

We feel it's important to always look back before you move forward. Don't get us wrong; we love moving forward and tackling the next thing, but reflecting on past experiences allows us, as educators and school leaders, the opportunity to debrief and deeply understand "what went right and what went wrong." If we look back, we can recognize some keystone moments in education.

The rise of standardized testing . . . the move toward Universal Design for Learning . . . accessibility needs and goals . . . copyright and digital citizenship . . . student ownership . . . relationship building . . . all of these things are happening and being discussed in a majority of traditional classroom settings. But in March of 2020, that all came to a crashing halt as educators around the globe were forced to become extremely familiar with these two terms: *synchronous* and *asynchronous* learning.

Synchronous learning

REMEMBER

Synchronous learning is simply the type of learning that is happening for students live or in real time. Though it is customary for student learning to happen within a classroom of some kind, face to face with a teacher, the pandemic further reminded all learners and educational leaders that the learning doesn't stop there, and if done right, the learning experiences can happen in any number of settings.

Synchronous learning was one of the most intimidating and mis-strategized teaching elements during the pandemic. Many teachers were told that they would have to *go live* with students learning from home. This premise, though relatively simple from a technology standpoint, became the *new normal*. For the record, we despise the term *new normal*.

As many teachers were teaching within a fully remote model, with no students physically in the classroom, many were asked to function in a hybrid model, which meant they had students both in the classroom with them and others at home. This scenario is, to us, one of the most mis-strategized and tragic practices to come out of the educational world during the pandemic. However, politics aside, the majority of teachers are all better educators now for having made their way through whatever learning scenario they faced.

The need to move synchronous, or live, learning into a virtual or remote platform was a crazy change and adjustment for many educators worldwide. It required educators to learn new technology that they had either never used before, or had only used sparingly prior to the pandemic. Their entire knowledge base, strategies and tactics, classroom management skills, and general comfort level were blown to smithereens! On top of all that, they were doing it in real time. Regardless of the institution, no one was absolutely prepared for the pandemic. We all had serious adjustments to make. The kids were there, waiting to learn.

Unfortunately, we saw, in a painful number of occurrences over the past couple of years or so, many educators trying desperately to cram a square peg into a round hole. Many teachers, particularly those who had not learned about blended learning prior to the pandemic or those who had not worked with any sort of LMS before, truly struggled to get to a place where they could even feel like they were functioning or treading water as teachers.

"We did our best," as they say. We discovered new ways to accomplish learning. We cried, laughed, sang, and danced. But the feeling of not having the ability to adjust and create for students is one that no educator in the world will ever fail to conquer again. How crazy is that? Teachers had to overcome the obstacle of teaching during a pandemic that rocked this world to its core and had dire impact on everything and everyone, and they *still* made a positive impact on learners. We will go ahead and get mushy for a moment:

> Educators are truly a group of epic super heroes!

Synchronous learning became basically every meme on the Internet that related to anyone working or teaching remotely. Every joke about a Zoom call, a Google Meet, a teacher who can't hear, a teacher who taught an entire lesson on mute and the kids didn't say anything, the weird things seen in the backgrounds of people's houses, and the downright ridiculous things seen and heard accidentally during synchronous learning, *that* is what we educators have battled through.

"Marcus! You're on mute!"

WHY WE NEED TEACHERS

Many educators have now taught within a number of different learning models — in-person, hybrid, and remote — in both synchronous and asynchronous formats. Within this reality, the logical next question the uninformed may ask is, "If you don't need to be face to face to learn, then why do we even need teachers?" Believe it or not, people say this. Those people may have had a bit too much to drink, but we hear this sort of talk. You may have a neighbor or a loved one who says something similar. And this is the same person who says, "What are you complaining about? You get the summers off."

These folks don't understand the full value of the teacher. The power of you! If anything, the divergence of learning modalities like remote, hybrid, and face-to-face only reinforces your value. You are the professional who has the skill, expertise, and ability to teach in nearly any modality, to nearly all types of learners. So, yeah, you get some time off in the summer to gather your sanity. You deserve it.

Asynchronous learning

REMEMBER

Asynchronous learning, on the other hand, is the concept that the learning experiences educators create for their students can happen effectively wherever they are, with little to no teaching or learning in real time. What we often saw in districts during the pandemic was that educators would create content in the form of lessons, videos, and so on, that would be viewed by students at some other time throughout a given day, and that those students would still meet due dates for assignments to be submitted.

As with a remote or hybrid synchronous learning model, asynchronous learning was an equally hefty task for educators to learn and execute. Some aspects were the same in that they still had to learn brand new technology, they had to quickly become adept with new tools and platforms, and they had to struggle through all the growing pains that come with learning.

TIP

We think that this struggle is a crucial point we can take away from the pandemic. Remember how challenging, depressing, infuriating, frustrating, and rewarding all that learning was for you as an educator? Our learners go through all of those same emotions nearly every day, regardless of the time, place, or mode of learning. We truly believe that the pandemic has ultimately made us all better at our craft, but never forget those emotions you felt about *learning something new* when you encounter learners in your classrooms who are struggling to *learn something new.*

If you were lucky enough to be familiar with the practice of a flipped classroom prior to the pandemic, then it is likely asynchronous learning was something you felt a bit more comfortable with.

According to the Flipped Learning Network at `https://flippedlearning.org`, a flipped classroom approach is defined as the following:

> Flipped Learning is a pedagogical approach in which direct instruction moves from the group learning space to the individual learning space, and the resulting group space is transformed into a dynamic, interactive learning environment where the educator guides students as they apply concepts and engage creatively in the subject matter.

In both flipped learning and asynchronous learning models, the educator does a great deal of what we call *up-front work*. This work includes lesson planning, but also includes a great deal more in terms of creating digital content in the form of

» Presentations

» Manipulatives

» Individual, small group, and large group activities

» Quizzes and assessments

» Projects

» Videos

» Lectures and tutorials

That is a big ask when nearly all of this planning was done differently prior to the pandemic.

In flipped learning, the teacher is ultimately doing the teaching, but students work with that learning asynchronously so that deeper practice, discussion, tasks, and so on, can be done in a synchronous manner. For example, in a high school Algebra class, students may use Canvas LMS to watch a lesson by the teacher on a particular topic tonight at home in preparation for tomorrow's class when they will complete an assignment, take a quiz, and so on, with the teacher present. The pedagogy is "flipped" because historically, the homework was done . . . you guessed it, at home!

We found the most successful teachers during the pandemic were those who took this flipped classroom mindset and applied it to the remote-learning modality. Rather than lecturing students during the synchronous learning time, they pre-recorded those lessons and shared them with students ahead of time so that the synchronous time could be more impactful by enabling students to interact, collaborate, work, and ask questions.

Hearken back to Spring 2020. There was a lot going on worldwide, and many of you heard something like this from your administrative leaders, "Do what you normally do, but in a digital form." If you're not laughing out loud right now, then we clearly haven't done a good job of expressing our sarcasm. The point is, it sounds simple enough. *Just make everything digital.* We all know the inherent impossibility in that. We also have learned that so much of what we used to do in our classrooms can actually be reimagined or even improved drastically by implementing the correct piece of technology.

REMEMBER

We also learned that some skills don't need technology. This was a huge realization by many educators. So many of us wanted to do what was best for our students. We knew things were going to have to be different, but many of us got very caught up in the technology, only to realize that some things are just fine the old way. Again, the square peg versus the round hole issue was at play here. In an asynchronous learning environment, teachers were too often trying to make the old things happen in the new world of learning. It was profoundly clear during those early days of the pandemic that all educators needed to become more mobile, more flexible, more digitally adept, and more compassionate.

It's Go Time!

The current educational landscape may be the most critical moment for users who are new to Canvas LMS, new to blended learning, or new to this perceived to be recent focus on technology in the classroom. Let's start with that: the *perceived to be recent* focus on technology in the classroom.

Though it is true that there is an ever-growing number of educators in the K–12 through higher education settings that have taken on roles or titles such as instructional designer, instructional coach, technology coach, technology integrationist, innovation coach, digital learning coordinator, digital learning director, and so on, the content on which these roles focus has been around for quite a long time. One thing we have noticed over the past decade or so is the proliferation of these types of roles in the K–12 setting, specifically. Where many schools have had instructional coaches for years, many of those roles are either being massaged into including more technology, or in other cases even being changed into a more tech-centric role. Still yet, district after district continue to attempt to add these roles due to a number of factors that again, existed before the COVID-19 pandemic forced educators to move to online and hybrid learning models.

TREADING WATER

As we note in Chapter 1, Marcus worked as a high school English teacher in a relatively small district during the greater part of the 2010s. The school had adopted Canvas LMS primarily to help with the weather issues faced during the winter months. In this rural community in Indiana, you could expect numerous delays and cancellations throughout the winter months due to "blowing and drifting snow." So the district made an extremely forward-thinking decision to adopt Canvas LMS to help with that issue. When the district had to continually postpone and delay events such as the graduation ceremony at the end of the school year to make up all of those missed instructional days, it became clear that something had to be done. Thankfully, there was Canvas.

During the district's first couple of years with Canvas, teachers were doing much the same thing that many of you may have been doing in your early years with Canvas: treading water. Teachers got *some* training to get them started, but most were functioning only within the Announcements and Assignments features, and maybe a few used the Quizzes feature. Most used text-only directions and added minimal media integrations outside of the occasional hyperlink to a YouTube video. Most primarily used Canvas to house content digitally and communicate with students on inclement weather days.

Though it was true that it was a smaller district, the district did in fact already have 1:1 devices in its K-12 schools, and it was really effective at investing in technology for that time, but the training was lacking. Who has seen this movie before? The district is able to spend the money on technology that could be impactful for learning, but the implementation or roll-out seems to lack the proper support. Or, another common story is that all of the technology support happens early in the adoption, but doesn't extend past those first few months.

We all know that support must be an ongoing process and plan of attack if it is going to lead to foundational teacher and learner success. The point of all this is to exemplify one case where a district, not unlike thousands of others worldwide, missed an opportunity to be on the cutting edge of technology integration, and instead, treaded water.

In thinking about these types of roles within your districts, it becomes clear that these people tend to be the techy teachers, right? Did they get some sort of magical gene that you didn't get? Did they have some different education that prepared them for technology in the classroom? The answer is, probably not. Those folks are simply wired in a different way, not a better way, but a different way. They generally have a willingness to tinker, to click on things and see what happens, to break something and ask for forgiveness later. You may be one of these people, but if you aren't, you definitely know someone who is. That person is your "go to" helper, your confidant, your "thank goodness you're here, I need help" person.

The truth is that these folks, at least those of a certain roughly middle-aged generation anyway, did not have any training that differs from any other educator. They were simply fearless clickers, independent learners, possibly a bit compulsive in that they refuse to not "figure it out," and likely wired to be helpful to others.

In our roles in districts during the pandemic, we found out very quickly that the best way for us to make impactful change and improvement was to assist teachers in their ability to harness the power of Canvas LMS to help with both synchronous and asynchronous learning approaches. Luckily, Canvas LMS makes both learning modalities possible, and even comfortably attainable for even the *least* techy of us.

REMEMBER

You heard that correctly. The *least techy* of any of us can feel comfortable inside this LMS. It is always true that Canvas LMS was built to do everything, but that doesn't mean that you need to know *everything*. Just finding a few tools to put in your toolbelt should do the trick and that is why when we show educators a new tool we always focus on the two to three things we are really passionate about and hope that those things transfer over to very obtainable skills by educators. The goal is always to take quick action and make real connections in your classroom.

Helping Learners in the Digital Space

Possibly one of the biggest misconceptions we have seen over the past few years is the belief that online course design needs to be, for lack of a better term, a piece of artwork. One of the things educators love to do is create and maintain visually appealing elements in the classroom. Now we both taught at the secondary level, and we could probably combine our interior design skills into a shot glass, so bulletin boards and general classroom decor was not our strong suit. However, we see you teachers out there who create these amazing bulletin boards, maintain them, update them, and theme them to the point where they are Instagram-worthy.

Now take that mentality and apply it to the digital space within Canvas LMS. Here is where the general misconceptions begin and ultimately, can become troublesome. Do we want our learners to be engaged in the content we create in Canvas? Of course! Do many of you have amazing design skills, creativity, and artistic eyes? Absolutely! The challenge is that these skills have to truly be harnessed within a digital learning space because too much of a good thing can actually inhibit learners from learning at all.

Incorporate the basic elements of instructional design

For our purposes in this chapter, we divided the basic elements of instructional design into three categories: learning objectives, learning activities, and assessments. We recognize that the discussion that follows doesn't come anywhere close to even scratching the surface of what instructional design is (instructional designers may scoff at us). However, we avoid getting too deep in the weeds here and instead focus on how you can keep some of these items in mind when you design in Canvas LMS.

Learning objectives

All educators know this term. Though you or your district may refer to learning objectives using some other term — maybe *outcomes* — the point is that we all recognize that everything we do in our classrooms should be designed and driven toward some sort of objective, outcome, or goal. Learning objectives can be as simple as, "The learning objective for this lesson is to introduce students to Frederick Douglass as a prominent and hugely important figure in American History," to something more standardized such as, "The learning objective for this lesson is to introduce mathematics standard 4.5.5 (Computation)." However you slice it, objectives drive design within Canvas LMS.

Learning activities

Learning activities are both the fun part of Canvas and probably the part that requires the most innovative thinking and design by educators. There are certainly plenty of learning activities that translate very easily from what you've always done in your classroom into a digital platform like Canvas. For example, a multiple choice quiz on paper is, for the most part, the same learning activity when built within Canvas LMS.

However, what if your favorite activity of the entire year was when students designed a front page of a newspaper on posterboard? Can you still do that project in the "new normal" of teaching using Canvas LMS? Do you have to completely redo everything you've ever done in your class? The answer is wholeheartedly "no!" This is where that mentality of the ever-evolving learner comes into play. Lifelong learners, like you, do what Marcus's old show choir teacher always said: "You cope and adjust!"

Designing learning activities within Canvas can be tough, not because it is difficult to use, but because rethinking how we teach and why we use certain activities is challenging. Introspection is tough. We hope this book gives you some ideas on how to rethink some of your favorite learning activities in order to make them awesome within a digital space.

Assessments

Assessments come in many different shapes and sizes. From formative assessments to state mandated summative assessments, we know that we are likely testing our students too much. In Marcus's experience in the classroom and as a corporation test coordinator, he progressively learned how to better assess student learning. His ability to formulate questions and question types that truly measured student knowledge and understanding was a skill that took many years to evolve. Canvas allows you the luxury of focusing on building fair and accurately measurable assessments because you don't have to worry as much about all of the old logistics.

Create a visual experience

TIP

Just as you want to have a nice atmosphere in your classroom, perhaps with some very Instagram-worthy bulletin boards, many teachers have that same desire when designing digital content for their students. However, we say this now and we say it multiple times throughout this book: A good rule of thumb when it comes to course design in an LMS is to keep it simple. Don't spend hours upon hours creating artsy home pages if you haven't already created quality learning content.

REMEMBER

As technology has come to the forefront of education over the past decade or so, we've learned that we can most definitely do more harm than good for our students if we don't consider the strengths and weaknesses of the technology platform. Simply trying to make activities fit into a technology framework is not proper use of educational technology. It's the whole "square peg in a round hole" scenario. (See Chapter 5 for best practices for turning your course content into visually immersive learning experiences.)

FEELING OVERWHELMED? YOU ARE NOT ALONE

Thousands of educators are in exactly the same space you are in right now. Canvas LMS is either brand new to you or to your district, and knowing that you aren't the first educator to ever experience something, and certainly won't be the last, is a great start. It is a daunting task to know the jungle in front of you, but we are here to help motivate you and give you some subtle nudges through all the thick shrubbery and bamboo fields.

Leveraging Canvas for All Learning Styles

As educators, we have all been taught — sometimes through the harsh realities of the classroom — that every student learns in different ways. Obviously we have seen the research and we have learned different strategies for reaching our visual (spatial), aural (auditory), verbal (linguistic), and physical (kinesthetic) learners. And even more recent studies have developed additional learning styles to add to the mix.

So the question or challenge is this: How can an educator, responsible for the learning of anywhere from 2 to 2,000 learners, meet all of those needs most — if not all — of the time? The painful truth is that we probably can't. It is unlikely that you can adequately fulfill all the learning needs of every type of learner in your classroom all of the time. So what do we do? Where is the silver bullet?

You saw this coming: There is no silver bullet in education!

TIP

The closest thing to a silver bullet is simply the true and authentic belief that to best serve students, you, as an educator, must constantly be learning yourself. You must never settle or become complacent in your craft.

When thinking about learning styles and how educators can best tackle those challenges within Canvas LMS, we believe the tool provides all educators with the options necessary to reach all learners. The challenge for you is in continuing your learning, honing those Panda Powers, and finding that delicate balance within Canvas that can lead to authentic learning for your students. Within Canvas LMS, there is a way to meet those learning styles with ease. Table 2-1 outlines how Canvas LMS can be harnessed to address each type of learning style from visual and aural to verbal and physical learners.

REMEMBER

As a Panda Cub, a Panda Teen, or even if you're a Panda Jedi, the aim is to rethink learning and leverage Canvas LMS in a way that can lead all of our diverse learners to success. You will hear a mantra throughout this book that goes something like this: "Canvas LMS makes X much easier for you and for your learners." This is an absolute truth. It is undeniable.

However, if you're new to Canvas LMS, feeling frustrated or challenged with technology, or just wish you could do it the "old-fashioned way," you probably scoff at the ease of Canvas now. Hang with us! If you're a Panda Cub, you may be a bit clumsy at first, but with practice you become more adept. As a Panda Teen, you have the basics down, but you tend to try new things and get yourself into more trouble. And as a Panda Jedi, you're looking for the next great thing to try within Canvas LMS.

TABLE 2-1   **Learning Styles and Canvas LMS**

Type of Learner	What Canvas Offers
Visual (spatial) learners	Canvas is full of visual options from adding images, diagrams, and videos from outside sources or those you create yourself. You can design pages to whatever extent you desire. The visual learner has a wealth of accessible opportunities within Canvas LMS. Chapter 5 discusses how to incorporate visual elements into your course designs.
Aural (auditory) learners	Canvas provides both video and audio options throughout the platform. One option we love most is the ability for teachers to provide feedback by recording audio messages in addition to typing our feedback using the Media Recorder. Check out Chapter 5 for more on using this tool for aural learners.
Verbal (linguistic) learners	There is no shortage of opportunity for our speakers and writers to thrive within Canvas. Students can record video and audio for many submissions as well as within discussions, and they can do all of this within the platform without the need for additional third-party tools.
Physical (kinesthetic) learners	This type of learner can pose a challenge within the digital learning space, but once again, it comes down to the inherent flexibility of Canvas. These learners can show understanding through video, and teachers can provide digital manipulatives that allow students to drag and drop and build within Canvas. And with a bit of ingenuity and a few common household items, these learners can build, record, and share, all within Canvas. Chapter 10 takes a deep dive into creating content in Canvas and selecting various assignment submission types.

Whatever level you are at right now, relaxed is probably not an emotion you are always feeling. The ease comes after the work has been done. That's why you're reading this book. We have to put in the up-front work in order to reap the rewards of learning and student success later.

2

Welcome to the Jungle

Discover how to log in to Canvas LMS and find your way around the Canvas Dashboard.

Figure out the Global Navigation Menu and using the Options menu to update user settings and notifications.

Create your first Canvas course and update course settings.

Become familiar with accessibility and usability issues and how to ensure your courses positively impact all students.

Find out how to create a visual learning experience with the Rich Content Editor.

Tour the Canvas Inbox and discover tips for implementing a deliberate communication plan.

Explore the Canvas Calendar and see how to adjust calendar views, course colors, and integrate the Canvas Calendar with others.

Chapter **3**

The Panda Primer

As an aspiring Canvas Panda, it's time to get your paws dirty and get a bit more comfortable with the Canvas LMS environment, or what we Pandas often call the "Canvas ecosystem." In this chapter, you discover the basics of logging in to the Canvas LMS client. You then survey the lay of the land to understand basic navigation via the Canvas Dashboard, how to create and edit your profile, and how to manage user settings and notifications.

The Lowdown on Logging In

Before you can use Canvas, you have to log in. Now, before you get all defensive and silently think, *Dude, c'mon! I can log in to the darn thing already!*, we want to make an important point here.

TIP

Because you may have separate accounts, or *instances*, of Canvas — whether you attend multiple schools or teach in two different Canvas environments for different groups — one of the more challenging elements some users may face is knowing which instance to log in to. For example, we currently work within a few different instances of Canvas: one for school, one for our Indiana Canvas Users Group, and another one for the Canvas Advocates group. Each of those instances has a different set of *credentials* — usernames and passwords — that we use to log in. So, if you use Canvas in more than one environment, just be sure to keep straight which credentials get you into which of your Canvas accounts.

Logging in to your school's, district's, or institution's instance of Canvas starts when your information technology (IT) department provides you with the specific URL for you and your fellow staff to use to access the application on your computer. Every instance of Canvas has its own unique location. We have seen plenty of new Canvas Pandas become quite frustrated after they attempt to log in to the wrong Canvas instance, or others who have been so confused as to where to log in that they resort to doing a Google search for "Canvas login page" (and still can't find where to log in). For example, a site-specific login page is shown in Figure 3-1.

Single Sign-On

Email Address

Password

Login

Secured by Duo

FIGURE 3-1:
A site-specific Canvas login screen.

If you need to find your school's login page, navigate to the Canvas login page on the Instructure website at www.instructure.com/canvas/login/free-for-teacher, as shown in Figure 3-2. From this page you can search for your school's specific login page in the search box that appears under the heading, "If Your School Uses Canvas . . . ." If you are using a free account (or want to create a free account) you can log in to that account from this page, too.

Each instance of Canvas LMS has its own, unique login page. One of the very first things you should do is bookmark your school's Canvas login page(s) within your Internet browser. Then you won't have to keep searching for it via the main Canvas login page.

REMEMBER

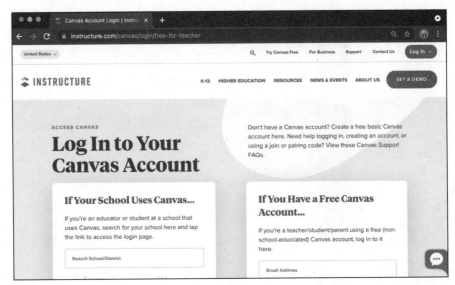

FIGURE 3-2:
The main Canvas login page from the Instructure website.

Though you can also access Canvas LMS via a mobile app, and we talk briefly about the various mobile app versions later in the book, Canvas LMS is primarily used via the web-based version. So, you are going to use an Internet browser such as Google Chrome to get to your Canvas login page. In most cases, you do not need to download or save any additional software in order to use Canvas. The truth is that most Canvas LMS login pages tend to look pretty similar to each other. Therefore, it is up to you to be sure you're attempting to log in to the proper one. Otherwise, you will most definitely draw the ire of your local tech geeks when they realize that you've been telling them that you can't log in to Canvas, but the true reason you can't is because you're not on your district's or institution's Canvas login page to begin with. Think of it like this: You have the proper key to get into the house; however, if you are at the wrong house, that key won't work.

Once you've logged in to your Canvas account, what you see depends on a number of different factors that are, at this point, mostly out of your control. Hey, isn't that fun? Depending on how your IT department has set things up for your district, you could see anything from a nearly blank screen, like what you see in Figure 3-3, to something more robust, like the screen shown in Figure 3-4.

Depending on those IT factors we spoke about earlier, you may actually see a screen that includes all sorts of things . . . or nothing at all. You may see courses already, you may see different elements added to the Navigation bar on the left side of the screen (which we talk about later in this chapter), and you may even see a prebuilt home page with a color scheme that matches the color scheme of your school, university, or school district.

Now that you're logged in, it's time to check out your home within the Canvas ecosystem: the Canvas Dashboard.

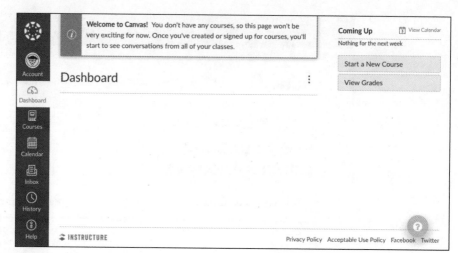

FIGURE 3-3:
An empty Canvas
Dashboard.

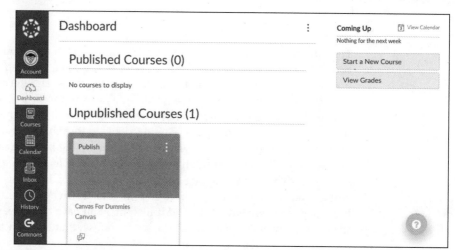

FIGURE 3-4:
A pre-populated
Canvas
Dashboard.

Getting Comfortable with the Canvas Dashboard

No matter what you see upon logging in — an empty screen like what is shown in Figure 3-3 or a prepopulated, color-coordinated home page like Figure 3-4 — your next step is to get to know the user interface and the basic navigation from the Canvas Dashboard.

REMEMBER

The Canvas Dashboard is a Panda's favorite place. It is your home within the Canvas ecosystem, and it is the first screen you see when you log in to Canvas LMS. No matter what you're doing in Canvas, whether you lose your way or just need to take a moment to harness your Panda Powers, the Dashboard is where you can easily see all of your courses, your to-do list, upcoming events, and more.

The Global Navigation Menu

When looking at your Dashboard in Canvas, the most important location is the Navigation bar on the left side of the screen, known as the *Global Navigation Menu* (see Figure 3-5). Located on the left side of every page in Canvas, this is where you can move from the Dashboard to view your Account, Courses, Calendar, Inbox, History, and added services you may have access to like Commons, Studio, and MasteryConnect. A Help option also appears at the very bottom of the menu.

FIGURE 3-5:
The Global Navigation Menu.

Account

Clicking the Account option from the Navigation bar opens an additional menu full of all sorts of goodies, as shown in Figure 3-6. This is where — if your school's or institution's IT department allows — you can change your personal user settings, add or modify your profile picture, and set up some pretty powerful options for how Canvas works for you.

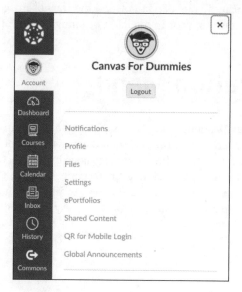

FIGURE 3-6:
The Account options.

Profile

In the Profile section, you can add and edit your profile content to make it more specific to you by adding such information as a biography and links to websites you may own. You can edit your name, display name, default language, preferred time zone, and so on. As a teacher, you usually have access to adjust all of these profile settings. However, it is common for these to be locked for student users. For example, we prefer to keep our students identified by their first and last names within Canvas, rather than allowing students the ability to change their name to whatever they want. Oh, the humanity!

The most important element here is that you can choose to add an image to your profile. Adding a profile picture is very helpful because it can assist students, parents and guardians, and staff in identifying you and your Canvas content in the future.

Settings

Settings is next on the list. This is where, as the kids say, "things get real." The Settings section (shown in Figure 3-7) is where the information as it pertains to your individual account is stored. You can adjust this content by selecting the Edit Settings button that appears in the right sidebar. By editing your settings, as shown in Figure 3-8, you have the ability to make account-level changes that stick with you as a user.

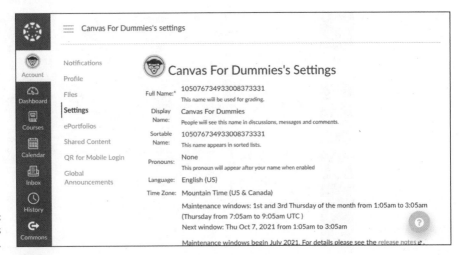

FIGURE 3-7:
The Settings
screen.

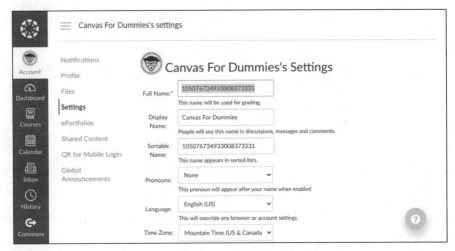

FIGURE 3-8:
Editing user
settings.

Farther down the screen are the Registered Services and Approved Integrations sections, which may be controlled by your IT department, but you can choose to integrate other services like Google Drive, Skype, and Twitter here. Generally speaking, we advise teachers to let their IT professionals dictate to them what may need to be adjusted here under Web Services and Approved Integrations. As aspiring Canvas Pandas, this is a good opportunity to let our beloved Panda computer geeks handle the extra-techy things.

FEATURE SETTINGS

Moving down the page, the next section you see is called Feature Settings, as shown in Figure 3-9. Here you can control some of the aesthetics of your courses. These options can get a bit tricky but we have some tips.

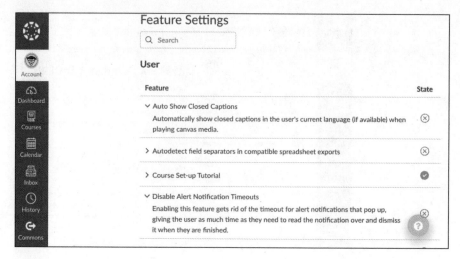

FIGURE 3-9:
User-level feature settings.

TIP

If you're asking us, we suggest *disabling* (turning off) the following Feature Settings options:

>> Course Set-up Tutorial (unless you are brand new to Canvas and want the extra help)

>> Disable Alert Notification Timeouts

>> Disable Celebration Animations

>> High Contrast UI

>> Underline Links

If you're asking us, we suggest *enabling* (turning on) the following:

>> Auto Show Closed Captions

>> Disable Keyboard Shortcuts

>> Microsoft Immersive Reader

For the remaining spreadsheet options, if you're asking us, we disable them because we don't use a ton of spreadsheets in our Canvas instances. If you anticipate using spreadsheets within Canvas regularly, then we suggest enabling all of those settings to be safe. Again, you can *always* come back and adjust these settings. No worries, Panda Cub.

WARNING

As we note earlier, you have the ability to turn on or off the Course Set-up Tutorial in this section. If you are brand new to Canvas and are reading this amazingly written, inspiring, and informative book, while also learning about your Canvas instance on your computer right now, you may choose to toggle off the Course Set-up Tutorial. But it's up to you. Keeping the Course Set-up Tutorial toggled on launches you into tutorial suggestions and "how to's" every time you log in to Canvas. Based on your comfort level with Canvas LMS, this option may be helpful in these early stages of learning. However, it may become a bit of a nuisance as your Panda Powers strengthen and your confidence grows. When that happens, simply come back to Feature Settings in the Account section and toggle off the Course Set-up Tutorial. Like most settings and preferences within Canvas, the lovely Panda Pros provide you with a short description to help you along in making these decisions. The great news is that nothing here is permanent.

WAYS TO CONTACT

Finally, in the Ways to Contact section, which appears on the right side of the Settings screen, you can add additional contact methods such as additional email addresses and even your cell phone number. Providing a cell phone number here enables you to receive text notifications. So, you have the ability to get text alerts based on your notification preferences, which we describe how to set up shortly.

Notifications

Clicking the Notifications link brings you to the Notifications Settings screen, where you see all of the contact email addresses and/or phone numbers you provided in your Profile earlier. For each type of notification available within your Canvas instance, you can easily toggle on or off whether you want a notification or not. So, you have the ability to completely customize where you receive notifications (cell phone, email, not at all) and how regularly you receive those notifications (right away, daily, weekly, or never). It is a regular occurrence for Canvas administrators to have users ask, "How do I turn off all these email notifications? I don't want an email every time a student submits an assignment." The Notifications section is where you can own notifications and get ahead of the game. No unwanted texts or email for this Panda! Notifications is one of the most important spots to visit early in your Canvas journey. You are in full control of how, where, and how often you receive all types of notifications.

TIP

Make your notification decisions early and then live with them for a month or so before making changes. I like to set a calendar event for myself to "Check notification settings in Canvas" as a reminder to go back and revisit what I like and what I need to change moving forward. As with everything within Canvas, these decisions should be deliberate, but they are not permanent.

Additional categories

Within the Account section of the Global Navigation Menu, you may see some of these additional categories: Files, ePortfolios, Shared Content, My Badges, Folio, QR for Mobile Login, and/or Global Announcements. These options vary based on your school district's set-up. If you have questions on any of these settings, reach out to one of your IT professionals.

Courses

The Courses section is where you see a list of all your published and unpublished courses. Clicking the Courses option in the Global Navigation Menu opens a menu of your courses, as shown in Figure 3-10. Selecting the All Courses link from this window opens a listing of your courses where you can customize the order in which they appear. Select the star icon next to a course name, as shown in Figure 3-11, to ensure it is visible on your Canvas Dashboard. This works both ways, too. Deselect the star icon to remove a course from view on your Dashboard. For example, maybe you create a course, perhaps a sandbox course just to try things out, and then decide you don't want to see that course in your Dashboard view. You can come here and easily click the star to remove it as a favorite.

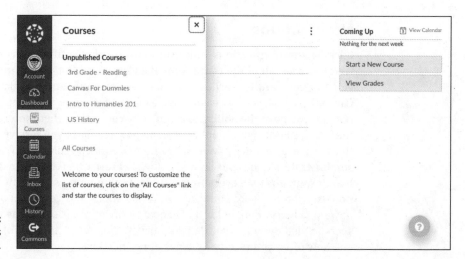

FIGURE 3-10:
The Courses window.

FIGURE 3-11:
Customizing
which courses
appear on your
Dashboard.

Calendar

When you click the Calendar option in the Global Navigation Menu, you are presented with a full-screen view of your Canvas LMS Calendar. We speak a lot about how intuitive Canvas LMS is. Calendar is a great example of that because the Canvas Calendar is designed exactly like most other common online calendars you may have used. You can quickly get your bearings here in terms of adjusting your calendar view by Week, Month, or Agenda. You can also adjust colors for each course's calendar events. And as is often the case, when you see a + (plus) button, that indicates you can create or add something new. We go into detail on using the Canvas Calendar in Chapter 7.

Inbox

The Inbox option on the Global Navigation Menu takes you to a full-screen view of the Canvas LMS messaging Inbox. This is where — you guessed it —you do a great deal of your teacher/student communication. The Canvas messaging environment is very similar to what you see in other commonly used email platforms. For much more on the Canvas Inbox and communication in Canvas LMS, see Chapter 6.

History

The History option on the Global Navigation Menu opens the Recent History page, which lists the most recent pages you viewed in Canvas. It includes page history for the past three weeks, listed in chronological order. Here you can see the date and time you last accessed the page.

Viewing your page history is one way to easily get back to a page you may have been working on. Note that any page removed from a course still appears in your page history, but the link to it isn't valid.

Help

At the bottom of the Global Navigation Menu is the Help option. Select this option to access . . . wait for it . . . help! Are you stuck? Do you have a question about how to accomplish something within Canvas? Is no one answering their phones or responding to your email cries for help? Click here to see a list of resources to assist you. Depending on what level of support your district or institution has provided for you, you may see different options here. Figure 3-12 shows a few of the options you may see.

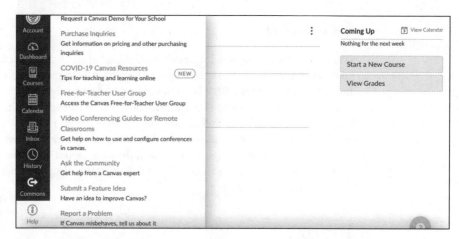

FIGURE 3-12: Help menu options.

TIP

If you are a Canvas LMS administrator, you can add your own domain-specific support links for your district or institution within the Help section. One common strategy is to create a document for users with "Top FAQs" or "Quick Fixes" that may be common in your schools or specific to your domain's set-up. Basically, you can now direct FAQs here for custom support.

Using the Three Dots, er, Options Menu

Another important spot on your Canvas Dashboard is the Options menu, or what Marcus often calls the "three dots menu." You can find the three dots menu toward the upper-right corner of the Dashboard and directly to the left of the To

Do list. Marcus has been incessantly teased by fellow Pandas for his use of this term; however, he uses it because that is exactly what it is. Now, some of your more eccentric Canvas users may call the Options menu any of the following: a kabob, stacked pickle, skinny snowman, the Options icon, vertical dots, the more menu, deer tracks, the pickle stack, the traffic light, jelly beans, the pea pod, or panda poop. Full disclosure: Most of these are made up, but we can confidently say that kabob, skinny snowman, and the Options icon are all commonly used. The Options menu is shown in Figure 3-13.

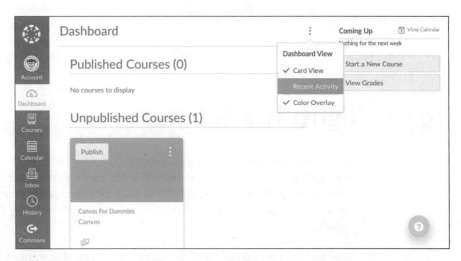

FIGURE 3-13: The Options menu expanded.

Clicking the Options menu icon on your Dashboard reveals settings that enable you to adjust your Dashboard view as well as turn on or off the color overlays on your course tiles. The color overlays are simply a colored filter that appears over the top of your course tile. Originally, this was the only visual way to discern one course from the next, outside of the course title. These days, the ability to add images, designs, and GIFs to the course tiles has created less of a need for the color overlays. Unless, of course, you want your course to wear rose-colored glasses. See what we did there? To change the color of a course overlay, click the Options menu in the upper-right corner of the Course Card to reveal the color choices, as shown in Figure 3-14.

In addition to adjusting, adding, or removing color overlays from the Options menu, you can also adjust your Dashboard view. Card View is the most common and arguably the most intuitive view to choose. However, you can change your view to other options if so desired. Selecting Recent Activity lists all recent activity from all your published courses. To revert back to Card View, simply click the Options menu and choose Card View.

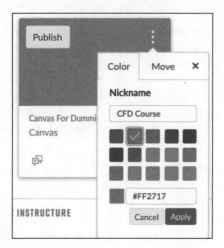

FIGURE 3-14:
Changing a
course tile
color overlay.

To the Right: The Sidebar

As you are navigating your way around the Canvas LMS Dashboard, take a look over to the right side of the screen. "To the right, to the right. All you need to know is to the right of the screen." For Marcus's ego, please reread the last sentence to the tune of the opening of the song *Irreplaceable* by Beyoncé. You're welcome.

Here on the right side of the screen is the sidebar, which includes two handy sections: the To Do list and the Coming Up section.

To Do

The To Do section appears in the upper-right corner of your Canvas screen. This section can be a very helpful spot for both educators and for students to quickly know what is on the immediate horizon. Any user can simply view that information here, or click on the item. Clicking the item takes you directly to that task. For example, the To Do section shows teachers exactly what needs grading at any given time, and by clicking the item, they are taken directly to SpeedGrader where they can grade and provide feedback on the submission. (We dive into using SpeedGrader in Chapter 11.)

As the teacher, clicking the "X" removes that item from your To Do section until there is another student submission. The To Do section is somewhat of a love/hate section for users we have talked to and worked with. For us as educators, we love it! However, some criticisms we've heard pertain to students who may rely too heavily on the To Do section by using it to go straight to the assignments and bypassing the course content. So, see how it works for you and your students. You be the judge.

Coming Up

Just below the To Do section is the Coming Up section. This is a quick snapshot at what's ahead in the course. It lists your course assignments that are coming due within the coming week. There is also a View Calendar link here, which takes you directly to your Canvas Calendar.

As you continue your Canvas journey, you will become more acclimated to your surroundings. As you do so, you will find yourself really appreciating elements within the Canvas Dashboard.

Chapter **4**

Where the Magic Happens: Setting Up a Course

The real reason you're probably reading this book is to create better courses, faster. Maybe you've figured out for yourself how to set up a course, but you know there must be steps you're missing. Or maybe you don't even know where to begin. This chapter is for you!

In this chapter, you start your journey to course-creation mastery by first creating a practice, or *sandbox*, course. As you learn new ways of delivering digital content, and as you experiment with what you learn in this book, the sandbox is where you can try things out without worrying about any of it affecting your students. You'll want a sandbox course no matter what. Surprisingly enough, we continue to find that teachers we talk to have somehow never heard of a sandbox course. If that's you, welcome to one of our favorite tips within Canvas LMS: Always keep a sandbox course where you can play, tinker with design, and preview content. More on how to do that soon.

Once your sandbox course is set up, you then take a look at how you can demonstrate your creativity with your course tiles, how your students will view the set-up of your courses, and how to ensure your links work and your courses are accessible, usable, and foster greater "learnability" among all of your students.

Creating Your First Course

TIP

Before you create and publish your first course in Canvas LMS, it is a good idea to create a sandbox course in which to try things out. A *sandbox course* is a sample course that students do not have access to. It is a practice area where we tell teachers they should "go play and try to break stuff." Every teacher should have a sandbox course.

As we have said, and will say throughout this book, each district's or institution's set-up of Canvas LMS will be different. Hopefully you have the ability to create your own course from your Dashboard. However, if you do not, it should be as simple as a phone call or email to your IT department to either have that function enabled for your entire domain, or to at least ask them to create one for you. The sandbox course is where you can try the new things you learn in this book, the new things you see while searching the #CanvasFam hashtag on Twitter, the new strategies you learn from fellow Pandas in your school or district, or the new ideas you discover on other social media platforms. The sandbox is your place to play and learn. Dance like nobody is watching!

The good news is that the steps to create a real course you eventually share with students are exactly the same as creating a sandbox course. Keep in mind that if you can create your own sandbox course or if you have to ask for one to be created for you, that course is never published. But we're getting ahead of ourselves. Let's look now at how to create a course.

Creating your first course can seem intimidating, but it requires nothing more than these five steps:

1. **Go to your Dashboard and click Start a New Course, as shown in Figure 4-1.**

The Start a New Course dialog box appears, as shown in Figure 4-2. Here is where you enter a course name, decide on the appropriate content license, and determine whether this course should be private or publicly visible.

Click to start a new course

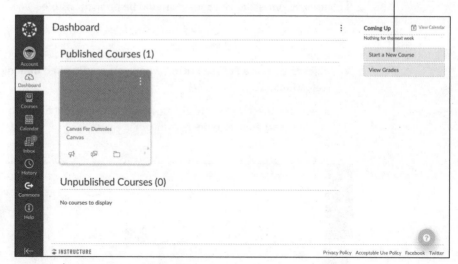

FIGURE 4-1:
The Start a New
Course button in
the Canvas
Dashboard.

FIGURE 4-2:
Start a New
Course
dialog box.

2. **Enter the name of your course.**

If you're creating a sandbox course to, as we mention earlier, break stuff without fear, name this course "Sandbox." If you're creating a course that you intend to go live and populate with student users, then name it something logical like "Sophomore English/Period 5" or "Intro to Shenanigans & Tomfoolery 101."

3. **Select the appropriate Content License.**

Choose Private (Copyrighted) from the drop-down menu if you're creating a sandbox course. If you're creating a course for students to access, click the question mark icon next to "License" and view the various options available to you. Select the licensing option you feel most comfortable with.

4. **Indicate whether the course should be publicly visible.**

If you're setting up a sandbox course, do *not* check the box asking for you to make this course publicly visible.

5. **Click the Create Course button when you are finished making your selections.**

Once you select the Create Course button, you are sent to the course home page to start adding content, as shown in Figure 4-3.

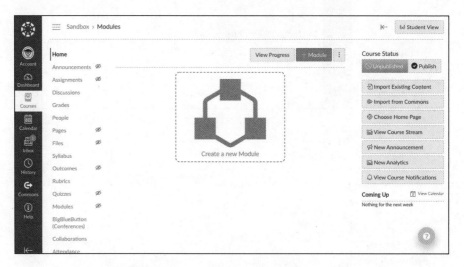

FIGURE 4-3:
The new course home page.

Ta-da! That's all there is to setting up a new course. Now that you have created a sandbox course (or a course that you intend to be published and available for students), it is time to change that course tile to something fun.

We dig deeper into adding course content in Chapter 5. Now, however, head back to the Dashboard by selecting the Dashboard option in the Global Navigation Menu so that you can make some adjustments to the course tile. Figure 4-4 shows the newly created course tile in the Dashboard.

REMEMBER

When you create a sandbox course, you are creating a course that *you* control. It is not seen by anyone until you publish it. As shown in Figure 4-4, this new course appears in the Unpublished Courses section of the Dashboard.

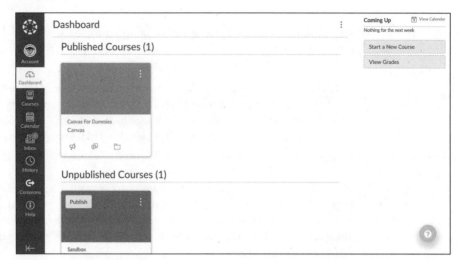

FIGURE 4-4:
The Canvas Dashboard with the newly created course.

Getting Creative with Course Tiles

Course tiles are the visual representation of each course you teach. Course tiles all start out looking the same. They are bland squares with a course title, and what is called a color overlay. Though some folks keep their course tiles blank and use the color overlay available in the Options menu to differentiate between courses, the cool kids add images or GIFs to course tiles. This is a great way to engage learners in your course, help set your course apart from other courses on user Dashboards, and express a bit of personality into the online space.

Marcus remembers when this feature became available to all Canvas users. He read about it in the Canvas release notes, tested it out, and then put together a quick tutorial for the teachers in his district. He can honestly say that few other emails have received the level of "love" that this email did from teachers. Marcus has probably shared thousands of tips and tricks, hacks, and workarounds to make teaching life better and easier for teachers over the years, but when this tutorial came out, teachers legitimately lost their minds!

TIP

Though many of you may find an appropriately licensed, clip-art picture of a one-room schoolhouse to use as your course tile, we'd like to recommend a few ideas to keep your course tiles fresh and engaging:

» Regularly change the image or GIF in your course tile. Students begin to watch for it and it becomes something like an "Easter egg" or hidden surprise. Eddie has even offered extra credit to students who are the first to notice the change.

>> Consider changing the image or GIF in your course tile to associate with special events, course content, or even "inside jokes" within your course. Again, this is about student engagement.

>> Consider creating your own images on sites like Adobe Spark or Canva to then use those images as course tile images. Marcus had a senior English student once photoshop his face onto an image of a pontiff for a presentation about the novel, *Les Misérables.* Marcus downloaded that image and made it the course tile for the following month.

TIP

GIFs, which are simply animated images, are a really fun element to add as your course tile image. The great thing is that in "computer geek speak," an image file and a GIF file are treated the same way. You simply have to find a GIF you like, download it, and then upload it to your course tile in the exact manner you would do for a standard image.

Let's take a look at how to change a course tile image or GIF. If you do not have any courses yet, you can create a sandbox course to experiment in (see "Creating Your First Course" earlier in the chapter).

1. **From the Dashboard, click one of your course tiles to select one of your courses.**

   The course opens and you see the full Course Navigation Menu for that course on the left side of the screen, as shown in Figure 4-5.

REMEMBER

   The Course Navigation Menu includes links to different course areas that appear on the left side of the screen whenever a course is selected.

2. **Scroll to the bottom of the Course Navigation Menu and click the Settings link.**

   The Settings screen appears with the Course Details tab open, as shown in Figure 4-6.

3. **At the top of the Course Details screen, click the Choose Image button inside the rectangle to choose an image to add to your course tile.**

   The Choose Image screen appears, shown in Figure 4-7, where you can search your computer for any image or GIF you have downloaded and saved already. Alternatively, you can simply drag and drop an image to this space, or you can even search stock photos from Unsplash, which is a free stock photography website that has partnered with Canvas LMS to provide high-resolution images free of charge.

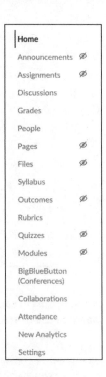

FIGURE 4-5:
The Course
Navigation Menu.

FIGURE 4-6:
The Course
Details screen.

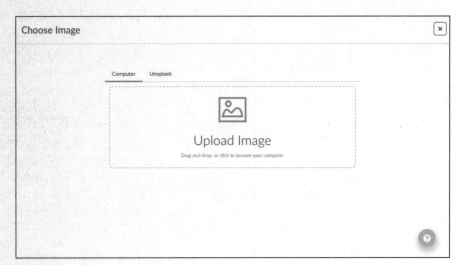

FIGURE 4-7:
The Choose
Image screen.

4. **To search Unsplash for a stock photo, click the Unsplash tab at the top of the Choose Image screen and type your search in the Unsplash Search box (see Figure 4-8).**

   Once you upload an image or GIF from your computer or chosen one from Unsplash, it is automatically applied to the course tile square on the Course Details screen so that you can preview it.

   If you don't like the image, no problem. Just click the Options menu in the upper-right corner of the course tile to either choose a new image or simply remove the one that you don't like, as shown in Figure 4-9. Repeat as many times as needed to find the image or GIF that is just right.

5. **Once you are happy with your image, scroll to the bottom of the Course Details screen and click the Update Course Details button to save the image to your tile — if you don't, it won't.**

   The course tile for your course now displays the image on your Dashboard.

WARNING

There are additional course settings in the Course Details tab, but most of them are "hands off" for most teachers. Most of the remaining settings on this page should only be changed or adjusted if dictated by your IT department.

Now that you've updated your course tile for this course, it's time to look at updating additional course settings. Let's do that next.

FIGURE 4-8:
Searching
Unsplash for tile
images.

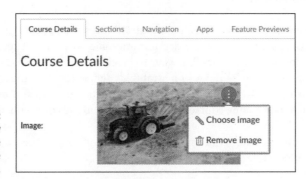

FIGURE 4-9:
Choose a new
image or remove
the image
altogether.

IF THEY THINK YOU'RE CRAZY, YOU'RE DOING IT RIGHT!

Our personal favorite example of incorporating a GIF image on a course tile occurred a few years ago when Marcus taught an eighth-grade technology class. He mentioned the movie, *The Never-Ending Story,* and not one student had ever heard of it. That was the real tragedy! However, he told them all to watch the movie over the weekend. The course tile the following week was Marcus's face placed on top of Bastian's face while he rides Falkor. We're not gonna lie. That was pretty ingenious.

Updating Course Settings

With your newly added tile image adding some flair to your course, direct your attention now to the top of the Course Settings screen where you find the following tabs across the top: Course Details (where we changed the course tile in the previous section), Sections, Navigation, Apps, and Feature Options. These tabs within your Course Settings allow you to further customize your course in how it looks, how it behaves, and how it functions. Let's start by digging into the Sections tab.

Sections tab

Sections is a spot where Canvas really shines in terms of course management. However, as always, set-up depends on your school district or institution. So if you do not see a Sections tab, it is likely locked down or disabled by your IT department. If this is the case, contact them to explain your goals for using Sections within your course.

The Sections area enables teachers to distribute students into groups within the current course. Certainly there are innumerable ways a teacher may choose to group students and innumerable ways to label these groups. So grouping students in this way needs to be done in a strategic, deliberate, and thoughtful way. One example is to use the Sections option to group students into sections of those who are enrolled in the same course, but actually attend the course on alternating days.

REMEMBER

Keep in mind that students can see the group names you choose, so be judicious in how you describe them.

No matter what your situation, to create different sections within your course, simply type a name for the section in the Add a New Section dialog box and click the +Section button. Then, you can add enrolled students to those sections as you wish, and you can edit those enrollments whenever you need. Editing sections is as simple as picking and choosing students and moving them from one section to the other, in much the same way you would group students in the classroom.

Navigation tab

Next up is the Navigation tab. This one is extremely important. When we say important, we mean the sugar level in Kool-Aid important! One of the most significant tenants of online and blended learning models is to be sure that the learning environment is as navigable, understandable, and intuitive as possible. Canvas gives teachers the ability to manipulate the course navigation here.

Basically, you are controlling what your students see in that left-side Course Navigation Menu. You can drag and drop items to re-order them, and you can disable items so that they don't show up in the Course Navigation Menu at all, as shown in Figure 4-10.

FIGURE 4-10:
Move and disable
items in the
Course
Navigation Menu.

For example, suppose you are not using the Syllabus feature within Canvas with your third-grade class. You can click the Options menu icon (the three dots menu) next to Syllabus and choose to either disable it or move it. This flexible navigation is so important for Pre-K through higher education learners. Take a few moments here in your course or in your sandbox course and edit the Navigation settings.

REMEMBER

Click the Save button at the bottom of the page to save your changes and remember that the changes you make here apply to the course you are currently in and *not* to all of your courses. Therefore, you need to follow this process for each course individually to customize course navigation. Also remember, nothing here is permanent. You can always come back and readjust as needed.

Apps tab

Move on over to the right at the top of the Course Settings screen and click the Apps tab. Apps are exactly what you think they are. Like on your smartphone, you can download and use apps in Canvas, too, and many of them are free to use. You can easily add an app to your course by selecting the name of the app and clicking the +Add App button. All the available apps within Canvas LMS are visible in the App screen.

YouTube is a great example of a free app that you can easily add to your Canvas course. However, there are hundreds of apps here in this list, many of them free, and some of them may be assets your school district pays for. In those cases, adding the app becomes a bit more complicated.

Take the Flipgrid app, for example. Flipgrid is a web-based tool that enables audio and video response. That is a basic and wholly uninspiring description because Flipgrid is awesome! However, when you click to add the Flipgrid app to Canvas, you find that it asks you for a Consumer Key and a Shared Secret. I'll be honest, though I don't harbor any strange connotations from a Consumer Key, I've always thought that looking for a Shared Secret sounded like something the CIA and FBI may need to be involved in. Nonetheless, this information is usually found by going to your Flipgrid account on that app's site. (In other words, you need to have a Flipgrid account already.) Once you log in to your Flipgrid account, you can find this information and enter it here in Canvas.

TIP

A number of other resources and even textbooks are available as apps that integrate and play nicely within Canvas. In the cases of apps that involve any sort of financial investment, I generally suggest that teachers get license/seat information from their IT departments. Often, IT automatically adds services to your Canvas account if it is a paid item or connected to textbooks. Once again, some of this falls to our recurring theme of, "this is best left to the IT folks."

Feature Previews tab

The next tab in the Settings screen is the Feature Previews tab (see Figure 4-11). Here you can make adjustments to various options that are available within this course, such as allowing extra credit or anonymous grading. Making adjustments is as simple as clicking the red X or the green checkmark to toggle these features on or off. Clicking the text of the feature itself expands that item and displays a short description of what exactly that feature is, as shown in Figure 4-12.

Again, we have great control and flexibility within Canvas. You can always come back to readjust these settings at a later date. And unlike in other areas, once you've adjusted any feature options here, you can simply navigate away without needing to save or update.

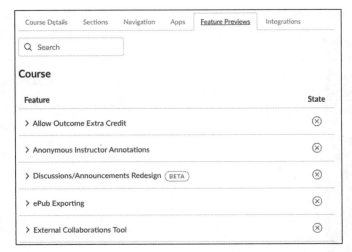

FIGURE 4-11: Feature Previews tab.

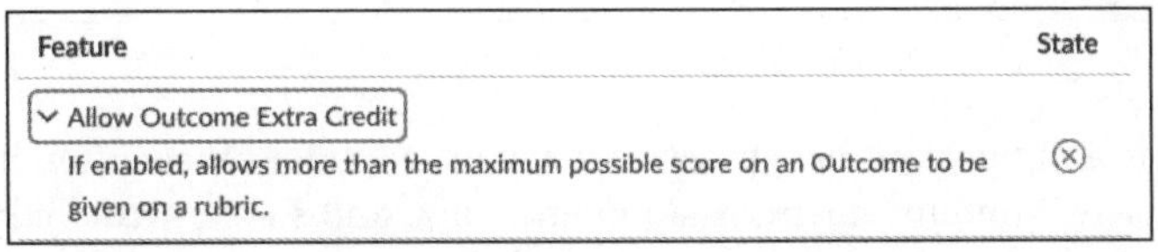

FIGURE 4-12: Expanded feature description.

Looking at Learning in the Student View

Likely one of the most commonly used elements within Canvas LMS is the Student View, which enables instructors to see the course as their students will see it. Within any course, the Student View button appears in the upper-right corner of the screen at all times. As shown in Figure 4-13, it even sports a cute pair of glasses. This button may quickly become a go-to tool for you as you design content within Canvas.

Educators are perfectionists by nature. We value an attention to detail and above all, we want to effectively guide students through their learning experiences within any learning modality (face-to-face, hybrid, remote or distance learning). With that in mind, it is always vital to have the ability to see things from the student perspective, and that is what Student View does.

When you click the Student View button, a fairly obnoxious fluorescent pink frame surrounds your entire Canvas screen. *Why are they calling it obnoxious? What's their beef with pink?* you may ask. We say "obnoxious" with the utmost love and respect in this particular case. It needs to be obvious when we are navigating within the Student View. We have seen situations where teachers have attempted to design content, create assignments and quizzes, or grade assignments while in Student View, somehow not noticing or realizing it.

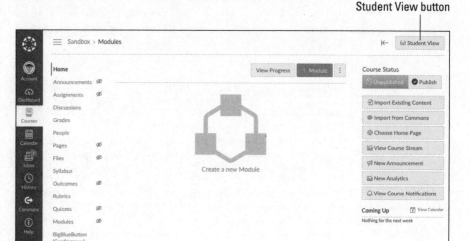

Student View button

FIGURE 4-13:
The Student View button.

TIP

It is an important best practice to visit the Student View often in order to see how a page, announcement, assignment, quiz, and so on, actually looks for your students. Some of you may be familiar with a very widely used BLMS (Barely Learning Management System) that rhymes with "Moogle Glassboom." Though great in many ways, it does *not* allow you to double-check your work like this. For those of us who are perfectionists with a side of anxious, we definitely appreciate and need the Student View for our own sanity.

REMEMBER

As you design a page, create an announcement, build an assessment in Quizzes, or basically anything else, always click the Student View button to check your work and to see the content exactly as your students will see it. When you are done, simply click the Leave Student View button located in the bottom-right corner and . . . boom! You're back to your Teacher View. Thank you, Canvas.

Validating Your Links

We've all been there. You spend countless hours building out content for your students. You worked hard to get everything in place. Design looks great, content is solid, and you get this email: "I can't open the link." Happens to the best of us at some point. But when you've spent countless hours keeping the good vibes going, nothing squashes the mood faster than now having to troubleshoot what link is broken and why it isn't showing the content you hoped your students will see.

Fortunately, built right into Canvas is the Link Validation tool. With this tool you have the ability to verify that all external links work the first time. As you navigate the jungle of Canvas, memorizing the path to the Link Validation tool is a way to ensure that your links are correct, thereby minimizing those panicked emails from students.

The Link Validator tool is found in the Course Navigation Menu under Settings. Let's walk through the process.

1. **From your Dashboard, open the course whose links you want to validate.**

2. **In the Course Navigation Menu on the left side of the screen, click the Settings link.**

   The Course Details screen appears.

3. **Click the Validate Links in Content option that appears in the sidebar on the right side of the screen, as shown in Figure 4-14.**

   The Course Link Validator screen opens, as shown in Figure 4-15.

4. **Click the Start Link Validation button.**

   The tool runs and lets you know how many broken links, if any, you have in the course. What's helpful is that Canvas not only displays the number of links, but also the content that is associated with that link.

   The "why is this broken" is extremely important in this case. Whether you're content has been deleted from another Canvas page, or the website is unreachable, the tool outlines ways to correct the problem. Correcting these broken links is as easy as selecting the broken link in question; the Link Validator tool takes you directly to the content.

FIGURE 4-14: Validating links in a course.

—— Click to validate links in your course

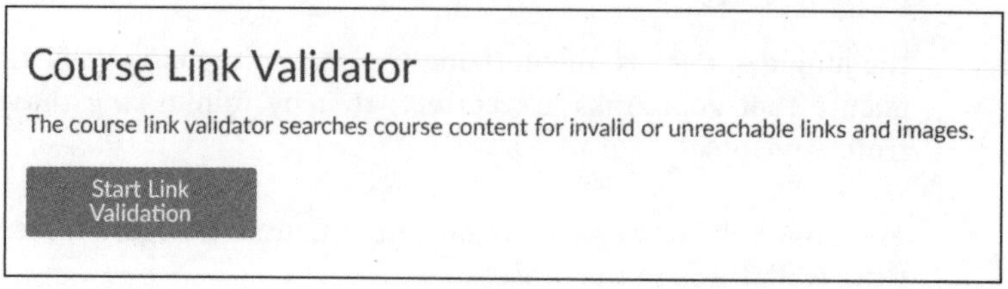

Course Link Validator

The course link validator searches course content for invalid or unreachable links and images.

Start Link
Validation

FIGURE 4-15:
The Course Link
Validator screen.

TIP

This tool is one of those "must haves, must remember" inside the LMS. The ability to not only recognize broken links, but also provide avenues to correct them quickly and efficiently is what really makes this stand out.

Checking for Accessibility, Usability, and Learnability

Let's be very, *very* clear to all you aspiring Pandas out there. This section will not be your only lesson on accessibility, usability, and the term we just made up, "learnability." The truth is that there are many, many other books out there that go into great depth and detail about Universal Design for Learning (UDL), accessibility, and what is intuitive for a learner in a digital space, like Canvas LMS. Consider this a friendly reminder that when we as educators are building content and lessons in an online space, we have to be aware of how that learning looks, sounds, and feels for our learners.

For the purposes of this book, look at accessibility and usability like this: When Marcus taught high school English, he used to teach the dreaded research paper. Every year he would have students offer up topics like "The Civil War" or "Rock Music." He would then launch into his usual diatribe about how those were impossibly large topics that needed to be narrowed down to something much more specific. So instead of an 8- to 10-page research paper on "The Civil War," he would suggest that students consider a topic like "The role of technology in the Civil War." This way, the topic became much more manageable and concise.

In much the same way, in this section we discuss the importance of accessibility, usability, and "learnability" within a typical Canvas LMS course only. We can only focus on some strategies and "baked-in" tools that can help you ensure that all of your learners are getting the most from their learning experiences.

REMEMBER

As educators, we want to positively impact all of our students. What we have continued to learn over the years is that there are so many different methodologies, strategies, and approaches to our teaching practices. And, along with those educational discoveries, we have also continued to learn more about our abundantly diverse learners. Our ability to fine-tune how we teach, creatively design learning experiences, and differentiate instruction to meet the needs of all of our students is, in a nutshell, what accessibility is to us. Luckily, Canvas LMS has a few truly amazing tools to help empower teachers and students alike.

Accessibility Checker

The Accessibility Checker is found anywhere you use the Rich Content Editor (RCE). The RCE is the textbox that includes all the buttons you would expect to see within a word-processing program like Microsoft Word or Google Docs, plus many more icons that assist you in designing content for students. Don't worry, we dig deep into using the Rich Content Editor to create content in Chapter 5.

Any time you see the Accessibility icon, as shown in Figure 4-16, you know that you can "check your work" as it pertains to ensuring all learners can have an equal learning experience designed by you.

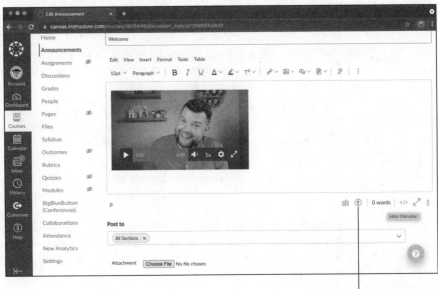

FIGURE 4-16:
The Accessibility Checker icon.

Accessibility Checker icon

The next logical question is this: What does the Accessibility Checker check for?

>> **Adjacent links:** If you link two adjacent links to the same URL, they should be a single link. Sometimes we mistype and add a space or an accidental character and that typo can cause issues.

>> **Heading paragraphs:** Headings should not contain more than 120 characters. Why you may ask? Well, headings are intended to be shorter pieces of text that lead learners into the rest of the content. So Canvas LMS has placed a character limit here.

>> **Image alt text:** *This is a big one!* Short for "alternative text," alt text is a short description of an image. All images you include should include alt text. (*Note:* Don't simply use the filename of the image as the alt text.) Chapter 5 goes into detail on adding image attributes, including alt text.

>> **Large text contrast:** You got cute in your design of a page, an announcement, or directions to an assignment. You are exasperated by students *not reading the directions.* So, in true passive-aggressive form, you decide to inflate that font size to about 50pt. to really get their attention. The checker reminds you that the contrast minimum must be 3:1 on text larger than 18pt. and bold text larger than 14pt.

>> **Sequential headings:** Be a rule follower, people! You start with H1 (the main heading, or heading 1), and move your way along to H2, H3, and so on down the line. You cannot skip heading levels. If you decide to be a Panda Rebel and get crazy with pressing the Tab key, Accessibility Checker calls you on it.

>> **Table captions:** If you insert a table, include a caption describing its contents. (For example, "Table includes a data set showing the students enrolled, their T-shirt sizes, and their mailing addresses.")

>> **Text contrast:** Accessibility Checker verifies your color choices for text compared to your background. It uses the same calculations as used by the WebAIM web-accessibility tool available online.

Once you click the Accessibility Checker icon, it runs and begins highlighting the issues found in your current work. When it has finished its check, a window slides out from the right side of the screen for you to view issues, apply fixes, proceed through all issues, and finally, confirm your fixes. Basically, the Checker runs you through the issues, provides suggested fixes, and all you have to do is click "Next." When you see the screen shown in Figure 4-17, you are ready to party like a panda!

Immersive Reader

One amazingly helpful feature that is baked right into Canvas LMS is Microsoft's Immersive Reader capability. Microsoft's Immersive Reader is a free tool that implements helpful techniques to improve reading and writing for people regardless of their age or ability.

Accessibility Checker

No accessibility issues were detected.

FIGURE 4-17:
The Accessibility
Checker screen
that appears
when no issues
are found.

As of this writing, the Immersive Reader feature works within Pages, Syllabus, Assignments (assignment instructions only), and the course home page (when appropriate).

Immersive Reader enables students to access a page within your course and simply click the Immersive Reader button to have that page read aloud to them. A number of different tools can screen-read for you or for your students, but Immersive Reader is one of the best options around. We love it because it requires just one click for the student (when available, it appears in the top-right corner of the screen), where most other options require an additional Google Chrome extension or a combination of keystrokes to enable a similar tool. For students, Immersive Reader is the simplest, most intuitive way to have a Canvas page read to them.

TIP

When making images accessible with Immersive Reader, be sure that each image you use on a Canvas page includes what is called "alt text" for Immersive Reader to be able to read. See Chapter 5 for more details on how to add alt text to your images.

Chapter **5**

Rolling in the RCE

The Rich Content Editor, or RCE for short, is where you'll spend a lot of your time when you start using Canvas LMS. The RCE is where you can add and format text and images and even record video to create a multifaceted learning experience for your students. Think of the RCE as the window into a learner's world of engagement. This is your creation space and the place where you as an educator get to display your skills. Remember that lesson you could sell tickets to? The one where students crave the next chapter in learning? That's the one you should focus on while trying out the RCE for the first time.

In this chapter, you discover why the RCE is important in every aspect of becoming a Canvas Panda. The information provided in this chapter will enable you to swing from tree to tree as you master the layout of the icons and buttons that you see and use each day. Once you've mastered the skills and basic concepts, we walk you through best practices for turning your course content into visually immersive learning experiences with the RCE.

Exploring the RCE

The Rich Content Editor (RCE) is a user interface designed to enable you to create and organize content within multiple setting in Canvas LMS. When demonstrating Canvas as a whole to aspiring Pandas, the RCE is always where we start because it touches every bamboo fiber of Canvas LMS.

After you've created your course and nailed down the settings and the basics of how you want the course to function (which we outline how to do in Chapters 3 and 4), your next step is to start creating *content*. You can create content in a number of places throughout the Canvas LMS platform, but that content is born by first inserting it into the RCE. Think of the RCE as your gateway to creating engaging content inside your Canvas world. You'll find it available in many Canvas pages including in Announcements, Assignments, Discussions, Pages, Quizzes, and your Syllabus.

As the rise of creating engaging and interactive content has graced our halls, so has the evolution of the RCE. Eddie always remembers his first experience with a word processor as a young student and how challenging it was for him to use at first. That first engagement with a word processor left him confused — there were just too many clickable elements — and he felt overwhelmed. But once he mastered the basic layout, he learned that he could create freely. So we can relate to how you may feel when you first open the RCE. It's a lot to take in and you may even think to yourself, *I may have bitten off more bamboo than I can chew.* That is obviously not true! As we authors evolved from using a typewriter and word processors to creating virtual learning content in Canvas, we learned that we are incredibly capable of putting all the pieces together, and you are, too.

In the following sections you discover how to create new content using the RCE and the components you'll need to arrange and organize your instructional content with your students in mind.

REMEMBER

As with most things inside the Canvas LMS platform, usage is highly customizable per district implementation and set-up. What you see on your platform may vary slightly from what you see in this chapter. Don't panic; this chapter is designed to share with you access on a very basic level.

Accessing the RCE

You access the RCE with a single click from within any of the following Canvas course areas: Announcements, Assignments, Discussions, Pages, Quizzes, and your Syllabus. All of these areas are accessible in the Course Navigation Menu that appears on the left side of your screen when a course is open.

To start creating content, you simply need to open the individual area inside your Canvas course to which you want to add content. For example, clicking the +Announcement button in the Announcements area (see Figure 5-1) launches the RCE. However, if you are interested in editing an element already created, click on the specific content to reveal an Edit button in the upper-right corner, as shown in Figure 5-2. Clicking the Edit button enables you to now edit that element using the RCE.

Click to open the Announcements section   Click to create an announcement

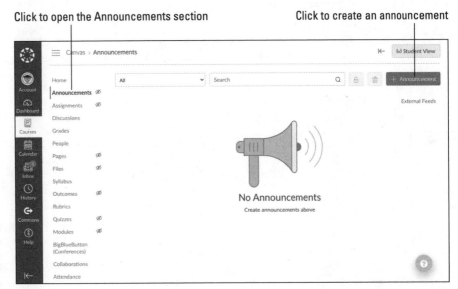

FIGURE 5-1:
Launching the RCE from the Announcements area.

Edit button

FIGURE 5-2:
Editing a created RCE element.

Finding your way around

The Rich Content Editor contains three main components that you should become familiar with:

>> The content area (editing window)

>> The menu bar

>> The toolbar

Check out Figure 5-3 to see each of these components labeled in the RCE. Then keep reading to find out more about each of these components.

Toolbar

Menu bar

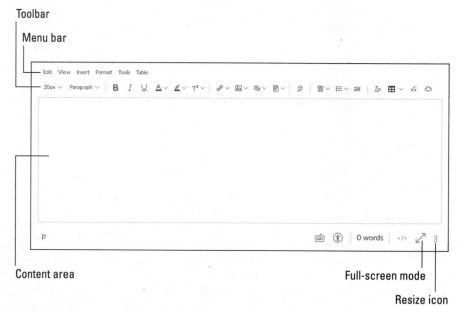

FIGURE 5-3:
The Rich Content
Editor.

Content area   Full-screen mode

Resize icon

The content area

By default, the content area, also called the editing window, is your blank canvas to start your creation of content. It's where everything starts and evolves.

The content area includes a WYSIWYG (pronounced "wizzeewig") rich text editor. A rich text editor is a tool used to create and format text in an online platform and is the basis of the RCE in Canvas. Using this tool within the content area you can format text just as you would in a word-processing program using familiar options like bold, italics, and underline.

You may be asking yourself, *What in the world is WYSIWYG?* WYSIWYG is a common computer acronym that stands for What You See Is What You Get. This just means that as you are editing, what you see on the screen is what will be replicated in the finished product. It's helpful to be able to create in this format. If you've used other word processors before, you've likely been using a WYSIWYG rich text editor without even realizing it.

You can expand learning opportunities for your students in many ways in the content area. For example, within the content area, you can add the following elements:

>> **Graphics:** You can create or add images.

>> **Hyperlinks:** You can add internal and external links.

>> **Media:** You can record video and audio directly.

>> **Plug-ins/LTIs:** Plug-ins and LTIs (which stands for Learning Tools Interoperability) are external tools that you can embed directly into your content using the RCE.

You can resize the content area by clicking and dragging the Resize icon, which looks like a collection of six dots. You can also open the content area in full-screen mode to allow for a better visual experience. (Refer to Figure 5-3.) To exit full-screen mode, click View from the menu bar and select Fullscreen.

One of the best features of the RCE is its autosave feature. If you happen to refresh your page while working in the content area or move away from the content you are working on before you save it, the next time you open the RCE you return to a "Found auto-saved content" message. You can preview the content and then select "Yes" to pick up where you left off. No lost work! This feature is particularly valuable to easily distracted, forever multitasking Pandas like us. Note, though, that the autosave feature only saves your work for up to one day, and it is only available on the same computer and browser you used to create the content, so you can't hibernate for too long before saving your work if you don't want to risk losing it.

The menu bar

The menu bar appears above the content area and displays the available menus and commands including Edit, View, Insert, Format, Tools, and Table. Some may find that these tools are easier to navigate with a keyboard and mouse, and some users may prefer using the menu bar over the toolbar that is found directly below it. In short, the menu bar and the toolbar provide many of the same capabilities, but can serve two very different audiences. Table 5-1 outlines the contents of the menu bar.

TABLE 5-1

The RCE Menu Bar

Menu Bar Option	What You Can Do
Edit	Undo content changes, redo content changes, cut, copy, paste, paste as text, and select all content
View	Expand the editor content area to the width of your browser and open the HTML editor
Insert	Add links (external URLs or to course content), images, media, documents, math equations, tables, embedded content, and horizontal lines
Format	Format links (bold, italic, underline, strikethrough, superscript, subscript, code), manage text blocks, select a font, change font size, change text alignment, change the direction of text, select a text color, select a background color, and clear all formatting
Tools	View word count statistics and embed content from an external tool or app
Table	Add a new table; format table rows, columns, and cells; view table properties; and delete tables

TIP

Did you know that you can view a list of keyboard shortcuts in Canvas? Clicking the Keyboard icon in the lower-right corner of the RCE or pressing Alt+F8 (PC), or Option+Fn+F8 (Mac) simultaneously brings up the list of shortcuts that can save you time when working with the RCE.

TIP

As with most content-editing platforms, your ability to copy and paste becomes invaluable. You've most likely created content elsewhere, such as in other programs or apps, or maybe even elsewhere within Canvas, and the RCE allows you to copy and paste text from other sources with simple keyboard shortcuts such as Crtl+C and Ctrl+V (PC) or ⌘+C and ⌘+V (Mac).

The toolbar

The toolbar is located beneath the menu bar and features much of the same functionality as the menu bar items but with a more graphical interface. Canvas is one of those platforms that gives you multiple ways to get the job done. It is never about which way is the right way; it's about which way is the right way for *you*. This flexibility is part of what makes Canvas great, but for new Pandas, it can be a source of early confusion or even frustration at times. This is where focus and Zen-like Panda patience comes into play. For more information about what the buttons on the toolbar do, check out the next section.

Mastering the toolbar buttons

As the great Willy Wonka once said, "Button, button, whose got the button?" Well the RCE has buttons — *plenty of them*. So we break them all down for you in Figure 5-4. Because Canvas LMS may be seen as a massive jungle of multiple pathways to accomplish simple and efficient tasks, the toolbar buttons continue that functionality to allow you to get things done quickly.

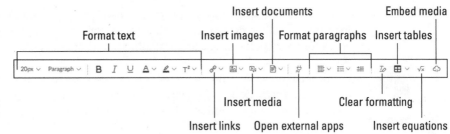

FIGURE 5-4:
The RCE toolbar buttons.

Table 5-2 offers a look at what all these buttons do and how they can help you format a great-looking page.

TABLE 5-2 ## The RCE Toolbar

Toolbar Options	What You Can Do
Paragraph formatting	Select font size and paragraph headings
Text formatting	Select bold, italic, underline, color, highlights, and subscript or superscript
Page formatting	Increase or decrease indents, also add bulleted and numbered lists
Links	Insert external links and links to other courses or content
Images	Upload images from your computer or select images from your course files or user images folders
Media	Upload media from your computer, select media from your course files folder, or directly record media
Documents	Upload other word-processing documents into your course
Apps	Add external apps (LTIs) in addition to the standard RCE tools

Creating a Visual Learning Experience

Now that you've been introduced to the RCE workspace, it's time to start painting learning experiences for your students by adding content. When we coach large groups of teachers on Canvas usage, we always talk about creating *experiences.* Students aren't easily engaged — you know this, I know this, everyone knows this! That's why creating a space that grabs attention is extremely helpful.

First impressions are always important, which is why so many school districts are focusing on course design in a digital space. By creating these learning experiences for your students, you are designing that first impression of your course.

REMEMBER

Think about how you want your students to feel when they click that Course Card, or when they first load up your course home page. You want to create an environment for them that is comfortable and easy to navigate.

Some of the very first steps to course design include adding image elements to the RCE. So let's dive deeper into the bamboo of image uploads.

Adding images to your course

There are a multitude of potential applications and advantages to adding images to your courses. Whether you are adding images to a Canvas page, assignment, announcement, or any other area using the RCE, visuals help learners. For example, you can use images

>> As reference material, such as a map, a diagram, or a schematic.

>> As writing prompts.

>> As supplementary information. (Marcus often provided students with images of artwork or architecture produced during the same time period as a piece of literature he was teaching. Often, this sort of supplementary material led to some really great learning opportunities.)

>> To assist English-language learners in strengthening language acquisition.

>> As scaffolding for vocabulary study.

>> As a visual break from too much text.

>> As a built-in "brain break" within any area in Canvas LMS.

Images can be uploaded to the RCE from two locations: from the toolbar or from the menu bar. Both accomplish the exact same task of adding images.

To upload images to the RCE, follow these steps:

1. **Select Insert ⇨ Image ⇨ Upload Image from the menu bar, as shown in Figure 5-5.**

   Alternatively, click the Images button in the toolbar and select Upload Image. The Upload Image screen appears, as shown in Figure 5-6.

2. **Drag and drop your image onto the Upload Image screen or click within this screen to upload a file from your computer.**

3. **Click Submit.**

   The image is added to the RCE where you can continue to add and format content.

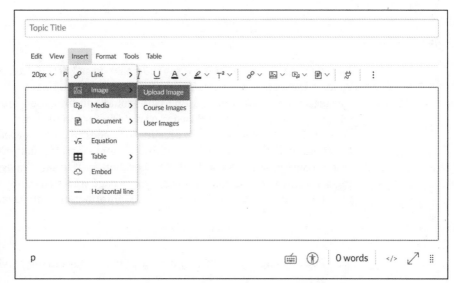

Including image attributes

We touch upon the importance of ensuring accessibility of your course content for all learners in Chapter 4. Image attributes, such as alt text, embedded options, and image sizing, are all things you probably never thought about in regard to your images when creating a document or building out digital content, but they are extremely important for accessibility within Canvas LMS.

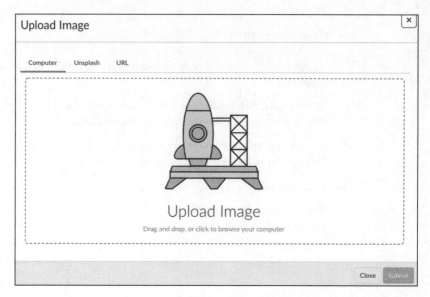

FIGURE 5-6:
The Upload
Image screen.

Alt text (short for *alternate text*) is a short text-based description of an image that appears that can be read by screen readers, or when an image fails to load. A crucial piece of accessibility and one you should add into your daily routine as an educator is giving simple and clear text descriptions to the images you add to your courses. For example, if we are serving the needs of all of our learners, we want our course content to "play nice" with a screen reader. It is better to have a screen reader read "image of a plant cell," rather than for it to say, "image." Simply telling a student that there is an image on the page won't help, but with thoughtful use of alt text, the student gets the needed information more clearly.

To add alt text to your images, follow these steps:

1. **Add an image to the RCE, as described in the steps in the previous section.**

2. **Click the image once to select it in the RCE.**

   The Image Options button appears, as shown in Figure 5-7.

3. **Click the Image Options button.**

   The Image Options window appears on the right side of the screen where you'll see a textbox for adding alt text. By default, the Alt Text field displays the image filename, as shown in Figure 5-8.

4. **Replace the filename with alt text for the image by typing a simple description in the Alt Text field.**

   If the image is decorative and does not require alt text (such as a banner or header image) select the Decorative Image checkbox.

Display Options are embedded by default. Most images you create will be simple embedded options, so there is no need to change this option.

5. **Click Done when finished.**

   The alt text is added to the image to be read with a screen reader tool.

FIGURE 5-7:
The Image
Options button.

FIGURE 5-8:
The Image
Options window
with the image
filename in the
Alt Text field.

Resizing images

When you add images to your course, the RCE embeds these images in their default size, which means your image size may vary. However, the RCE gives you full control of your image sizes if you want it. You can be specific about the size of your image by customizing the size down to the pixel, or you can choose from multiple image size presets.

To adjust image size, click the image in the RCE and then click the Image Options button, as shown earlier in Figure 5-7. In the Size area of the Image Options window (see Figure 5-9), select a preset image size from the drop-down menu, or add specific values for height and width (in pixels). Custom image sizes must be at least 10 x 10 pixels.

FIGURE 5-9:
Set image size in
the Image
Options window.

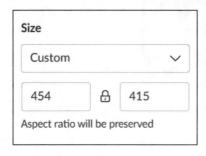

Once you've dialed in the perfect attributes, select Done.

TIP

It's always a good idea to preview your images in the Student View to ensure the image size is appropriate. You want your images to be clear. Clear enough that students can effectively view the difference between an airplane and a balloon, for example. To access the Student View, click the Student View button that appears in the upper-right corner of the screen. And for more information on using the Student View, check out Chapter 4.

TIP

If you would like more manual control over your embedded images, grab and drag the anchor points of your image inside the RCE and watch your image come to life by gaining width and height.

You're the Star! Using the Media Recorder

Several areas within Canvas support embedded media recordings that can be created inside the Rich Content Editor. The ability to add embedded video and audio (for all you shy Pandas) via the Media Recorder is a killer feature that brings personality and openness into your course design. (See Chapter 8 for more on why adding video and audio content via the Media Recorder can be a powerful way to build community, relationships, and connection with your students.)

After spending years as a classroom teacher educating students on the power of audio and video production, Eddie understands the power video in particular provided audiences externally. Once he realized that this feature was baked into the Canvas interface, he was floored by its potential and the creativity it gave even the most basic user. These short videos are the keys to the kingdom in education and can be what engages your students. Period. Full stop.

Although Canvas allows you to record for any length of time, we recommend you keep it short. Think about your audience and how long you believe they are willing to sit and watch your content. We like to use the analogy of what we call "The Reluctant Reader." A reluctant reader, which Marcus certainly admits to being, is the type of person who, before starting a new chapter, first looks ahead to see how long that chapter is. Reluctant readers then decide whether or not they can tackle that upcoming chapter. Your learners are very much this way. If they look at a video you produce in Canvas, and that video is longer than five to six minutes, you may see a huge dip in the number of students watching that video or finishing it.

TIP

The same way you chunk your content throughout the day to make it the most manageable for learners, you must do the same with video content. It is much better to provide five two-minute videos than one ten-minute video.

You start the Media Recorder by selecting the Insert Media icon from the RCE toolbar and selecting Upload/Record Media in the drop-down menu that appears. You can also access the Media Recorder from the menu bar by selecting Insert ⇨ Media ⇨ Upload/Record Media, as shown in Figure 5-10.

When you open the Media Recorder, the Upload Media window appears where you can upload content from your computer, just as you would upload an image. To record media, select the Record tab where you have additional options:

>> **Mic and webcam options:** The Media Recorder accesses your computer's default microphone and webcam. To change these settings, click the Mic or Webcam buttons at the bottom of the screen. As is always the case, if you have multiple devices plugged-in to your computer or laptop, you may need to tell the Media Recorder which one to use.

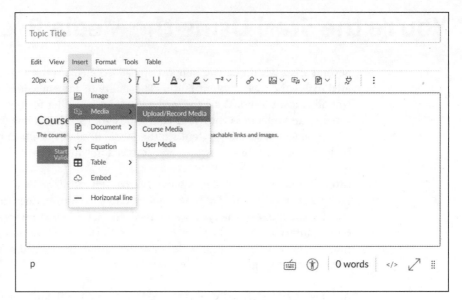

FIGURE 5-10:
Accessing the
Media Recorder
from the
menu bar.

>> **Audio-only recording:** To disable video recording, click the Webcam button and then select No Video.

>> **Record media:** To start a recording, select Start Recording.

>> **Finish media recording:** Once you start your recording, you can restart or finish your recording by selecting Start Over or Finish.

>> **Preview recorded media:** You can watch your recordings back, create a title, and save the recorded message.

Once your video or audio file is saved, it is embedded into your course content in the content area of the RCE.

WARNING

The Safari browser does not support recording media at this time. We recommend using Chrome or Firefox when recording media to the RCE.

The Media Recorder offers you a number of options to connect with students. One of Eddie's favorite examples of utilizing the Media Recorder is when after introducing the tool to fellow teachers, he received a call from one of them who was absolutely thrilled that he could provide a welcome message to his students on a day he was absent. "It's like I'm still with them, even when I can't be." To us, this sort of realization, discovery, and exuberance is just a small part of why we love Canvas LMS.

Practicing with an Announcement

An easy way to see the RCE's capabilities in action is to start by creating a course Announcement. Creating an Announcement is simple and doesn't require any heavy lifting for new users. It's also a fairly low-risk way to experiment with the RCE because any mistakes you make along the way can easily be repaired and replaced without breaking anything attached to it in other Canvas spaces.

Let's practice by opening an Announcement and introducing our students to our class by adding in an image, some text, and a recorded media element.

1. **Select Announcements from the Course Navigation Menu on the left side of your Canvas screen.**

2. **Click the blue +Announcement button located in the upper-right corner of the screen.**

   The RCE is launched, enabling you to create a message, as shown in Figure 5-11.

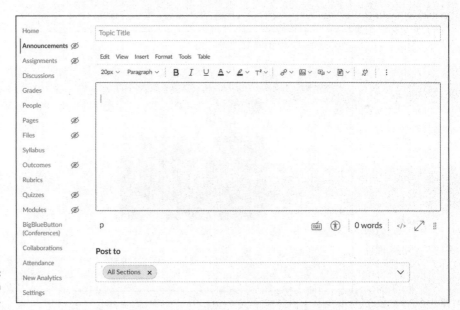

FIGURE 5-11: The RCE in Announcements.

3. **Create an Announcement title and then click inside the content area.**

4. **Add an image to the Announcement by selecting Insert ⇨ Image from the menu bar (or selecting the Insert Image icon from the toolbar).**

5. **Choose to upload an image from your computer (Upload Image) or an image that has already been added to your course (Course Image).**

   Once you've selected an image, it displays inside the RCE.

6. **Add text by single-clicking inside the RCE and typing at your available cursor.**

   A simple "Welcome" should suffice.

7. **Record a video welcome message by clicking Insert ⇨ Media from the menu bar (or select the Insert Media icon from the toolbar).**

8. **Select Recorded Media and record a simple 5- to 10-second message.**

9. **Select Finish and then Save when you are done recording your message.**

   Once saved, the media file is embedded directly into the RCE, as shown in Figure 5-12.

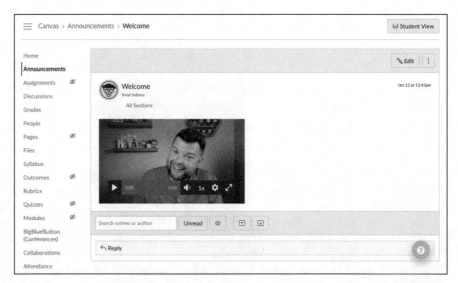

FIGURE 5-12:
An Announcement with an embedded media file.

You've done it! You've just completed a task using the RCE and created an inviting and welcoming announcement to your course. These messages bring a ton of personality into your course and expand relationships with your students virtually.

The Canvas RCE provides more than just the "bear" necessities to survive in the Canvas jungle; it also gives you a place to add interactive elements that can set you apart from the pack when organizing and building out your instructional content.

To take a deeper dive into the RCE, visit `https://community.canvaslms.com`.

Less Is More: Aesthetics and Logical Learning

This is where things can get very controversial. Each one of us has our own style. Some of us like to spend hours digitally designing a page in Canvas using the RCE to really jazz everything up. We take pride in creating this digital work of art complete with Bitmojis, movable objects, and almost anything we can imagine short of a "scratch-and-sniff" area (which, to be clear, would be the worst thing to have in a digital learning ecosystem).

One of the elements we love most about Canvas LMS is the flexibility it provides. You can create almost anything visually, from interactive home pages to the fanciest buttons you ever did see. But, just like Mom always said, "Just because you *can*, doesn't necessarily mean you *should*."

What you'll learn from some of the best Canvas LMS courses is that regardless of the age of the learner, less is more when it comes to design. We like to prioritize the design process within Canvas LMS this way:

>> Make your design intuitive and easy to follow.

>> Eliminate "clicks" where possible.

>> Dress it up a bit, if you like.

Now, when we say "dress it up a bit," we don't mean for you to go nuts spending hours and hours on your home page adding interactive slides, informational slides, instructions in the Rich Content Editor, or whatever. We like to keep the "fashion" of the learning environment "conservative with a splash of personality." The flexibility of Canvas LMS is what allows all of us, as educators, to have the freedom to teach in our own ways.

Think of your design within Canvas LMS like the bulletin boards in your classrooms. We ultimately want to convey information as clearly as possible, but we also realize that our learners tend to benefit from a little extra "splash" of personality here and there.

KEEPING THINGS CLEAN AND STREAMLINED

The RCE is a built-in organizational tool that can be a great way to embed content, but also a great way to keep all of your course pages clean and streamlined. Whether you are embedding video, adding header icons, or dumping in math formulas, the RCE enables you to design content that follows an instructional flow with the learner in mind. What do we mean by "clean and streamlined" you may ask? For us, it is all about creating intuitive, clearly navigable learning experiences for students. Leveraging the RCE to embed a YouTube video directly into an assignment is better, for example, than simply providing a hyperlink to that video. We always want to try to keep learners within the Canvas environment. Hyperlinks either cover the current Canvas tab and navigate you to the YouTube video, or the link opens in a separate tab. Either way, your design and use of a hyperlink is actually hindering the learning experience by adding unnecessary complications. Embed the content using the RCE and your learners "stay put" within the learning ecosystem, they avoid distractions, and they avoid unnecessary clicks.

Another example of clean and streamlined content is to insert a diagram or map directly into a page, announcement, or assignment rather than providing that diagram or map in any number of other ways. We know we may sound like a broken record here, but trust us when we say that a great rule of thumb for all Canvas users is to always consider the best way to deliver the needed content and materials and be sure to keep learners in the platform as much as possible — don't send them to outside links that open a new tab. It's just easier.

Keeping the learner in mind is key in all design work you accomplish inside Canvas. Keep your content organized, highlight, and use rich text formatting to provide prompts to learners for accessibility, usability, and learnability.

In our time teaching in Indiana, we have encountered some truly amazing educators. Two of our good friends used to do a session that discussed how to properly design in a digital space. They themed their session after the popular reality television show called "What Not To Wear." Since attending that session, their analogy has been stuck in our heads because it just makes sense and speaks to so many educators. It goes something like this:

> When designing content in a digital space with the amount of flexibility available in Canvas LMS, you as the teacher want to approach design like a time-honored fashion rule from Coco Chanel, that, frankly, we had never heard of until we attended this session. Chanel recommends, "Before leaving the house, a lady should stop, look in the mirror, and remove one piece of jewelry." We don't wear much jewelry, but we think anyone can understand the message Coco Chanel was delivering.

When we consider this fashion advice and connect it to our design of content within Canvas LMS, or anywhere else in a digital environment for that matter, consider this: When you think your page, presentation, document, or manipulative is done, stop! Look at it again and remove one unnecessary design element before publishing to your course or sharing it with learners.

TIP

Before finalizing your new content, ask yourself these questions:

>> Do I really need to change font size or color there?

>> Is that image necessary for the learning?

>> Is there anything on this page that is there simply to fill white space?

>> What part of this lesson design may be more distracting to learners than helpful?

>> Can learners read the text in that color?

Finally, to ensure that what you have designed for learners is logical and easy to follow, we simply suggest that before publishing, go to Student View and try to navigate in the same way a student would. Give this newly designed page, module, assignment, and/or announcement a test run from the student perspective.

We know what you're probably thinking right now: *These jokers keep talking about design. Blah, blah, blah. I don't want to design anything!* Or maybe you're thinking, *I don't have time to make everything cute.* Or maybe even, *I know how to teach . . . I don't know how to design. And, though I see the value, I would just rather not try to learn all of this digital design stuff.* We get it! Don't forget that we are a couple of middle-aged dudes from Indiana. Our design skills were lackluster at best, and may even be lackluster now. However, if you're not wanting to tackle the learning behind good digital design, we have an amazing solution for you. Mosey on over to Chapter 13 where we take a spin through the Canvas Commons marketplace where you can share and find cool Canvas resources already created for you.

Chapter **6**

You've Got Mail in Canvas Inbox

You're likely familiar with the use of email in your school district. As an instructor, email can be both a blessing and a curse. Being able to communicate with your students (and their parents) through email is a great way to build relationships and keep everyone in the loop, but it can be cumbersome to manage your personal email, your work email, and your communication with students in a centralized location.

With Canvas Inbox, the built-in messaging tool in Canvas LMS, you can keep your communication with your students inside Canvas, which means those course-related emails never have to leave the platform. Ever! This is a good thing. In this chapter, we discuss how to use the Canvas Inbox and how it can help you achieve communication greatness in Canvas LMS.

Exploring the Canvas Inbox

The Canvas Inbox messaging tool is a great way to communicate with a group, an entire course, or individual students. The Inbox is found in the Global Navigation Menu on the left side of your Canvas screen, as shown in Figure 6-1. The Inbox can help you communicate effectively with all of your students across all of your Canvas courses. As instructors, we love using these features for quick access to:

>> Send messages to an individual student in a course.

>> Send messages to everyone in a particular course.

>> Send messages to a select group of students.

>> Reply to messages from others.

>> View or add to submission comments.

Click to open Canvas Inbox

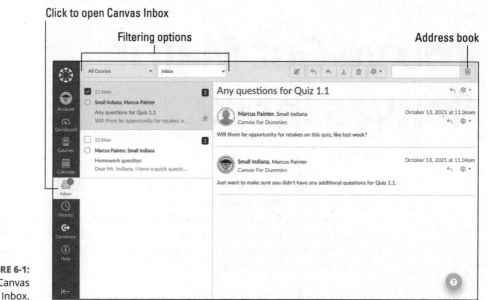

FIGURE 6-1:
The Canvas
Inbox.

TIP

Using Canvas Inbox, you have the ability to run almost all of your communication with your students and other instructors within your courses without needing to leave the Canvas environment. No more constant switching between the LMS and your work email to keep in contact with your students.

Filtering

With Canvas Inbox, you can filter by course, read or unread messages, starred messages, messages that have been sent and archived, as well as any submissions comments on assignments that have been created. To filter your Canvas Inbox, you simply need to use the two drop-down menus located on the top-left side of the screen, as shown earlier in Figure 6-1.

The first filtering drop-down menu, shown in Figure 6-2, lets you search messages from the following three categories: All Courses, Favorite Courses (these would be the ones you have clicked the star next to and are also the ones that you should see on your Canvas Dashboard), and Concluded courses. Obviously, for current messaging, you most likely will stay in either the All Courses or Favorite Courses sections.

FIGURE 6-2:
The Canvas Inbox
course filtering
options.

You may be saying to yourself, *Self! Why would I ever have any need to search messages in Concluded Courses?* One example may be to locate correspondence between you and a student that happened toward the end of a semester-long or year-long course that has recently concluded. As we all know, sometimes our students don't have quite the sense of urgency about their grades until the grades are finalized. That is when we often have students reaching out to ask those questions. You know the ones . . . "Why am I failing the course?" "What can I do to raise my grade?" And so on. The ability to dig into the messages within those concluded courses gives us the safety net that may sometimes be necessary in disputes about grades or past attempts at communication.

The next filtering drop-down menu, shown in Figure 6-3, is one that may be more familiar because it is similar to what we are accustomed to seeing in any other email client. The options available here enable us to filter messages by the following types: Inbox, Unread, Starred, Sent, Archived, and Submission Comments.

REMEMBER

Whatever filter you apply in the first drop-down menu applies to whatever you choose in the second drop-down menu. For example, if you choose Favorite Courses in the first drop-down menu and Inbox in the second drop-down menu, you will only see messages that pertain to your Favorite Courses (those that are starred and appear on your Dashboard) that are currently in the Inbox and nothing else.

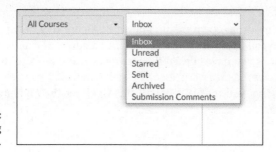

FIGURE 6-3:
More filtering
options.

Address Book

Now that you know a bit about how to filter the Canvas Inbox to see the messages you want, the next step is to think about sending and receiving messages. One of our favorite features inside the Inbox is the ability to quickly message groups or individuals who are enrolled in your courses. As shown in Figure 6-4, you are able to drill down to not only a specific course, but also individuals enrolled in the course.

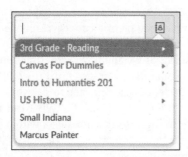

FIGURE 6-4:
Using the built-in
Address Book to
search for all
students in a
course or
individual
students.

To access the Address Book, click the Address Book icon, which is located in the upper-right corner of your Canvas Inbox and — you guessed it — looks like a little book. Dare we say, an address book? The Address Book is populated with all of the users currently enrolled in your courses, regardless of role. So you are able to see students, teachers, observers of the course, and so on. Note that once students are no longer enrolled in your course, they are no longer included in your Canvas Address Book. Only current students show up here. Once a course has ended, you can no longer send a message to that student via the Canvas Inbox.

Conversations

The Canvas Inbox is divided into two main panels: conversations that pertain to your selected course appear in the left panel, while all of the messages within a selected conversation appear in the right panel, as shown in Figure 6-5. To open a conversation thread, simply click the message in the left panel to select it. All messages related to that thread appear on the right.

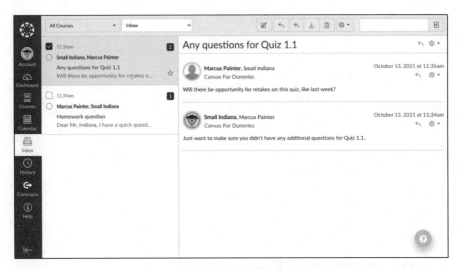

FIGURE 6-5:
Viewing
conversations in
the Inbox.

You also have the ability to manually mark conversations as read or unread as well as mark them as a favorite, as shown in Figure 6-6. To mark a conversation as read or unread, select or deselect the dot to the left of the conversation. To mark a conversation as a favorite, select the star to the right of the conversation.

Mark as read or unread

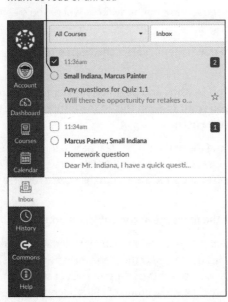

FIGURE 6-6:
Marking
conversations.

Within each conversation in the right panel, selecting the gear icon gives you even more options. Here you can choose to Reply all, Forward, Archive, Unstar, or Delete an entire conversation, as shown in Figure 6-7.

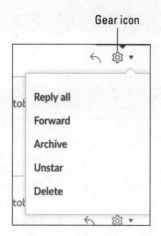

Gear icon

FIGURE 6-7:
Conversation
options.

Composing a Message

Now that you're acquainted with the look and feel of the Canvas Inbox, it is time to compose your first message. Select Inbox from the Global Navigation Menu to open the Canvas Inbox and then follow these steps:

1. **Click the Compose Message icon, as shown in Figure 6-8.**

    The Compose Message window opens, which is where you create your message (see Figure 6-9).

2. **In the Course drop-down menu, select the course to which you want to send a message.**

3. **Click within the "To:" textbox and begin typing names to add a recipient(s), or if you want to send this to the entire course, simply begin typing the course title here.**

    You are able to choose the entire course, teachers within this course, (co-teachers), or just students within this course. Of course, you can also use the Address Book to help locate a recipient from the course roster, as shown in Figure 6-10.

4. **Add the subject of the message in the Subject field.**

    If you are sending a message to multiple students and would rather not share the group list to each student, select the "Send an individual message to each student" checkbox to hide the entire user group list of students to others. If you are sending the message to a group of 100 students or larger, this option is checked by default.

Compose Message icon

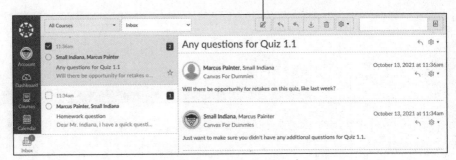

FIGURE 6-8:
Click to compose
a new message.

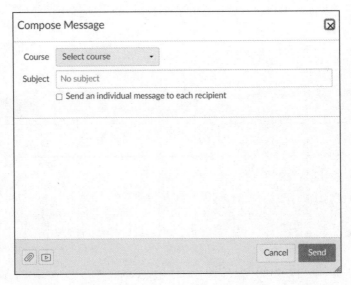

FIGURE 6-9:
The Compose
Message window.

5. **Type your message in the message window (see Figure 6-11).**

   Unfortunately the Rich Content Editor (RCE) not available in Canvas Inbox for you to use to compose your messages, but there are two options that may benefit you. (Be sure to check out Chapter 5 for more on using the RCE.)

6. **If you want to include an attachment or a media file, select the appropriate icon and follow the prompts to add your file.**

7. **Click the Send button.**

   Woosh! Your message is off into the Interwebs, flying through cyberspace directly into the Inboxes of your students. Now it's up to you to keep the communication going.

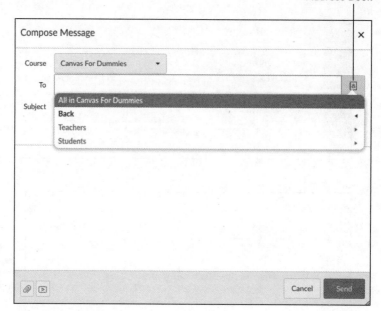

FIGURE 6-10:
Using the
Address Book in
the Compose
Message window.

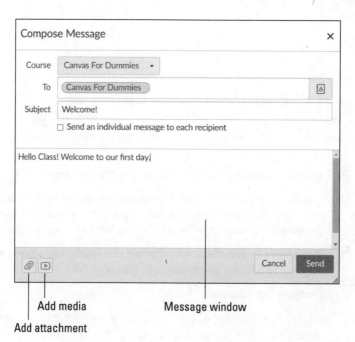

FIGURE 6-11:
Adding text in the
message window.

Add media

Add attachment

Message window

Considerations Regarding Communication

TIP

When talking about communication between teachers and students, it is vital that we as educators all are deliberate and aware of what we say and how we say it. As we note in the previous section, you can direct messages to specific groups of users, and by clicking "send an individual message to each recipient," you can ensure that each recipient of your communication doesn't see who else is included in that email message. This step is extremely important when we think about differentiated instruction and the communication to those groups. It can be quite complicated for teachers to differentiate instruction for learners' varying needs, and to also easily communicate with those students in a way that is respectful and doesn't create discomfort or embarrassment. The truth is that there are more students who do *not* want to be seen and treated differently within the classroom, than there are students who do. Therefore, if a student has special accommodations, discretion is vital.

Along the same lines, discretion in our communication becomes extremely easy when we use the filtering option to create communication. You can communicate similar messaging to a small group of learners without them knowing who else is included in this group. For example, suppose you teach fourth grade and you have tiered reading groups. Ideally, you want to differentiate learning tasks to be appropriate for each reading group. And you will need to communicate with those groups about specific details and expectations, because what applies to your struggling readers group may not apply to your strong readers group. Canvas Inbox provides you the most discrete and compassionate way to communicate with those groups without singling them out, drawing attention to which group they are in, or subjecting students to any undue stressors within the learning environment.

We have both seen how this approach to communication provides a much more caring, supportive, and deliberate avenue for communication with students. All of this goes back to one fundamental point we stressed earlier and focus on throughout this book: Connections with students are made easier with tools within Canvas LMS. Once you try differentiating communication to specific groups of students within Canvas Inbox, we promise you'll be hooked.

REMEMBER

What if you need to communicate more globally across multiple courses? For example, suppose you are an Algebra I teacher and you want to simply message all of your students across multiple courses with the same content? If you are sending a message to a group of 100 students or larger, your message is automatically sent individually, and this option is checked by default.

Should You Delete or Archive?

Most Pandas would agree that keeping their little corner of the Canvas jungle as neat and tidy as possible is a worthwhile goal. However, in regard to communication within Canvas Inbox, there is a great debate on whether you should delete or archive messages, and each district and college or university has its own guidelines. *Archiving* a message puts the message into a folder that can be accessed later. This message is "stored for later," but out of the Inbox. *Deleting* messages removes them from Canvas Inbox altogether and they can no longer be accessed.

REMEMBER

Each K–12 district or higher-education institution may have policies in place for communication with students. Please make sure you follow all school, district, college, or university guidelines as they pertain to deleting and archiving all communications.

You can delete messages at any time when you no longer need them. You can delete individual messages or multiple conversations at once by clicking inside the checkbox next to those messages and then selecting the Delete icon, as shown in Figure 6-12. Before the Canvas Inbox deletes the selected item(s), a confirmation dialog box appears asking you to confirm deletion, as shown in Figure 6-13. Click OK to confirm.

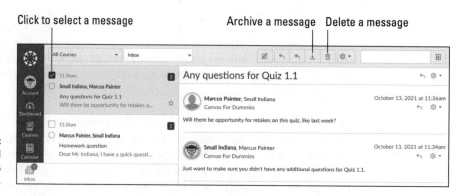

FIGURE 6-12:
Delete and Archive messages icons.

FIGURE 6-13:
Confirm deletion dialog box.

TIP

Any new messages sent by your students within a conversation you deleted will still appear in your Inbox.

Deleting a message isn't the only tool at your disposal for clearing up your Inbox. Archiving a conversation is a great way to move messages out of your Inbox without fear of losing important information contained within them. Just a note: You cannot archive *sent* messages currently in Canvas Inbox.

The archiving process is much like the deletion process. To archive a message or a group of messages, select the message or messages you wish to archive and then select the Archive icon in the Inbox toolbar shown earlier in Figure 6-12.

TIP

A favorite feature of archiving conversations is the ability to view these messages in the filter option drop-down menu. By selecting the Archived option in the Inbox drop-down menu, you now can see all of those messages you've cleaned up from your Inbox.

Implementing a Deliberate Communication Plan

In this section, we present some ways to use the Canvas Inbox to increase and improve your communication with your students. We believe communication plays a crucial role in building community, but we also recognize the dangers of too much access. In today's world, you can't be too careful when it comes to sending messages to students. The potential pitfalls, misunderstandings, intentional or unintentional tone of voice associated with one-to-one communications with students, parents, guardians, and even coworkers can be enough for some educators to avoid digital communication altogether. In rare cases over the years, we have heard fellow teachers go so far as to state that they avoid communication home to parents and guardians because they have felt that it only fosters additional *drama*. We believe that employing a couple of educational practices can help this challenge of communication.

TIP

We believe, as most educators do, that there must be a balance in the *amount* and *type* of communication from teacher to students, and teacher to parents and caregivers. It can't come as a shock that if you only communicate home to caregivers about negative issues with their child, the extra communication breeds more of that *drama* we mentioned earlier. *Duh!* This is where we, as educators, have to be deliberate about having a communication plan. How are we going to approach parent contacts? How often and what type of one-to-one student contact will we endeavor to have each week, month, or grading period? Heck, we have worked with some districts that have explicitly stated minimum communication requirements for teachers to execute and document on a weekly, monthly, and quarterly basis.

You may not need to sit down and design an extremely detailed communication plan. However, that may work for you. You may decide to come up with a plan within a Google Doc or Microsoft Word document. Marcus depends on his online calendar to remind him of his communication plan. He typically schedules events on his calendar like the following:

>> Canvas message my most outstanding student(s) and/or classes from the past few weeks and let them know I see them.

>> Canvas message my struggling students. Offer further support, maybe a pep talk.

>> Canvas message a student who needs to be noticed, even if that student isn't excelling or failing academically. Don't forget the middle!

>> Canvas message any student with whom I shared a connection this week.

>> Contact parents with positive information.

TIP

Add a calendar event randomly for a week or two from now. It doesn't matter what day it is. Call it your *Good Vibes Reminder.* We stole this one from an amazing educator named Stevie who, when feeling defeated, exhausted, and frustrated with teaching, makes a concerted effort to contact a student or a caregiver just to celebrate them. We love this idea and we love that Stevie has a plan to counteract any bad vibes with powerfully good ones.

These are just example calendar events or reminders to consider implementing to strengthen communication. You can put these items on your personal calendar as weekly or monthly reminders to yourself, and not to be seen by students, of course.

For Marcus, putting these types of events on his calendar acted as reminders to carve out time and to be deliberate about communication. Maybe you're an uber-computer geek and love spreadsheets — go for it! The point is to make it part of your weekly and monthly routine because if something is important, we want to make it part of a routine. Communication is important, but it is also hard work. Thus, educators have to really laser-focus in on what our goals are and what we need to do to make those goals reality.

TIP

Whatever your situation may be, communication with compassion and balance is vital. Students must feel that connection with you, even if they aren't the most disruptive or most exceptional student in the room. Why should *those* students get all the attention, right?

What about young Marcus? He's the middling student who earns A's, B's and an occasional C. He is mortified to speak in class. However, he is always engaged and pays close attention. He meets deadlines and gives his best effort. He blends right in and falls right through most cracks. How are you going to ensure that *he* feels seen, recognized for his efforts in class, and is not forgotten?

We whole-heartedly believe that Canvas provides educators with the tools to drastically improve communication. Canvas Inbox centralizes our communication without need for additional third-party tools. We love that once again, the things we need are right there at the tips of our Panda paws whenever we are using Canvas LMS for communication.

CONNECTING WITH YOUR STUDENTS IS KEY

Whether you are a veteran educator or a first-year student teacher, connecting with your students is a key element in driving community and fostering relationships in your classroom. Building connection through communication happens to be a passion of ours. We have spent countless hours with educators around the world talking about how a single message can make an impact on a student's day or life.

Lucky for us, that ability to message and remind students of upcoming deadlines, events, and schedule changes has always been *baked-in* to the tool we love. However, don't forget that our communication with students must go beyond simply being informative. Students don't need a teacher for that. Students need teachers who provide the information associated with learning, but more important, students need that human connection, compassion, coaching, support, and belief that we, as educators, can provide through quick notes and messages within Canvas Inbox. Those quick check-ins are far more powerful than any grade you can give. This approach to communication goes back to what we discuss earlier in this chapter about establishing a specific communication plan for your school year. That plan must include a focus on fostering connections through messaging, in much the same way you do in person.

As middle school and high school teachers, we both focused a great deal on engaging students in conversations, asking them how they are doing, asking them about their outside school activities, and so on. Those interactions are the ones students remember. We can further support those relationships with our messaging in Canvas Inbox. Think of communication in Canvas Inbox as the digital fist bump, high five, hug, or elbow tap.

Your Secret Weapon: Using the Media Recorder

In the section, "Composing a Message" earlier in this chapter, you may have noticed that when you select the Media File icon to attach a media file to an Inbox message, you are presented with what we feel is a pretty killer feature: the Media Recorder. (We first take a look at this tool in Chapter 5.) The Media Recorder is built directly into Canvas Inbox, and it is what sets Canvas Inbox apart from your current communication platform.

TIP

Creating video or audio recordings within your messages allows you to be *you*. We believe that using the Media Recorder for communication within Canvas Inbox takes the guesswork out of communication and interpretation and enables you to level up your communication game and build better relationships.

Let's think about something we have all experienced in our personal and professional lives: interpreting the tone of written text. You know exactly what we are talking about. Let's kick you a couple of scenarios and we dare you to dispute them:

> **Scenario 1:** You teach seventh grade language arts. You have five other teachers on your team. Prior to your scheduled team meeting or department meeting, you receive an email from the team lead that says the following:
>
> "At tomorrow's meeting, we need to discuss your progress, or lack thereof, on curriculum map alignment, rethink your formative assessments for next quarter, and we also need to be sure to confront the issues surrounding our upcoming state testing schedule."

Seems mundane enough, right? Whether it was intentional or not, there are some somewhat confrontational words and phrases here, and definitely some connotations. There is some unpacking that could happen when reading this email. You see some possible sarcasm, but you are unclear if it is indeed sarcasm or a bit of a jab. You see words like "rethink" and "confront," which leave a great deal of ambiguity about the messaging, as well. We have all received this type of email and commenced in attempting to interpret the true meaning of those words. In the end, it is unclear, we are unable to decipher the tone, and we are basically paralyzed with anxiety until the meeting.

Now, that example involved educated adult professionals. How would a similarly worded email or message be interpreted by one of your students? What if that student is a struggling reader? What if that student is an English as a Second Language (ESL) student? Our point is this: We, as educators, can take the burden of interpreting the tone of text off of the plates of our students by leveraging the Media Recorder within Canvas Inbox.

TIP

We have found that recording yourself on video and with audio takes so much of the guesswork out of the equation for students. They know when you're being sarcastic or joking because they get to see that wink of an eye, or that wry smile. They better understand your tone because they can hear every inflection of your voice. Using the Media Recorder for communication could very well be the most impactful element in the entire LMS!

Scenario 2: A text conversation between Marcus and his wife.

Marcus: Hey, I think I'm gonna go for a long bike ride. I know we were supposed to go meet your dad for dinner though. Can I skip it?

Carrie: Fine.

Is it fine? Of course, it's not! There is a tone. There are a lot of underlying thoughts and feelings here, and I think we have all probably experienced something like this in our lives. What was communicated in text was clearly not the actual vibe or tone, right?

Again, transpose this into your classroom communication. Long story short: Our text-based communication is not enough. It is not going to provide the proper level of understanding for students. We can communicate much more efficiently when we use video.

Marcus' rule of thumb is: If your instructions require more than three steps to accomplish, then you must include a video along with your text instructions. As former technology coaches in our districts, we both have taken this approach. What does it accomplish for teachers? It allows you to ensure that your communication is clear and concise. It saves you time, because, let's face it, those long, multistep emails are hard to compose. And, most important, video engages the viewer more than text does on a screen.

What does using video to communicate accomplish for our students? It provides them with additional pathways toward understanding because they can now read the message, hear your voice, and see your face. It also provides students with a built-in workflow.

TIP

When students have a video available to them, whether it is a quick note, a check-in, information about upcoming due dates, or instructions for today's assignment, the video allows students to Watch:Pause:Do:Review. They can watch the video, pause when necessary, do what needs to be done, and have the ability to review for their own understanding.

Implementing a deliberate communication plan like Marcus's calendar event approach we discuss earlier, while always recognizing tone, intent, and using the Media Recorder inside the Canvas Inbox can help convey compassionate and thoughtful communication with students and caregivers alike.

Chapter **7**

Using the Canvas Calendar

We get it. You've got calendars, upon calendars, upon calendars. You have an online calendar through your institution, a planner on your desk, the calendar on your smartphone, a refrigerator calendar at home, and maybe even a day-to-day tear-away calendar with cute little pictures of kittens and quotes that say things like "Hang in there!" and "The day will be purrfect!"

Adding yet another calendar to the list may feel a bit overwhelming, but the Calendar in Canvas LMS is more than just a place to remind you (and students) when items are due. It can be your go-to tool for maintaining a timeline for the smallest of projects to organizing information as vast as the entire roadmap of the course that year.

Throughout this chapter, you discover the fundamentals of how to use the Canvas Calendar as well as how the Calendar integrates seamlessly into other tools and features within Canvas. You also see how having students use the Calendar can help teach them valuable life skills around accomplishing tasks and meeting deadlines. Students are always being asked to multitask. As a former student yourself, you too had to devise plans, create procedures, and depend on outside sources to accomplish tasks. Today's learners are not that much different. In fact, Marcus has joked often about how today's learners actually believe they are great multitaskers, when, in actuality, their "multitasking" is better described as doing a bunch of things at a subpar level. As a relatively new triathlete, Marcus has told friends, "Why be average at one sport, when I can be below average at *three* sports?"

Canvas Calendar provides a fortified solution to help students prioritize workflow, meet deadlines, and become better multitaskers.

Exploring the Canvas Calendar

The Canvas Calendar can help you and your students organize, prioritize, and manage current and upcoming events and assignments. Acting as a central location for all of your course assignments and events, it is a great way to view all of your upcoming tasks at a glance.

The Calendar is accessed by selecting the Calendar option in the Global Navigation Menu on the left side of the Canvas screen. When selected, the main Calendar window appears, as shown in Figure 7-1. The view defaults to month view, but you can choose to view the calendar in week or agenda view as well.

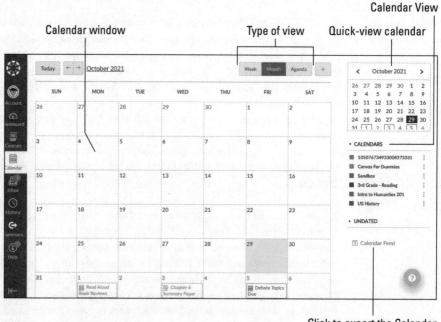

FIGURE 7-1: The Canvas Calendar.

Calendar is a global feature in Canvas, meaning it includes all assignments and events for all courses in one place, regardless of whether you are in week, month, or agenda view. Your calendar can be filtered by course as well by selecting and deselecting the course in the Calendar View section that appears in the sidebar on the right side of the screen. In addition to the calendars for each course, this section includes all calendars with the Canvas Calendar. All calendars are identified by a separate color.

If you have ever used any other digital or web-based calendar, this interface is probably familiar to you, which is yet another reason to love it.

You can add both *events* and *assignments* to the Calendar. Both can be added at any time and are created by selecting the + button that appears in the top-right corner of the Calendar window. (More on creating events and assignments later in this chapter.)

As is the case with any other calendar, an event can be a variety of things for teachers and learners. We often see educators leverage the events item on the Calendar in any or all of the following ways:

>> Create basic quiz and exam reminders for the week

>> Note any changes to the schedule for the week (for example, "Meet in the auditorium for the Drug and Alcohol Awareness Convocation")

>> Set reminders to students about due dates for larger projects (such as adding events as reminders leading up to a big due date)

These sorts of items are considered *non-graded events*, as opposed to an assignment, which appear on the course Assignments page or in the Gradebook. Think of these events as reminders to students to read content before coming to class for a group discussion, for example. Again, Canvas LMS provides the necessary tools to effectively and efficiently communicate with our students.

TIP

By creating a non-graded event within your Canvas Calendar, what are you actually doing? You're providing the same type of support and scaffolding within the platform that you do in class. If students were staring off into space, dreaming of playing Roblox or planning their next TikTok or Instagram post, they may have missed what you just said in class. Now, you have leveled support built in to your Canvas course as well.

Adjusting Calendar Views

We believe the only true way to save your sanity in any calendar application is to get familiar with ways to filter your view. This can be especially true for the Canvas Calendar. The default display is always to show you *all* the courses you are either enrolled in or teaching. This can lead to a calendar that is an absolute mess. In the same way you have to maintain your corner of the Canvas jungle by cleaning up your Canvas Inbox, you'll want to do the same here in the Canvas Calendar.

Selecting calendars and changing course colors

As shown earlier in Figure 7-1, on the right side of the Calendar is the Calendar View, which contains the list of courses you are associated with. The colors of each calendar in the Calendar View are assigned by default, but you can change that color by selecting the Options menu (the "three dots menu") to the right of the course name (see Figure 7-2). So if you want to further customize these calendars you have that ability.

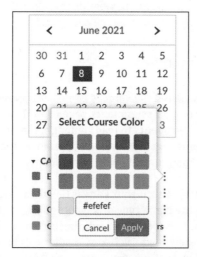

FIGURE 7-2: Selecting the Course Color in the Calendar View.

To turn a particular calendar "off" (in other words, to no longer view its contents in the main Calendar window), just click the colored checkbox next to the calendar to deselect it, as shown in Figure 7-3. This "grays out" that course's calendar in Calendar View, and the items are no longer shown in the main Calendar window.

Click to turn a calendar on or off

To turn a calendar back "on," just click the checkbox again. Using the same approach, you can also turn calendars on and off to, for example, only view a particular course's calendar. All in all, turning on and off calendars from view is a great way to filter what you are seeing based on your needs in the moment.

REMEMBER

You can only add or edit Calendar items in calendars that are turned on (in other words, those that aren't deselected in the Calendar View). We discuss how to add events and assignments later in this chapter, but it is important to remember that any adjustments to Calendar items can only occur in calendars that are selected — turned on — in the Calendar View.

Choosing week, month, or agenda views

You can adjust the view of the Calendar window by selecting a weekly, monthly, or agenda view at the top of the Calendar window.

Week view is exactly what it sounds like, Pandas. Here you see your Calendar events and due dates listed by time vertically, and by day horizontally, as shown in Figure 7-4. Week view is nice to "zoom in" a bit and get a good look at what's happening for any or all of your selected courses for that given week. We like this view as it is a good way to reflect on the pace of things in a given week. Are you getting too monotonous in your cadence throughout the week? Are you, the teacher, feeling bored? Maybe it's because you have been stuck in a routine and need to "shake it up" a bit? If so, the week view is a nice place to possibly notice that and adjust.

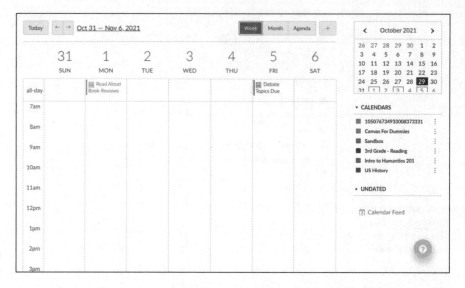

FIGURE 7-4:
Week view.

Month view, of course, is the gold standard of Calendar views (see Figure 7-5). It's what the vast majority of folks look at most often. Just remember that you have options. Options aren't scary or frustrating if you understand why they exist. In Canvas LMS, Calendar views provide you and your learners the ability to zoom in and out depending on how you want to focus your attention as you look ahead.

Figure 7-6 shows the Agenda view, which you can think of as a sort of daily view that runs vertically. In this view you see Calendar events and due dates listed by day and date from top to bottom like a scrolling list. Some users love it, some users, not so much. Marcus thinks this view is nice to look at during a given day, but he always finds himself clicking back and forth between Agenda view and the Month view.

Canvas is built to help you be more efficient. There isn't a single best way to use the Calendar function. It is always up to you to decide how you want to customize or filter your views inside the tool.

REMEMBER

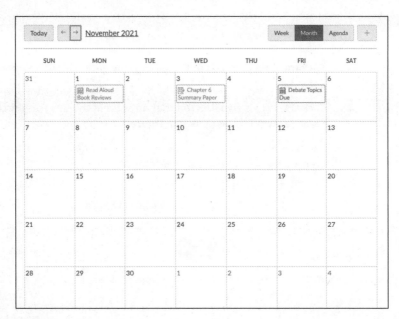

FIGURE 7-5:
Month view.

FIGURE 7-6:
Agenda view.

Adding Events

Adding an event or assignment to the Canvas Calendar is as easy as a few clicks, and both involve a similar process.

To add an event to your Canvas Calendar, follow these steps:

1. **Click the Calendar icon in the Global Navigation Menu to open the Calendar.**

2. **Click the + (plus sign) button that appears in the upper-right corner of the Calendar window, as shown in Figure 7-7.**

   Alternatively, you can click inside any date in the Calendar window. The Edit Event dialog box opens, as shown in Figure 7-8.

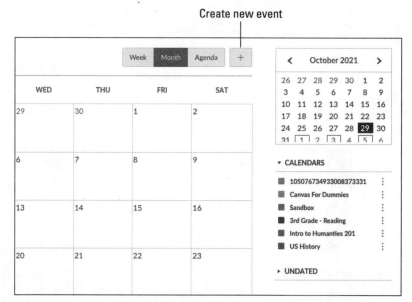

FIGURE 7-7:
Using the + button to add a new event.

3. **Select the Event tab and fill out the required information.**

   To create an event, you simply need to give it a title such as, "Convocation." Next, set the date and time frame for that event. If there is a location, add that. Then, you can choose to which calendar(s) to assign the event.

4. **When you are finished adding the event details, click the Submit button.**

   The new event is added to your calendar.

TIP

You can add additional resources and links to create a slightly more detailed or engaging Calendar event by selecting the More Options button in the Edit Event dialog box. This button opens the Rich Content Editor (RCE), as shown in Figure 7-9. So now if you like, you can create an event that includes all the magic available within the RCE. Simply add the event details in the RCE and then select Create Event. The event is then added to your calendar. See Chapter 5 for more on using the RCE.

FIGURE 7-8:
The Edit Event dialog box, where you can add new events and assignments.

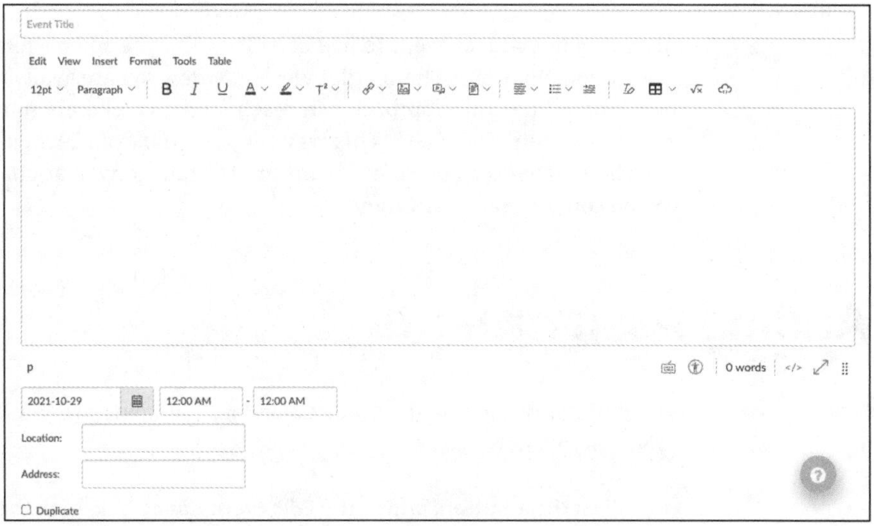

FIGURE 7-9:
More Options opens the RCE.

An added bonus to creating an event in the RCE is that you are able to duplicate that event on any schedule you like. Select the Duplicate checkbox at the bottom of the RCE to set how often you want the event to reoccur (see Figure 7-10). You can create recurring events on the Canvas Calendar and even number them if you choose.

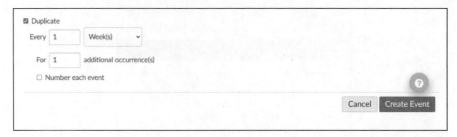

FIGURE 7-10:
Creating a
reoccurring event
in the RCE.

As you may have already discovered from reading this book, both of us are huge proponents of finding any and all ways to connect with students within a digital space like Canvas LMS, and we use Calendar events for just this purpose. Marcus commonly creates Calendar events that provide helpful information about an upcoming quiz, exam, or project. Being a video geek, he'd create event titles along the lines of, "Don't Miss This!" or "ICYMI" and then include a helpful video either from YouTube or of himself providing additional support, hints, or helpful content for an upcoming assessment.

TIP

Also, why not add an event to just say "Hi!"? Maybe add a short reminder to students about your office hours that week or when you are available to provide extra help. Sometimes this approach can reach students who are too nervous or shy to ask for the help they need. This way they see the event, when you are available, and then just show up. No awkward or stressful conversations needed. Students can be complicated, can't they?

Adding Assignments

To create an assignment within Calendar, the steps are similar to creating an event. Here's how:

1. **Click the + button, and in the Edit Event dialog box, click the Assignment tab, as shown in Figure 7-11.**

   Here you are able to create what we like to call a "quick add" assignment. Not many bells and whistles here.

2. **Give the assignment a title and due date, choose which calendar to add it to, and choose which assignment group you want the assignment to be in.**

   To select the assignment group for the assignment, click the down arrow next to Assignments in the Group textbox to open a drop-down menu of options. (See Chapter 10 for more on creating assignments groups.)

3. **Toggle the Publish button on and then click the Submit button.**

   The assignment is added to your calendar.

FIGURE 7-11:
Adding an
assignment.

This is a sort of quick-and-dirty approach to creating an assignment within Calendar, and let's face it, educators are detail-oriented beings. We want to be absolutely certain that what we provide to learners is exactly what we want and how we want it. So once again may we recommend clicking the More Options button here as well?

When you click the More Options button when creating an assignment within the Calendar, you are taken to the conventional Create New Assignment screen where you can add all the bells and whistles you want to make sure your students know exactly what to do and how to do it. Be sure to check out Chapter 10 for more details on creating assignments. Consider this the assignment *appeteaser.*

WARNING

Some new Pandas become confused by this ability to create an assignment from within Calendar. Canvas is flexible and enables you to create an assignment in multiple different locations. However, no matter where you create an assignment, being diligent about the content, settings, and due dates is vital.

REMEMBER

No matter how you create an assignment or where within Canvas LMS you create an assignment, if you give it a due date, it shows up in the Calendar for both you and your students auto*magically.*

Change Dates Here, Sync Everywhere

We recognize that many of you may have already created assignments on the Assignments page in the Courses area of Canvas, and the Calendar has a great built-in feature that allows you to adjust those assignment due dates with just a few clicks of the mouse.

If you open the Calendar window and select an assignment, you can click and drag it to any date on your calendar. If you want to further schedule out these assignments, you can click the assignment to open it and adjust the due dates. This is a quick way to make date adjustments to content because once that change is saved in Calendar, it is filtered across the entire platform. That means the Gradebook, Assignments, and To Do tabs are automatically in sync. This approach to adjusting deadlines is extremely efficient and likely to be a common practice for you as you continue your Canvas journey.

WARNING

Note that the Until date — the date after which students can no longer submit the assignment — does not automatically adjust when you update an assignment's due date in the Calendar. To adjust this date, you need to open the assignment and manually update it.

TIP

Regardless of where and how you create an assignment, going to the Calendar and clicking on that assignment is one of the quickest, most efficient ways to adjust that assignment after it has been created. Need to quickly change the due date? Go to the Calendar, click the assignment, edit the date, and submit. Boom!

No matter how you create your lesson plans, we all know that within minutes of you starting to teach that plan, you are making adjustments to it due to the nature of teaching. We all create these lesson plans and curriculum maps as exactly that: plans and maps. Invariably, our plans can and will change, and we adjust to the new plan. Often when you follow the map to get from Point A to Point B, you realize there is an obstacle in the way. No problem. You reroute and still get there. This flexibility and adaptability is ultimately what makes educators so amazing.

With all that being said, the ability to simply drag and drop and quickly adjust details of an assignment within the Canvas Calendar is the equivalent to what Marcus used to do when teaching. He would create his lesson plans two weeks in advance and simply write down the plan for each day in a spiral notebook. Inevitably, within the first ten minutes of his first period on Monday, he would already be drawing big, obnoxious arrows in his notebook, moving the things that he didn't get to accomplish to the next class period. Canvas Calendar allows you to do the same thing, and because it syncs everywhere, nobody is ever confused about the changes that are made throughout the course of a day, week, month, or quarter.

Integrating the Canvas Calendar with Other Calendars

Let's be real for a second. Calendar in Canvas is fantastic, but probably underutilized. Why? Likely because we all have a calendar application we currently use and like (or are at least used to) and having to juggle more than one calendar can be challenging, even for the most techy of us Pandas.

Because of this, Canvas has made it easy to integrate and sync your Canvas Calendar to your favorite tools. Whether you are a Google Calendar user or have a calendar application on your desktop, you can subscribe to your Canvas Calendar.

WARNING

Things are about to get techy. We don't go through every nuanced step in the process of adding the Calendar into other tools, but we offer steps to get you started. Be sure to check out your calendar app's user guide for more information.

The basic steps to integrate your Canvas Calendar into a third-party calendar app are as follows:

1. **Open your Canvas Calendar from the Global Navigation Menu and select the Calendar Feed link (refer to Figure 7-1).**

   This brings up a URL that you can then import into your favorite third-party calendar app, as shown in Figure 7-12.

2. **Within a third-party calendar app of your choice, open Settings and look for a place to add a calendar using a URL.**

3. **Copy and paste the URL from the Calendar Feed dialog box into the calendar app and follow any additional prompts as needed.**

4. **If you need to download an ICS (iCalendar) file, click the "Click to Calendar Feed" link and follow the prompts.**

   Once you've pasted the URL into your calendar app of choice, you can begin to see all of your Canvas Calendar events and reminders populate within your other calendar app. Though it may sound like strange techy voodoo, this is a pretty common strategy for professionals to get all of their planning into one streamlined, centralized location.

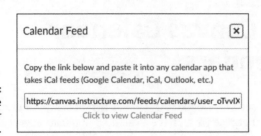

FIGURE 7-12:
Copying the
Calendar
Feed URL.

The Power of the Calendar to Teach Life Skills

As lifelong learners ourselves, we understand the importance of creating and adhering to habits that continue to improve our lives, make us more successful, or make us more happy Pandas. Organizational skills are those skills that take practice, and using the Canvas Calendar with students is a great way to encourage them to start working on their time-management skills.

We believe that part of our duties as educators is to always try to support not only the content learning of our students, but also the *act* of learning as well. And the best part of focusing on these sorts of life skills, or what some may call *soft skills*, is that we educators don't necessarily have to teach them directly. We can simply teach through modeling the best practices, which in this case, in the consistent use of a calendar.

TIP

It is absolutely recommended that as you may encounter the need to adjust events on your course calendar, you go ahead and show students how you do it. In this way, you are accomplishing a number of things. First, you are simply showing your own *edu-flexibility*, and yes, we just made that word up. Second, by modeling the clicks to change something in the Canvas Calendar, you are teaching the skill to your students. Finally, you are revisiting your own work and showing your learners the bigger picture. Think of this as a moment to zoom out from today, to the week or month. What a great way to continue to support and provide context to your students.

REMEMBER

As educators, it is our responsibility to help instill these life skills not only within our fields of study, but also because these skills are invaluable toward all learners' success in their current and future lives. The ability to schedule events, create reminders, follow expectations, visualize both the micro and macro levels of the work ahead, and the ability to meet deadlines are infinitely valuable to students of any age. By using Canvas Calendar, students practice that ability inside a tool that doesn't require extra learning on their part. Again, Canvas Calendar provides the tool for us and, again, it's right where we need it, when we need it.

DON'T FORGET THE TO-DO LIST!

Of course, we also have the to-do list at our fingertips to help keep our Panda lives in order. As we discuss in Chapter 3, The To Do section appears on the right side of your home page within a given course. We think of the To Do section as a cleaner and neater form of sticky-note reminders. Now, believe it or not, the To Do section causes quite a bit of controversy within the world of Canvas. Some Pandas love it, use it, and depend on it. Other Pandas wish it didn't exist at all. This is the point where you should be picturing a bunch of educators marching down a street in the dead of night, brandishing torches and weaponry to battle over the To Do section.

Regardless of which side of the To Do section fence you land on, there is no disputing the basic value of having this element available for both teachers and students alike. The battle generally becomes whether you choose to use the To Do section or whether you choose to keep track of things by other means. Some folks use a notes app on their smartphone, like Google Keep or Microsoft OneNote. Some have work spaces at home or at work that look as if about nine million sticky notes were loaded into a T-shirt gun and shot directly at their desks. And still there are others, we won't name names, who write things on their hands! No matter what, we're sure we can all agree that having a to-do list is better than not having one.

3
Living That
Panda Life

Find out how using the Canvas LMS communication tools can directly influence engagement in your classroom.

Discover how the Media Recorder can help foster communication by letting students hear your voice.

Become familiar with modules — the backbone of the learning experience in Canvas LMS — and how to create and edit modules in your courses.

Figure out how to add instructional content to pages and build meaningful discussions.

Find out how Canvas SpeedGrader can help you efficiently evaluate individual students and group assignments, giving you more time to spend on teaching.

Chapter **8**

Communicating the Canvas Way

Whether you're a district administrator, school counselor, building administrator, teacher, football coach, or the prom committee sponsor, the communication tools within Canvas LMS help you make learning personal for your learners, help you streamline communication within your schools and institutions, and help you clearly communicate with stakeholders. How often have you thought, *This meeting could've been an email!* Follow that statement with a hard eye-roll and we can all relate.

In this chapter, you take a look at the communication tools available in Canvas LMS and how they can help all Pandas communicate clearly in the forest of learning. You start by looking at the easiest way to get new course information to your students — Canvas Announcements — and then taking a look at how using the Media Recorder in your day-to-day Canvas life can help you better connect with students. There is no better way to build community, relationships, and connection with your students than by letting them hear your voice when they are learning remotely.

Creating Canvas Announcements

Want to know the easiest way to get new information to your students? The answer is Canvas Announcements. Announcements are simply "posts" that show up for specific courses you teach.

You may already be familiar with what that little red dot means in the corner of apps on your smartphone. It's a notification! Well, announcements within Canvas are similarly easy to understand. Whenever there is an announcement for a course, the Announcement icon appears in the lower-left corner of the Course Card, as shown in Figure 8-1. And whenever there is a new announcement, a little red notification dot shows up on the Announcement icon.

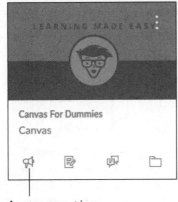

FIGURE 8-1:
The Announcement icon on the Course Card.

Announcement icon

Now that you know what an announcement is and where you can easily notice new ones, let's walk through how to create an announcement for one of your courses in Canvas LMS.

To create an announcement in your course, follow these steps:

1. **Navigate to your Course Card from the Dashboard, as shown in Figure 8-2, and click it to open the course.**

2. **Click the Announcements link in the Course Navigation Menu.**

   The Announcements window opens, as shown in Figure 8-3.

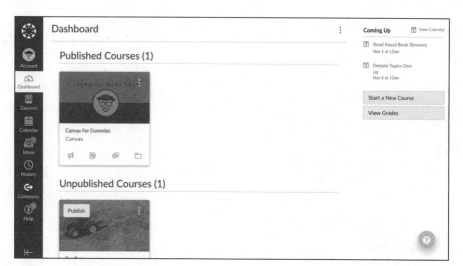

FIGURE 8-2:
The Course Card
on the Canvas
Dashboard.

Click to open Announcements

FIGURE 8-3:
Open
Announcements
from the Course
Navigation Menu.

3. **Click the +Announcement button that appears in the upper-right corner to open the Create New announcement window shown in Figure 8-4.**

4. **Type a title for the announcement in the Topic Title field.**

   And you guessed it — we are back in the Rich Content Editor (RCE).

5. **Type your announcement text in the content area of the RCE.**

   You have all the RCE functionality available to you here within an announcement. (For more on working with the RCE, see Chapter 5.)

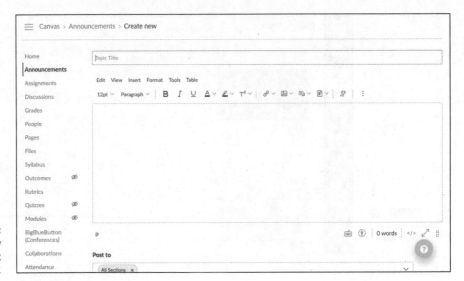

FIGURE 8-4:
The Create New
announcement
window.

6. **Specify which section(s) of your course should receive the announcement in the Post To drop-down menu, as shown in Figure 8-5.**

    By default, Canvas Announcements sends announcements to all sections of your course.

7. **(Optional) Add an attachment to your announcement by selecting the Choose File button and navigating to the file you want to include.**

8. **Select any special options for the announcement in the Options area.**

    A few options are displayed to allow you to accomplish a number of tasks we think are pretty killer features, such as:

    - *Delay posting:* Allows you to schedule the announcement for a future time and/or date.

    - *Allow users to comment:* Turns on commenting (but don't worry, they can never be anonymous).

    Additionally, you can have your students reply to the post before they can see additional replies.

9. **When you've finished your announcement, click Save.**

Once you click Save, that announcement is available (visible) to the students in that course. They can either click the Announcement icon with the red dot notification, or click the Announcements link in the Course Navigation Menu on the left side of the course screen.

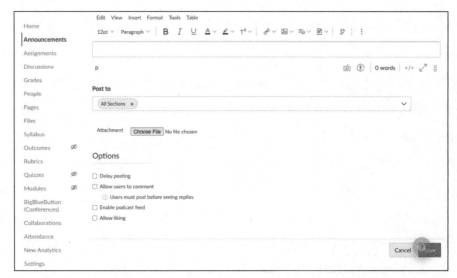

FIGURE 8-5:
Select which
courses should
receive the
announcement in
the Post To
drop-down menu.

Multiple courses, same announcement

As much as we love the flexibility within Canvas LMS, one thing Marcus struggled with for years was the need and desire to send the same announcement to multiple courses. In his case, he often needed to publish the same announcement to his three sophomore English courses or an announcement to both of his AP English courses. For years, he would open two tabs of Canvas and copy and paste the announcement contents from one course to the other. Talk about tedious.

Thankfully, the days of copying and pasting are long gone. Now, it is as simple as a click or two to copy an announcement directly to another course. It's almost too easy.

To send one announcement out to multiple classes, follow these steps:

1. **Click the Announcements link from the Course Navigation Menu to open the Announcements window shown in Figure 8-6.**

2. **Navigate to the announcement you want to duplicate and click the announcement to open it.**

3. **Select the Options menu ("three dots menu") in the upper-right corner of the announcement.**

4. **Select Copy To, as shown in Figure Figure 8-7.**

   The Copy To dialog box opens, as shown in Figure 8-8.

FIGURE 8-6:
The Announcements window.

FIGURE 8-7:
Selecting Copy To from your announcement.

FIGURE 8-8:
Selecting courses to copy the announcement to.

5. **Click the drop-down arrow in the Copy To dialog box to select the courses you'd like to copy the announcement to.**

6. **Click Copy to send the announcement to the additional courses.**

TIP

Can this particular awesomeness help our K-5 Pandas, too? It sure can. We have a large number of K-5 educators who are in fine arts, rotationals, or what we have called them here in Indiana, Specials Classes. Elementary-level physical education, music, and technology teachers all can capitalize on the ability to quickly copy an announcement from one course to another. And, obviously, if you teach multiple sections of a course in grades six through higher education, this communication element within Canvas Announcements is an absolutely wonderful thing.

Timing and scope of announcements

Not only does Canvas LMS provide an efficient, easy-to-use, and intuitive communication platform with Canvas Announcements, but also it provides the gift of flexibility for all users.

When we talk about the concept of the *timing* of announcements, what we are really talking about is an educator's ability to customize and focus announcements in ways that best help learners, fellow educators, and community members. Often, we, as educators, post announcements to our courses in a similar manner to what we would do without an LMS. Or in our experience, when something pops into our heads, we just say it to our students so that we know we've reminded them.

TIP

We are total fanboys of Canvas Announcements because it is the easiest "lift" in Canvas LMS. It is the entry point and the one thing all new Pandas can immediately leverage to help make learning personal for students. Again, because of the RCE, the options are almost endless for teachers. Don't be intimidated by the options, the flexibility, and the freedom. This book is about introducing you to the basic elements of Canvas LMS and inspiring you to function with fidelity in Canvas, while also learning how to continue to be curious as you make your way on your Canvas LMS journey.

Schedule announcements

The greatest advantage within Canvas Announcements may be the ability to schedule them. Again, the built-in flexibility of Canvas LMS allows us, as educators, the freedom to rethink and reevaluate how we do things in our classrooms. Working with Canvas LMS as long as we have, we have had the advantage of realizing that scheduling out announcements can provide a yellow brick road of pertinent reminders for learners.

For example, if there is a big test coming up this Friday, you can simply set an announcement for Monday and maybe another one for Thursday. Maybe it is as simple as, "Don't forget that we have our big *Macbeth* exam on Friday!" And of course, as all educators have the tendency to do, we reference the upcoming exam a few dozen times a day during class. However, what we really love is the concept of timing and focusing those scheduled Canvas LMS announcements.

TIP

Try scheduling some of those announcements to publish *during* your class and wait to see who is engaged. Marcus has even gone so far as to schedule hints and guidance concerning the classroom discussion. That announcement can be scheduled to publish before class begins and can act as a sort of guiding question for students. Pose a question as an announcement that is published during your class and during a time when students may be on their devices.

Create Easter eggs

We adore the idea of creating Easter eggs using Canvas Announcements. Simply create an announcement, schedule it to publish during a time when students are likely to be using their devices, and instruct them to do something, pose a question, share an action item, and then sit back and see who discovers the Easter egg first and acts on it. Regardless of your learning environment, Canvas needs to play an integral role. It provides teachers like you the ability to clone yourself and become more effective, efficient, and impactful on student learning.

This example is just one of many that help you use announcements in an unconventional, but fun and effective way.

Vary the type of announcement

Another proven approach to using Canvas Announcements is to be less standardized with your announcements. Because you have the RCE at your fingertips in announcements, you have an absolute wealth of possibilities in the types of communication you do. For example, rather than posting a basic reminder for the upcoming *Macbeth* exam, you could post a short YouTube video that covers a key concept or moment that is covered on the exam. Marcus has done this to tease what the essay question was going to be on an exam. Therefore, students who were engaged in the Canvas LMS course and saw the announcement and watched the video, were better prepared for the exam on Friday.

Target specific groups

Yet another application of Canvas Announcements is to consider the ease of publishing those announcements to different groups within a course or to multiple courses at once. If you have created sections within your course for the purposes of differentiating instruction or creating reading-level groups, for example, you can create and publish announcements that are specific to those sections. What a great way to foster connection to all of your learners and customize your communication. In the same way that you may assign different content to certain sections within a course, you can customize your communication as well.

Be careful with how you name those groups because students can see them.

As we've shared numerous times before, Marcus is the Canvas LMS "OG," or *original gangsta.* (Apologies for our blatant and Dad joke–level attempt to sound cool.) Marcus thinks back to days of yore when announcements in Canvas were simply text-only. Fast forward to around 2017, and he started leveraging Media Recorder within his high school English Canvas courses. What he loved most was the fact that he felt that he could cover more content, be more engaging, and make learning more personal for students with a video, than he could with a long, drawn-out text-based announcement.

One of the simplest ways to "level up" your announcements is to simply add audio and video content. Let's take a look at how that works and why it is one of our favorite Panda Powers.

A CANVAS ANNOUNCEMENTS USE CASE

Eddie always remembers his first time using Canvas Announcements with his fellow teachers when his school first purchased Canvas. Before then he had been searching for a tool that would not only relay information, but would also allow him to show his glowing and effervescent personality (place winking emoji here). Although a number of third-party tools accomplish these goals, he never felt completely satisfied with the results. So before typing a single word into that first announcement, he clicked the option to "Add Video, Media Recorder" (which you get to check out later in this chapter). He recorded a short video in his closet — a makeshift studio created for recording our podcast — and welcomed the educators to the professional development course he had built in Canvas.

Within minutes, he received numerous comments from his teammates discussing the video. This more personal approach to communication established a safe space where all ideas were welcome and a place where all information and expectations were known. Before they knew it, a full-blown discussion had broken out on the ways Canvas Announcements would close the communication gap in his fellow teachers' classes. There were feelings of immediate comfort, connection, and safety, all established simply by Eddie turning on his camera and microphone.

Media Recorder: Letting Students Hear Your Voice

Your voice is more powerful than text on a screen.

We don't think that's a bold statement. However, with our cultural dependence on smartphones, it can be a forgotten medium to focus on communication with our voices. Think about how often you call people versus how often you text or email them. To be honest, we find ourselves receiving mostly spam phone calls, and if we do get a call from an actual human who exists in our contacts, we are generally expecting it to be an emergency. For all of these reasons, we urge Pandas to focus on utilizing the Media Recorder within Canvas Announcements in order to make learning personal in a more tactile way. Students need and deserve to hear your voice, its tone, its tenor, its undulations, its soothing qualities, its excitement, its energy.

Is a simple text-based announcement sometimes all that it takes to convey your information? Of course! However, we have found both in our own experiences, and in the hundreds of examples we hear from Canvas educators worldwide, that the Media Recorder plays a huge role in their successful day-to-day use of Canvas.

TIP

For more information about the how to's and the clickity-clicks of using Media Recorder, see Chapter 5.

We often sing the praises of A/V (audio/video) content when speaking to guests on our Canvas podcast: When talking about text versus media, it just seems obviously more powerful to use audio and video when possible. Tone matters. Connotation matters. Facial expressions and voice inflection matter. So to us, implementing the Media Recorder into your day-to-day Canvas use only makes sense. It helps everyone. You can be more efficient as an educator with your time. You can be more personable and connect with students. Students get the visceral experience of seeing and hearing you, even when you may not be in the same physical space. They get the added advantage of being able to have multiple senses met within their learning.

TIP

We also urge you to "trim the fat" of your text-based announcements. Trim them down to bullet points in much the same way we urge students and teachers to do when delivering a presentation in front of a group. Let your *talking* do the talking with the Media Recorder. Your students will not only thank you for it, but they will also benefit from the opportunity to continue to improve on reading skills, listening skills, following instructions, being an active listener, taking ownership of their learning, and interpreting verbal and non-verbal cues. Aren't these all skills we want our kindergarten through higher education students to improve upon?

Beyond that, using the Media Recorder also makes serving students with accommodations easier. And to top it all off, if you teach where you have English-language learners, then you know how important all of these aforementioned skills are. Think about how quickly your English-language learners will improve when you empower them with this type of consistent communication.

Building Compassion and Relationships

Over the past years, the concept of Social-Emotional Learning (SEL) has come to the forefront within education. SEL is the practice of integrating and considering social and emotional skills into your classroom curriculum. Some districts have attempted vast SEL initiatives and see great results with students. Though SEL can sometimes be a somewhat controversial topic, we believe that Canvas, once again, helps us meet our students' educational, social, and emotional needs with ease.

The truth is, if you need a tutorial video, a fancy LMS, or a fancy third-party technology platform to teach you how to show compassion for your students, then maybe this jungle ain't for you, Panda.

What we *do* know is that many educators who have found themselves now entrenched in technology that they are uncomfortable with, find it difficult to "be themselves" within a platform like Canvas. It goes back to the old "Teacher Toolbelt" idea. Most of you likely have been teaching long enough to know what it was like to be a teacher before a global pandemic forced most of us into a remote-teaching model. You have those tools in our toolbelt. If Marcus is acting like a lunatic in your classroom, you know how to calm him, how to redirect him, and how to get him back on track. What you may have struggled with over the past few years is the idea that if Marcus acts up while you are on a Zoom call with remote learners, you may feel that you are helpless. Everyone has felt this type of helplessness as a teacher.

The real challenge you now face is this: How can you best use technology to make yourself the best teacher you can possibly be for your students? How can you use Canvas in equally powerful ways to communicate with your students both inside and outside of your classroom? How do you connect with your students when you can't always carve out time for individual conversations during the school day or during class?

REMEMBER

What we know to be true is that students don't remember teachers for how quickly they graded their last quiz or the outstanding design of that algebra test. "Mr. Painter was my favorite teacher because he created the most rigorous tests and graded them so well and so quickly!" said no student ever. They remember us, they are inspired by us, they look up to us because of how we let them know and believe that we truly care. You can still accomplish all of those things within Canvas in a face-to-face, hybrid, or even fully remote-learning modality.

TIP

Put a recurring event on your calendar to message 10 to 15 students using Media Recorder each week. You don't have to have an agenda, a list of action items, or anything. Just speak to them with respect, with care, and with compassion. You may quickly see that this has a huge impact on them in a positive way.

Elevating Communication with the Mobile App

We haven't yet spoken about the Canvas LMS mobile app. Some of you, particularly those of you teaching in primary grades, may be living within the Canvas mobile app if your students are using iPads as their classroom device. However, everything we have discussed and will discuss throughout this book is almost entirely focused on the teacher experience on the web-based version. With that being said, one of our absolute favorite uses of the app for teachers is the ability to simply communicate when you think about something.

Remember all those meetings that would end with, "Okay, before we go, does anyone have any questions?" Of course you didn't have any questions at that moment, but about three minutes into your drive home, 14 questions suddenly pop into your head. The mobile app has saved Marcus from his own terrible memory hundreds of times. All too often he would wrap things up at school, think to himself, *Self, I think you can safely call it a day and go home,* only to realize during his commute that he had forgotten to remind his fourth-hour class that they are supposed to report to the auditorium for a convocation tomorrow instead of coming to class. In cases like these, where you have that moment of clarity, that realization at the most inopportune moment, or that great idea while on your evening walk, the Canvas mobile app is your savior. In cases like these, it's as simple as pulling out your smartphone, opening the Canvas mobile app, and sending that reminder announcement.

You can check out details on setting up the Canvas mobile app on your smartphone by visiting `https://community.canvaslms.com`. And in Chapter 17, we discuss ten great ways to use the Canvas mobile app. As your Panda Powers continue to grow, one of your best weapons is resourcefulness. We love the app for its ease of use, convenience, and "on-the-go" ability to make great use of your "in-between time" throughout the day.

Chapter **9**

Grazing through a Forest of Modules

E ducators are many things, and the one thing most of us are, either naturally or out of necessity, is *organized.* Therefore, if you are an organizational freak (if you were the only kid in fourth grade who asked for a label maker for Christmas, for example), this is going to be your favorite stop on our journey through the Canvas forest. Or for those of you who are currently reading this book while sitting behind a desk riddled with hundreds of sticky notes, you at least aspire to be organized! Either way, you're in the right place.

As a new Panda learning Canvas LMS, *modules* provide that structure you need to make your teaching and learning organized, manageable, and self-contained. And they mimic organizational strategies we are already accustomed to implementing in our personal and professional lives. You have folders in your Google Drive. Those folders hold things. Canvas has modules. Modules hold things. Except modules can do so much more than just hold the contents of a day's, a week's, a chapter's, or a unit's worth of learning. They can be simple or complex, they can be self-paced or controlled with requirements, and they can even be gamified using badging. Talk to any experienced Canvas Panda and ask them, "What is one part of Canvas you just can't live without?" Invariably most respond, "modules."

In this chapter, you discover what modules are in Canvas LMS and the many ways to use modules in your courses. You find out how to create, edit, and add more modules. You also take a look at why you may want to include requirements in your module design and why gamifying your course may help those who need a little extra push.

However you choose to organize your content within modules, you will soon realize that modules are the king of the Canvas jungle.

The Backbone of Self-Contained Learning

In Canvas LMS, modules are the backbone of the learning experience and are the most powerful organizational tool you have at your fingertips. Some teachers approach using modules on a daily basis — students complete one module per day. Others zoom out just a bit and create modules on a weekly basis. Still others build modules not based on chronology at all, but on content. So some folks like the chapter-by-chapter, unit-by-unit approach. And in higher-education settings, we often see modules built on a much larger scale in which they mimic the syllabus and encompass an entire semester's worth of coursework.

REMEMBER

Flexibility can sometimes breed fear and maybe even intimidation. However, no matter how you decide to approach your use of modules, the goal is to provide clear and effective delivery of content. How you decide to organize that content is up to you, and never permanent.

With modules you are able to create self-contained learning environments within Canvas. (In other platforms, modules may be called folders, packets, or bundles.) They can range from a self-contained lesson for one day of learning all the way through to a complex, highly customized, differentiated, gamified learning experience. It's helpful to think of modules in terms of something more familiar. We all understand how a folder works in both the physical and digital form. We generally use a folder to hold things. As educators, you have anything from a physical file cabinet to an online Google Drive, One Drive, or the hard drive on your computer stocked full of the content you use and create as a teacher. Within those places, you have folders that hold content that (we hope) is organized in some way. For example, Marcus and Eddie are both Google Drive users, so both have Google Drives full of folders that hold related content. However, for the most part, once you go to a folder to find content, the contents within the folder can sometimes be relatively unorganized. The organization is in having the folder, but once in the folder, things can get muddy.

Translate that line of thinking to modules within Canvas LMS. Modules function similarly to folders, but add the superpower of organization, pacing, requirements, and even gamification. Self-contained learning!

For example, suppose Marcus is teaching *Of Mice and Men.* Today's lesson can be built within Canvas as a module. Within this module, Marcus has the ability to create and add the same elements he would use in a conventional lesson to this digitally focused Canvas module. He can provide an introductory document or video about the migrant farm workers to introduce the novel, he can add a discussion, he can add a short reading assignment followed by a short check for understanding using either an assignment or quiz, and he can even provide additional support or enrichment content based on the content in the module. The point is that this module can be created, populated with all the content he wants to provide students, and can be published for them to view and interact with.

Generally speaking, many experienced Canvas LMS users depend on modules as a way to *chunk content* (in other words, break content up into manageable portions for student learning), as a way to provide structure and organization to the learning, and as a way to easily manage the content.

Here are the types of content you can currently add to your module:

>> Assignments

>> Quizzes

>> Files (documents and media)

>> Pages

>> Discussions

Ready to see what a successful module looks like? Check out Figure 9-1 to see a module titled "Week 1." Don't worry, we walk you through the steps to build your module in the next section.

Before we dig into building modules, let's quickly discuss a few things to keep in mind as a new Panda. As you continue to learn more about Canvas LMS, you will invariably have more questions. This Craft of Curiosity is what we love about Canvas users worldwide. One question we often hear from newer Canvas users is, "What is the difference between me building a lesson for students using a page versus a module?"

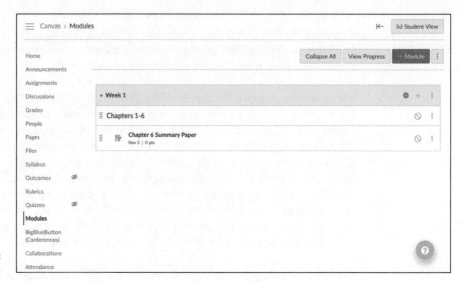

FIGURE 9-1:
A sample module.

Though there are a number of small differences that may or may not truly affect student learning and engagement, we feel the biggest advantage to using modules over pages is that a module allows you, the teacher, to have a bit more control over the pacing of the learning. Building a lesson within a Canvas page can ultimately lead to a lot of clicking on hyperlinks to take students to other things within or outside of Canvas. That can sometimes be unnecessarily complicated for learners. Too many new tabs are opened, and the possibility of covering up the original Canvas page is not ideal for any learner in a digital space, especially not young learners.

TIP

Using modules effectively can keep your students within Canvas, without extra distractions or navigational challenges. If you create requirements within your module (more to come on that later in this chapter), you can control the pacing of the learning and ensure that students are following the learning pathway that is best.

We have all seen it: We create an assignment or task for students and they try to do things in some random order that they have decided is easier for them, thus, likely missing the overall goal for the learning. Modules allow you to guarantee that students watch the video *before* taking the quiz, for example.

TIP

We state earlier in this chapter that we view modules as the backbone of Canvas LMS. Truly, our recommendation to all Canvas users — but specifically to new users — is to get to know the basics of modules and focus your efforts here. When it comes to lesson design, modules are like pizza: They can come in many different forms, but ultimately, they are always good.

Creating Modules

As you start to organize your thoughts around creating modules, it helps to think of them as a linear feed of what you'd like your students to accomplish in your course. You can even set your course home page to automatically load modules so that your students can access them directly upon clicking your Course Card in the Dashboard.

Here's how to create a module:

1. **Navigate to your Course Card from the Dashboard and click it to open the course.**

2. **Click the Modules link in the Course Navigation Menu.**

   If you've never created a module for this course before, an empty Modules window appears, similar to what is shown in Figure 9-2.

3. **Click the +Module button in the upper-right corner.**

   The Add Module dialog box opens, as shown in Figure 9-3.

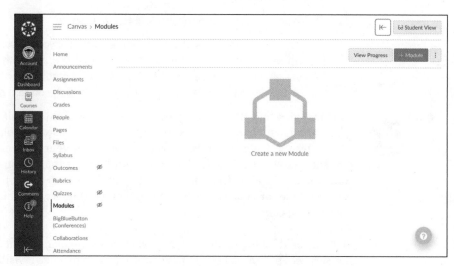

FIGURE 9-2:
An empty
Modules window.

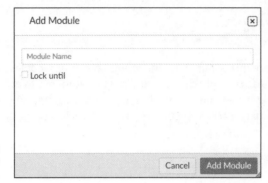

FIGURE 9-3:
The Add Module
dialog box.

4. Add a name for your module in the Module Name textbox.

What you name your module is important. See the sidebar, "What's in a Name?" for more.

TIP

You may see the "Lock until" option below the Module Name textbox. This enables you to lock a module until a certain date. This helps with managing the course content by automating access to each module, rather than making all modules available right away or risking forgetting to add a module at a later date when it is needed.

5. Click Add Module to add the module to your course.

The module you just created loads up at the bottom of your existing modules (if you have others), or as the first module in your course, as shown in Figure 9-4. Because all course modules are "housed" within the modules section of each course, the newest module is automatically added to the bottom of that list.

REMEMBER

New modules and the content you create within them default to *unpublished*, which means students can't see them until you choose to publish them. Make sure to hit the Publish icon when you are ready for your students to access this content. The Publish icon is shown in Figure 9-4. If there is one thing we both want you to take away from this chapter it is this: It is up to you to make the content available for your students to be able to view it. We call this *publishing* and *unpublishing* content.

You may be thinking to yourself, *Self, what does publishing content really mean?* For the purposes of Canvas LMS, to publish anything is to make it visible and available to your students within your chosen courses only. Nothing is going out to the Internet. Anything you create within Canvas needs to be actively published either immediately or by scheduling it to publish later. Publishing elements within a module is as simple as clicking the Publish button or clicking the Publish icon within a module.

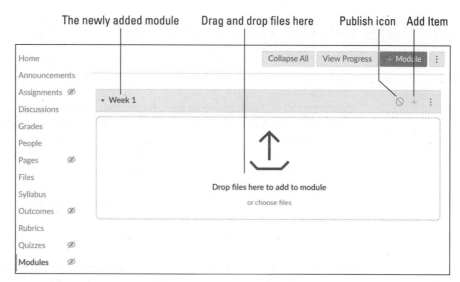

The newly added module   Drag and drop files here   Publish icon   Add Item

Drop files here to add to module

or choose files

FIGURE 9-4:
The newly added
Week 1 module.

REMEMBER

When content is published, a checkmark within a green circle replaces the grayed-out Publish icon, giving you an easy visual on what is published and what isn't. Published content is ready to rock! Unpublished content cannot currently be viewed or worked on by students.

WHAT'S IN A NAME?

When creating and naming modules, think of each module as a container or folder for your course — a place that houses additional content. We recommend breaking modules into units, subjects, weeks, days, lessons, or by content. How you name your modules is important. Computer geeks like us refer to such a structure as *naming conventions.* Establishing your own naming conventions will serve you well in Canvas as you begin to create lessons, activities, and modules for learning.

Sometimes, if you teach in a really great, forward-thinking, and proactive school district or institution, someone may have already established naming conventions for your entire district to follow. As former technology coordinators at the district level, both of us have seen the long-term importance of establishing strong naming conventions in Canvas LMS. To put it simply, after a few years of using Canvas without naming conventions, you'll end up with 37 "Vocabulary Quizzes" and you'll want to jump off a cliff every time you need to find the correct one.

Adding Content to Modules

Once your module is created, you can now add content to it. We discuss the nuances of creating the content to add to your module — pages, discussions, assignments, and quizzes — in the next chapter; here we look at the basics of how to add that content to our module once it's created. Adding content is simple and easy with a forest of options. If you are ready, let's dive in.

To add content to a module, follow these steps:

1. **From within a course, click the Modules link from the Course Navigation Menu.**

   A list of all the modules for a course appears.

2. **Locate the the module you want to add content to. (You may have to scroll if you have multiple modules already created.)**

   You have two options for adding content:

   - Clicking the Add Item icon (shown earlier in Figure 9-4)
   - Dragging and dropping files directly into the module

   The drag-and-drop menu is fairly straightforward, but it requires you to bring created content files in from your device. If you have files on your devices that you'd like to drag into the module from Windows Explorer (PC), Finder (Mac), or even Files (iOS/Chromebook), you can do that by locating your file in a separate window, clicking, holding, and dragging the file into this window.

REMEMBER

   The drag-and-drop option is only available if you are adding content to a newly created module, or one you haven't already added content to previously. If you are adding additional content to an existing module, the drag-and-drop option is not available.

TECHNICAL STUFF

   Canvas supports the most popular document file types, including but not limited to DOC, DOCX, PDF, PPT, PPTX, XLSX, XLS, and TXT. Canvas also supports the most popular image, video, and audio types, along with several others, including but not limited to BMP, GIF, JPEG, PNG, MOV, MPEG, AVI, MP4, MP3, and WAV.

3. **Click the Add Item icon.**

   The Add Item to [Module Name] window appears, as shown in Figure 9-5. You have a variety of options when it comes to adding content into your module: an Assignment, Quiz, File, Page, Discussion, Text Header, External URL, and External Tool.

   For this example, we'll add an existing assignment. If you need help on creating assignments, check out Chapter 10.

4. **Select Assignment from the Add Content drop-down menu, as shown in Figure 9-6.**

A list of available assignments appears that you can choose to associate with this module. You can also create a new assignment here as well. (If that's what you want to do, slap a bookmark in this spot and refer to Chapter 10 on creating a new assignment.)

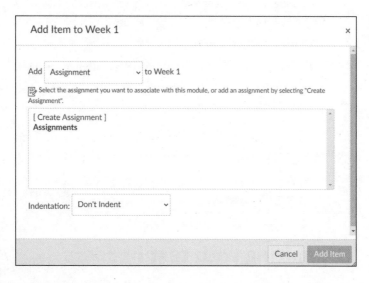

FIGURE 9-5:
Adding an item to the module.

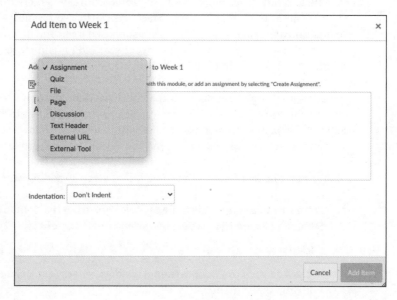

FIGURE 9-6:
The Add Content drop-down menu.

5. **Choose the existing content you've created from the list of available assignments.**

6. **Select the level of indentation desired for this particular assignment (see Figure 9-7).**

You can choose no indentation or to indent the item one, two, or three levels. Indenting an item within a module can help learners in a number of ways. Using indentation for content can create grouping and allow you to chunk content within a module.

7. **Click the Add Item button.**

The content you just added loads up at the bottom of the module.

FIGURE 9-7:
Selecting the indention level.

Organizing with text headers

As with so many other elements in digital learning, when creating modules and adding content to them, an integral factor is clarity. You want it to be abundantly clear within a module what learners are supposed to do and in what order they are to do it in. Modules provide the necessary scaffolding and structure for students to efficiently learn within the LMS.

One additional organizational tip that we have had educators discover and rave about is utilizing the Text Headers element within modules to further organize material. Choosing to add a text header within a module allows you to create very clear and obvious breaks in content, add simple directions, group items, and so on.

Adding a text header follows the same initial steps as adding any other content:

1. **From within a course, click the Modules link from the Course Navigation Menu and locate the module you want to add content to.**

2. **Click the Add Item icon.**

3. **In the Add Item to [Module Name] window, select Text Header from the Add drop-down menu.**

4. Type the text you want to add in the Header textbox and select the indentation level for the header (see Figure 9-8).

5. Click the Add Item button.

The header appears in the module, as shown in Figure 9-9.

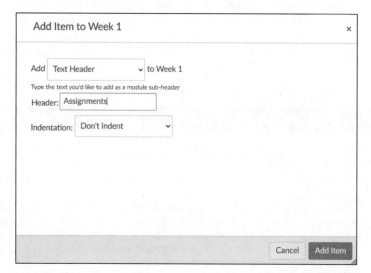

Add Item to Week 1 ✕

Add [Text Header ⌄] to Week 1

Type the text you'd like to add as a module sub-header

Header: [Assignments]

Indentation: [Don't Indent ⌄]

Cancel | Add Item

FIGURE 9-8:
Adding the text
header text and
selecting
indentation level.

The newly added text header

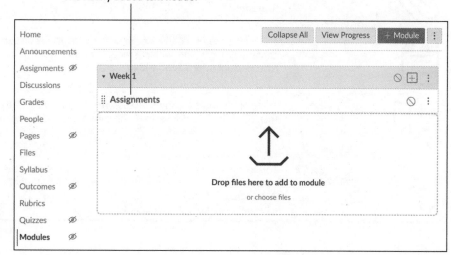

Home
Announcements
Assignments
Discussions
Grades
People
Pages
Files
Syllabus
Outcomes
Rubrics
Quizzes
Modules

Collapse All | View Progress | + Module | ⋮

▾ Week 1 ⊘ ⊞ ⋮

⸬ Assignments ⊘ ⋮

↑

Drop files here to add to module
or choose files

FIGURE 9-9:
A text header
within the
module.

Deciphering the icons

We all know that learners often try to peek ahead to see what to expect in their learning, how much work there is to do, or how much time they will be investing in their learning. In modules, each item you add includes an icon that identifies what type of content it is — a page, a file, a quiz, and so on. When students expand a module on The Battle of Gettysburg, for example, they can see at a glance that today's module includes a page, a file, a quiz, and a discussion.

Table 9-1 lists the commonly occurring module icons and what they mean.

TABLE 9-1   **Module Icons and What They Mean**

Icon	Name	Meaning
	Assignment	This icon denotes a Canvas assignment. Clicking this item takes students to the assigned task in order to complete it.
	Quiz	This icon denotes a Canvas quiz. Generally, these may be more "high stakes" and are often a way for educators to assess the learning that was to happen within the module. Sometimes quizzes can be used in a diagnostic manner, but more often, we see quizzes in a module acting as a way to measure the learning within the module itself.
	File	This icon denotes an item attached to a module. Files often include supporting materials, documents, maps, or resources that may be helpful to students.
	Page	This icon denotes a Canvas page, which can include all sorts of different content. Using a page within a module is often a way to redirect students to important information within the course.
	Discussion	This icon denotes a Canvas discussion. Also known as the Comment icon, this icon identifies discussions and comments within the module.
	External URL/Tool	This icon denotes an external link or tool is included in the module. Most commonly, we see educators link to websites for students to view or read. But, there are many options. Basically, if it has a URL, you can put it as an external URL/tool within a module.

Editing Modules

Take a look at your content inside the module. Is it being displayed correctly? Do you need to make changes? Maybe you'd like to move a quiz farther up in the timeline? It's easy to move things around within a module. You can either drag and drop the item into the desired location, or you can use the Options menu.

First, to drag an item into a new location, click and hold your mouse on the group of eight dots that appear to the left of the item you wish to move, as shown in Figure 9-10. When you hold these dots, you can drag a piece of content up and down the module. You can even move the item to an entirely different module.

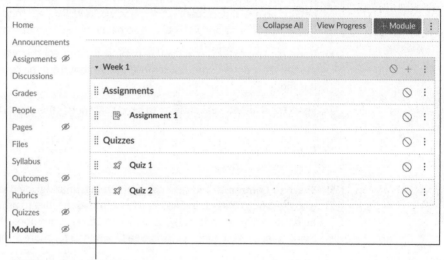

FIGURE 9-10: Moving content within a module.

Click and drag to a new location

TIP

The drag-and-drop option available when editing modules is just one of the many elements within Canvas LMS that is extremely intuitive and useful to most users. We often find that after we build a module and get all of the content we want placed into the module — pre-tests, videos, articles, tutorials, checks for understanding, assignments, and quizzes — we want to tweak the order of things. Organization here is no different than what we all do in classrooms every day.

In addition to drag-and-drop, you also have the option to quickly adjust module content by selecting the Options menu that appears on the right side of the content that was created, as shown in Figure 9-11. Editing inside the module content is a quick and easy way to make changes that are visible to the students such as indentation or editing the title. It also provides you with an easy way to interact directly with what you created. The following are some of the editing options available in the Options menu:

>> **Decrease indent:** Items decrease in indent by 1. This option isn't available if the item was created without being indented.

>> **Increase indent:** Items increase in indent by 1. This option isn't available if the item is indented out to its farthest point.

>> **Edit:** Allows you to adjust the title of the current item and its level of indention.

>> **Duplicate:** Duplicates the content and creates a copy of the module item.

>> **Move To:** This option allows you to easily pick the module container and options on exact placement. This option works well if your module page has gotten out of hand and you have to scroll multiple pages to drag and drop.

>> **Remove:** This option allows you to remove the content that was posted to the module. This option does not remove the content from the course, just from this module.

>> **Send To:** This option allows you to send content to other educators in your institution.

>> **Copy To:** This option allows you to easily send content to another course in your Canvas instance.

>> **Share to Commons:** Did you make something amazing you'd love to share with the world? This option allows you to spread the love to others who may be building similar content by sending it to Canvas Commons, the online marketplace for all things Canvas. See Chapter 13 for more information.

If set up, you will also see a Mastery Paths option in this list, which gives you the ability to establish prerequisites and connect those to Mastery Paths.

TIP

Many of these options are also available for the module as a whole, too. So you could create a module template you like and then copy it into the various sections of the module to keep a consistent format throughout. You can even share an entire module with another course as well as with colleagues. Talk about Panda Powers!

Click to open the editing options

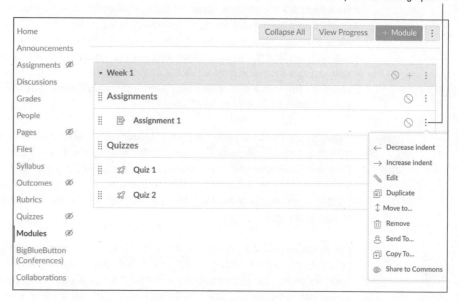

FIGURE 9-11:
Options menu items.

REMEMBER

Your thinking is the same in designing a Canvas module as it is when designing a lesson plan in general. It is important to remember that just because you are functioning and teaching using Canvas LMS, the platform is designed to make you better, to enhance what you do well, and to improve the learning experiences of your students. We believe that the best mentality to gain from this book is that Canvas is the game-changing platform that can unlock your teaching abilities, rather than any sort of challenge or obstacle to overcome. That is easier said than done, *especially* by the guys who are literally writing the book on learning to use Canvas LMS. So you're going to have to trust us. Once you've read this book, applied some of the advice and guidance we've provided, taught with Canvas, and had successes and failures, we are confident that you will see Canvas LMS as the platform that unlocked your teaching.

Pace Yourselves! Using Requirements and Prerequisites

We think adding requirements and prerequisites is the best part of designing modules in Canvas LMS. You can choose to design modules without any requirements, of course. Those modules will be completely self-guided. Self-guided and self-paced learning is generally great for adult learners.

However, for us, we have seen so many examples in K–12 classrooms where students don't take the proper or necessary time to focus on the work and instead, blow through things carelessly just to get the work done. Sound familiar? How many times has the first student to finish an assignment also been a genius? How many times have the first students to finish simply been the students most dedicated to finishing this annoying learning so that they can move on to playing video games or watching YouTube?

TIP

Regardless of your experiences with pacing within learning, we believe strongly in utilizing requirements and prerequisites within modules. They are exactly what they sound like: In order to proceed to the next item in a module, the student must accomplish something first — the *requirement.* And you can take it even further by setting a prerequisite that in order to move on to the next module, students need to complete another one.

For example, maybe you teach the novel, *Of Mice and Men.* Maybe you plan to begin reading that novel with students soon, but you want to ensure that some prior knowledge has been accessed by students first, such as of the novel's context and historical background. And maybe you have provided some sort of bell ringer or introductory activity to accomplish this. All of this happens simply within a module!

You may start with providing a website for students to visit that provides a basic "no spoilers" synopsis of the novel to peak their interest. Of course, once they've read that, you know that they will have questions concerning the time, place, and historical context. So you make viewing and reading the first website a requirement to the next part of the module, which is where you provide students a YouTube video from PBS about the Dust Bowl. Along with that video, you provide a simple list of guiding questions for them to answer within a Google Doc, or in a Canvas quiz. Or if your district or institution has Canvas Studio, you can combine those two things and have questions embedded directly into the video! Finally, now that students have read the article you provided and watched the video you provided, they can proceed to the last stage of the module where you provide a quick assessment using Canvas quizzes.

Setting requirements

Here's how to set up requirements within a module:

1. **From within a course, click the Modules link in the Course Navigation Menu to open the Modules screen.**

2. **Go to the module that has content that you want to add requirements.**

3. **Click the Options menu ("three dots menu") on the right side of the module name.**

4. **Select Edit from the menu.**

   The Edit Module Settings dialog box appears, as shown in Figure 9-12.

5. **Click the +Add requirement link.**

6. **Select the content items you want to be required and select what you want the student to do for the content item to be considered completed (view, mark as done, submit, score at least).**

   For younger learners, we recommend having students move through requirements in sequential order.

TIP

7. **Click the Add requirement link to add additional requirements.**

8. **Click Update Module when you've made your selections.**

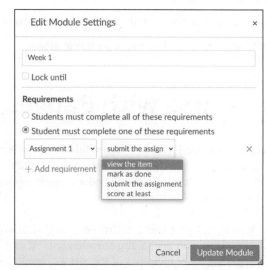

FIGURE 9-12: Setting requirements in the Edit Module Settings dialog box.

Leveraging requirements in this module won't guarantee that young Marcus doesn't still rush through the work in order to play online video games, but it inhibits that behavior. Requirements also allow you, the teacher, to better pace and plan for both in-class and outside-of-class work time. Again, Canvas helps you as a teacher as much as it helps learning.

Setting prerequisites

Another tactic to help guide students along the learning trajectory you've so carefully crafted is to use prerequisites to prevent students from jumping into a new module before they've completed all of the requirements from a previous module. The steps for setting module prerequisites is similar to setting requirements. Here's how:

1. **From within a course, click the Modules link in the Course Navigation Menu to open the Modules screen.**

2. **Click the Options menu ("three dots menu") on the right side of the module to which you want to add a prerequisite.**

    Note that you must have more than one module within a course to set prerequisites.

3. **Select Edit from the menu.**

    The Edit Module Settings dialog box appears.

4. **Click the +Add prerequisite link.**

5. **Select the module you wish to set as a prerequisite.**

6. **Click the Add prerequisite link to add additional prerequisites.**

7. **Click Update Module when you've made your selections.**

Gamifying Your Course with Badges

Maybe you're feeling really comfortable with modules by now. Maybe you've created them, leveraged them in multiple different ways via daily modules, weekly modules, thematic modules, or maybe even used a module as the container for a large project for your course. What's next?

Well, what's next may be badging and gamification. Gamification is exactly what it sounds like. As educators, you are taking the elements of gaming, specifically video games, and applying those concepts of incentives, leveling-up, challenges, and points to your teaching and learning. And, in this case, you're using Canvas LMS and modules as the vehicle.

TECHNICAL STUFF

For this discussion, we are using a program called Badgr, which is a free, open-source program for tracking student progress by issuing badges. You need your IT department to allow and add the Badgr LTI add-on to Canvas in order to use Badgr for badging within a Canvas module. Badging and gamification can be done without Badgr, but we speak specifically about Badgr as it has become the leading source of badging with Canvas.

Simply put, as a teacher using the Badgr LTI, you can award pre-created, open-source badges to students as they complete modules (one badge per module) or award badges for an entire course completion. Badgr has thousands of badges to choose from for both the K-12 and higher education settings. Additionally, you can create your own badges within Badgr if you are so inclined. Using this approach to gamification and incentivizing, you can imagine how many students will respond. They want that badge!

Once the Badgr LTI has been turned on by your favorite IT geek you see a Badges option in the Course Navigation Menu, as shown in Figure 9-13. The next step is for you to dig into how you want to gamify a module or even your entire course.

FIGURE 9-13:
When Badgr is enabled, the Badges option appears in the Course Navigation Menu.

WARNING

You need to create at least one module *before* attempting to assign and award any badges using Badgr.

TIP

You may choose to approach badging within modules based not on specific daily, weekly, quarterly, or semester-long content, but instead on additional skills within your course. For example, maybe instead of a badge awarded to students based on their completion of the Week 13 Module, students would have an additional module that is ongoing throughout the semester that focuses more on skills-based learning than the specific content. In a high school English class, for example, you may award a badge for completion of the Creative Writing Module, or the Speak Your Mind (Oral Communication) Module. In a United States History class, maybe students are awarded a badge for completing a module called Making

Connections to Today that asks students to make connections between our past and current events.

Now, because badging is somewhat of a *next-level* Panda Power, we won't get into the click-by-click instruction. However, a number of outstanding resources are available to get yourself started with badging and gamification within Canvas, specifically using Badgr and modules. Want to learn more? Check out the Badgr for Canvas Quickstart Guide at `https://support.badgr.com/en/knowledge/checklist-for-badging-in-canvas-courses`.

Another great way to find information is to search YouTube for "How to use Badgr with Canvas." We all know that some serious learning can and does happen from YouTube videos. How do you think Marcus changed out his kitchen faucet?

Chapter 10

Climbing the Deliverables Tree

f modules are the backbone of Canvas LMS, deliverables are the vertebrae. Pages, discussions, assignments, and quizzes make up the primary collection of deliverable elements that provide teachers and students with opportunities to assess and display learning. Generally speaking, pages are used more as a place for providing informational content to students, while discussions, assignments, and quizzes all provide avenues for students to demonstrate their learning and mastery of skills and content. As we climb the deliverables tree, you discover how to effectively design and leverage pages, discussions, assignments, and quizzes in your Canvas LMS courses.

In this chapter, you find out how to create and edit pages and add instructional content. You explore how to provide authentic and impactful learning opportunities. You also take a deep dive into the use of the discussion platform inside Canvas LMS to facilitate meaningful and collaborative discussions among your students. Let's start climbing.

Creating and Editing Pages

The Pages feature is an extremely useful tool within Canvas LMS for conveying information to students in your courses. There are always new and innovative ways to make use of pages in your Canvas courses, but the most conventional use is to create pages to hold important information.

To a novice Canvas user, it may seem that pages are the only places your course content lives. However, as we dive deeper in to the options Canvas LMS provides, you'll recognize that the Pages feature is just one of many tools at your disposal when designing learning outcomes. Educators often use pages as a jumping-off point in their course as a home page; some use it as a place to update weekly links to assignments; others may build an interactive syllabus to engage learners. All of these things can be accomplished in pages.

To create a page in a Canvas course, follow these steps:

1. **Navigate to your Course Card from the Dashboard and click it to open the course.**

2. **Click the Pages link in the Course Navigation Menu.**

   When you navigate to the Pages section of a course, you may see one of three things. If you have already set up a home page, the home page appears. Or, you may see a home page template that has been created by your district or institution that you are able to then edit to meet your needs. The third view you may see is a blank page ready to be filled, as shown in Figure 10-1.

REMEMBER

   The home page is designed to be a page that is seen when Pages is selected from the Course Navigation Menu. It is also your course home page. If your course has not been set up with a front page, you see a list of pages created instead.

   For this example, we are going to assume we need to create that first page.

3. **Click the +Page button located in the top-right corner of the Pages window.**

   The familiar Rich Content Editor (RCE) appears where you can add and format the content for your page (see Figure 10-2).

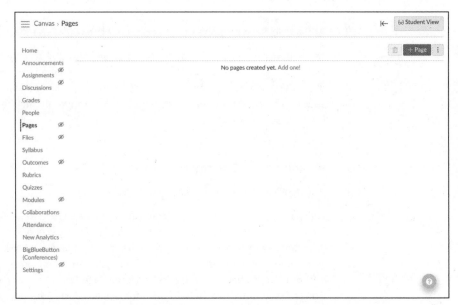

FIGURE 10-1:
An empty
front page.

FIGURE 10-2:
The Rich Content
Editor.

4. **Add a title for your page in the textbox at the top of the dialog box.**

TIP

As we state throughout this book, an important step toward long-term success with Canvas LMS is to establish consistent naming conventions and be mindful of the titles you choose. When it comes to naming your home page, being specific and including general dates and/or date ranges in the title is helpful. Here are some examples:

- English 10 Home Page (2022)
- Earth & Space Science (Sem. 1/2022)
- Earth & Space Science (Sem. 2/2022)

You get the idea. Consistent naming conventions also help to keep things clear for yourself year after year. We want to avoid the crazy scenario we've seen all too often in which three years from now you decide you want to use a page you created for a course "back in 2022" and you can't find it among your dozens of pages because you titled it "Home Page." How many of you have a Google Drive, OneDrive, or hard drive full of files titled "Quiz" and you have to sift through all of them every time you need one?

WARNING

However, for the regular pages you add to course modules that you may reuse semester after semester or year after year, a general rule of thumb is to *not* include dates in page titles. The reason is that if you add a specific date to your pages, when you flip to the new semester or school year, you then need to go in and rename every page within the module. That is both tedious and a waste of teacher time and energy. And if you don't update the dates, then students know how long it's been since you updated your course resources.

5. **Add the content for your page using the RCE.**

In addition to text, you can add page-specific content like links, images, files, and even create videos with the Media Recorder. (We cover everything the RCE has to offer in Chapter 5.)

6. **Choose your preferred page settings in the Options drop-down menu that appears below the textbox.**

You can choose to:

- Allow users to edit the page. One example may be to allow students within a course to share notes on a page or add their own content.

- Add the page to students' to-do lists. Adding the page to students' to-do lists is just another simple way to be sure that the most timely and pertinent content is easily accessible to students.

7. **Check the "Notify users that the content has changed" checkbox if desired.**

8. **Click the Save button or the Save & Publish button when you have finished creating the page, depending on your needs for the page.**

Whether you are finished with a page or have a few more tweaks, you need to save your work. *Save* allows you to create this page as a draft and only you, and possibly other teachers in the course can access and see it. *Save & Publish* allows your students to see the page when they select the Pages link in the Course Navigation Menu or if you have linked this page to a module.

We often hear teachers say that they don't understand why there are both choices or they question when it's best to use Save versus Save & Publish. As a rule of use, we often see teachers use Save simply to have the ability to create content pages in Canvas LMS ahead of time, maybe for upcoming units, and keep them invisible to students until they are needed. In both of our cases, we have created pages ahead of time and just used Save. Then, when we were ready for that content to "go live" to students, we would simply locate that page within the Pages section of a course, and click Save & Publish.

REMEMBER

Publishing your work is a necessary step if you want anything to be available to students. See Chapter 9 for more on publishing (and unpublishing) content.

TIP

Often, we see teachers use the Pages feature as a convenient place to provide content for students to access. Think of pages as a resource section. We love a good "one sheet." If we can boil content down to fit onto one sheet of paper, all the better! Along those same lines, teachers often create a page in Canvas and create a sort of "one sheet" there. For example, we like the concept of creating a Help Page for each week of learning where we put pertinent information, talking points, takeaways, vocabulary words, links to videos, websites, and so on for students to access. That page can be published on a set weekly schedule and unpublished at the end of the week if necessary. That Help Page can also be linked at any point within a module. As always, you can experiment with what you like and what seems to be most helpful to your students. A daily resource page may be a bit excessive for most settings, but maybe weekly, monthly, or by grading period would work? Flexibility is key, but honing your skills at building basic content within a page is going to be helpful in your Canvas journey.

WARNING

Remember, less is more when it comes to designing pages. Your top priority is always to convey content to students clearly. You can add plenty of aesthetic value to pages by embedding slides, images, buttons, and so on. Just constantly ask yourself, "Is this element I'm adding to this page helping my students learn?" If not, that element may not be necessary to include and may actually hinder or distract from the learning process.

Some additional considerations when creating pages:

>> Remember that whether published or unpublished, you can *always* make adjustments to pages. To edit a page, simply go to your course, click the Pages link in the Course Navigation Menu, click the page you want to edit, and boom! The page editor launches with the all-powerful RCE. Again, always click the Save button. Those changes are automatically pushed out to students and at worst, they may just need to refresh the tab in which they have Canvas open to see the updates.

>> As we state earlier in this chapter, we generally see the majority of pages being used to provide content, resources, and support materials to students. This content is often for reference purposes. However, that is not the only way to leverage pages within a Canvas course. Can you create an entire, self-contained lesson within a page? Sure! We have certainly seen it done, but we often find that there is a bit more work involved in this practice because you must build in the breaks and manually "chunk" the content on a page. This is why we prefer using modules for lessons versus pages. Modules inherently are designed to chunk the content. (Chapter 9 goes into the details on using modules.)

TIP

As educators you know your students the best. Do your students thrive and learn well looking at content on one screen, scrolling through that content as they learn and execute tasks? Or do they function better in a module where they see only the "task at hand" and cannot, in most design cases, proceed until they have completed one phase of the module and clicked Next? Pages versus modules is a preference conversation, but we suggest that conversation be had with students, so that you know what is working best for them.

Building Meaningful Discussions

The Discussions feature in Canvas LMS is a great way to create a more inclusive and accessible environment to get your students to talk, collaborate, and share and exchange ideas. As two former high school teachers, the idea of facilitating a discussion with the slight cloak of technology can be challenging to consider. Truthfully, it's hard not to scare easily when we use the phrase "message board," but believe us when we say that if Canvas Discussions are set up correctly, you have a safe, viable format for your students to express their ideas and thoughts within Canvas.

The other big benefit of leveraging the Discussions feature within Canvas is the ability, yet again, to bring more learners into the conversation who may otherwise stay silent. Not all of our students have a desire to contribute to a classroom discussion or conversation. Some may be completely mortified by the thought of it. However, we have seen time and time again that discussions have a way of allowing some of your more passive or even more reluctant students an opportunity to contribute.

Now that you know a bit about the Discussions feature, let's set up a discussion to create community and build relationships within your classroom. Here's how:

1. **Navigate to your Course Card from the Dashboard and click it to open the course.**

2. **Click the Discussions link in the Course Navigation Menu.**

   The Discussions window loads, as shown in Figure 10-3.

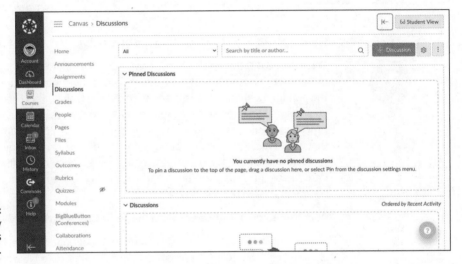

FIGURE 10-3:
An empty
Discussions
window.

3. **Click the +Discussion button located in the top-right corner.**

   You are now able to create your discussion with you guessed it, our good friend, the RCE (see Figure 10-4).

4. **Give this discussion a Topic Title.**

5. **Create content for the discussion using the RCE.**

   This content can include many things. Here are some ideas:

   - Pose a question or topic for discussion

   - Provide a video as a discussion starter

   - Provide a map, infographic, or document

   - Provide an image or piece of artwork

FIGURE 10-4:
The Create New
Discussion
window.

6. **(Optional) Add an attachment to the discussion.**

TIP

You can add attachments to discussions. Adding an attachment is as easy as clicking the Choose File button next to the word Attachment, locating the file in the pop-up menu that appears, and then clicking Open or Add depending on your device. We often see attachments added to discussions that include procedures, rules, or instructions for the discussion. Of course, any content that would further benefit students within the discussion could be included as an attachment as well. Maybe consider including a document with common introductory phrases, transitions, and ways to politely agree or disagree with comments within the discussion?

7. **Add discussion options as desired in the Options section.**

The Discussion feature comes with a laundry list of options from which to choose. See Table 10-1 for a breakdown of the options available and what you can control with each.

8. **To make your discussion available on a specific date, enter it in the Available From and Until textboxes, as shown in Figure 10-5.**

This setting is convenient for all those who want a thriving community of users discussing current events or even items that may be time-sensitive.

9. **Click the Save button or the Save & Publish button when you are finished.**

Once the discussion is saved and published, it appears in several places throughout Canvas, including students' to-do lists (if graded) and in the Canvas Calendar.

TABLE 10-1   **Discussion Options**

Option	Action
Allow Threaded Replies	Canvas defaults all discussions to a focused discussion. If you'd like to thread the discussion, you can do that by selecting this option. Threading replies in a discussion can lead to additional conversations within the larger discussion that are more specific and focused. This can be great! However, keep in mind that sometimes comments and replies may seem to get lost in the shuffle when allowing threaded replies. We like this option in high school and higher education settings where users are a bit more able to multitask.
Users Must Post Before Seeing Replies	This option requires users to reply to the discussion before they are allowed to see any replies. This is a nice option to use to ensure students think about the discussion prompt and come up with their own ideas before seeing what other students have posted.
Enable Podcast Feed	You can insert a podcast feed as a way to distribute this content to those who want to subscribe through an external channel.
Graded	If you are grading this discussion, make sure this option is selected. If this is an ungraded discussion, leave it unchecked.
Allow Liking	Students will be able to see a "like" icon within a reply and will have the ability to "like" a posting. This is a great setting to enable in order to recreate a situation where the most liked comment will bubble-up to the top. Therefore, we can see some positive reinforcement of great discussion points, as those with the most likes will move their way up to the top.
Add to Student To Do	This option is only available if the discussion is not graded. Enabling it adds the discussion to students' to-do lists on their course Dashboards. If the discussion is graded, the discussion automatically shows up on students' to-do lists.

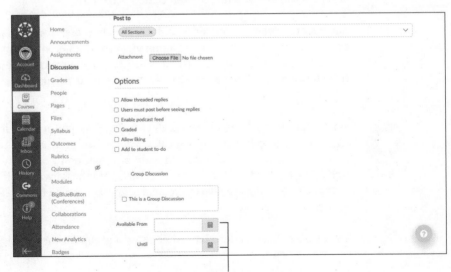

FIGURE 10-5:
The Available
From and Until
options.

Available From and Until textboxes

One final note on discussions. Students have the ability to use the Media Recorder within discussions. This is a huge factor to keep in mind when considering the use of the Discussion feature in primary grades. As the teacher, you can provide a prompt and have students simply reply using the Media Recorder, rather than typing a response. So, we can hear thoughts from learners of all ages. Additionally, allowing students to use the Media Recorder within discussions can be extremely beneficial for those who have verbal communication strengths but may struggle with writing.

Designing Assignments

Easily one of the biggest complaints we have heard from teachers learning how to navigate online or blended learning using Canvas LMS, or really any digital learning platform, pertains to the issue of academic integrity. Many teachers feel helpless when it comes to knowing whether or not a student's work has been submitted with integrity — basically that they didn't cheat. We could probably write an entire book on this topic alone.

To put it quite simply, from both a teaching perspective and a design perspective, the more difficult any assignment is to cheat on, the more likely you are to see students submit work *without cheating*. If you create a multiple-choice assignment in Canvas and give it to students as a homework assignment, let's be real: Many of them find a way to "collaborate" on that assignment. Maybe students text each other, or maybe they search Google for the answers. Either way, your assignment design is somewhat lending itself to this behavior.

Marcus even knew a teacher who did a Google search for a quiz, downloaded it, and put it into Canvas as an assignment. Imagine her shock and surprise when students did the exact same thing. They found the exact same quiz (it was the third result on the Google search) and the answer key! This may seem obvious, but it happens often.

Yet another reason why Canvas LMS is such a powerful tool for learning is due to its built-in flexibility and an educator's ability to create authentic learning tasks that accomplish the outcomes you want and that don't basically beg students to find a way to cheat. So, as we move forward into the Canvas Assignments feature, always consider how the design of an assignment can dictate the outcome in both positive and negative ways.

To get started, let's take a look at creating a group for these assignments.

Creating an assignment group

Assignment groups help you better organize the various types of assignments you may use in your course, such as "Weekly Readings," "Essays," and "Quizzes," and they are important if you are using a percentage-based grading system. Creating assignment groups enables you to determine how different groups of assignments are weighted in your course.

Here's how to create an assignment group:

1. **Navigate to your Course Card from the Dashboard and click it to open the course.**

2. **Click the Assignments link in the Course Navigation Menu.**

   The Assignments window opens, as shown in Figure 10-6.

3. **Click the +Group button located in the top-right corner of the Assignments page to create a Group.**

   The Add Assignment Group dialog box appears, as shown in Figure 10-7.

4. **Give your group a name and then click the Save button.**

   Once you've created your assignment group, you are ready to create an actual assignment that can be published.

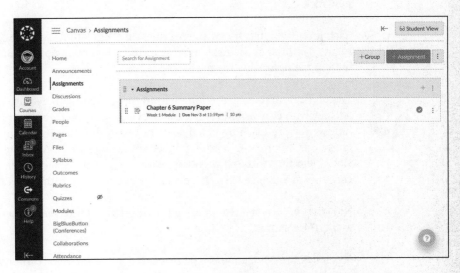

FIGURE 10-6:
The Assignments window.

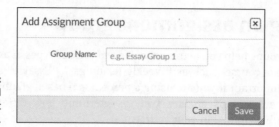

FIGURE 10-7:
The Add
Assignment
Group dialog box.

REMEMBER

Students can see the assignment group names, so be deliberate and judicious when deciding what names to use. In higher education it is often recommended that you match the assignment group names you have in your syllabus with the group names you have in Canvas. For example, if you have Discussions, Homework, Quizzes, and Exams listed in your course syllabus, then those would be the assignment groups you create in Canvas.

Creating an assignment

Fair warning: we're diving into the deep end with this one. The Assignments feature in Canvas LMS has a number of differentiation and accountability options for both teachers and students. Take your time when creating assignments and always remember that you can go back at any point if you get lost and need a refresher. And, you have this book to refer back to whenever you need additional guidance.

Each institution has its own set of rules and regulations when it comes to assignments, so think of the next steps as a guide to get you up and running quickly on building assignments in Canvas.

REMEMBER

You don't have to do everything within the Assignments feature right away. Your journey with Canvas LMS is not a one-, two-, or even three-year commitment. As long as you are teaching in a district or institution that uses Canvas, your Canvas journey is an ongoing learning experience. Embrace it. Attack your own professional learning through this book with vigor. This is the Panda Power that will continue to enhance what you do each and every day with students.

Now that you've created an assignment group, you're ready to create an assignment. Here's how:

1. **Click the +Assignment button located in the top-right corner of the Assignments window.**

   The Create New assignment window opens with the RCE available to add and format the content for your assignment (see Figure 10-8).

FIGURE 10-8:
Enter the
assignment
details in the
Create New
assignment
window.

2. **Give the assignment a name.**

3. **Enter the number of points available for the assignment in the Points field.**

4. **In the Assignment Group drop-down menu, select the assignment group you want to add it to or create a new group.**

5. **Select the grading type in the Display Grade As drop-down menu.**

   Types can be Percentage, Complete/Incomplete, Points, Letter Grade, GPA Scale, or set as Not Graded.

6. **Select the submission type in the Submission Type drop-down menu, as shown in Figure 10-9.**

   Submission types enable you to use a number of different formats for your assignments. You can choose No Submission, Online, On Paper, or via an External Tool. Check out the section, "Selecting submission types and entry options" for more information on the pros and cons of each type.

   If you select the Online submission type, you have a number of different online entry options from which to choose. (More on that coming up.)

7. **Decide how many submission attempts you want to allow in the Submission Attempts drop-down menu.**

   You can choose to allow unlimited submission attempts or limit it to a certain number.

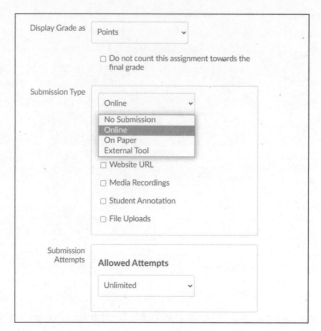

FIGURE 10-9:
Assignment
submission types.

8. **Check the "This is a Group Assignment" checkbox if you want to make it a group assignment, or choose to assign grades to each student individually.**

   Group assignments can be particularly helpful if you created groups in your course and those groups have differentiated assignments.

9. **Decide if you'd like to require a peer review of the assignment and check the "Require Peer Reviews" checkbox if so.**

   This option gives your students the ability to review each other's work. You can manually assign or have Canvas assign the peer reviews. As a former high school English teacher, Marcus regularly utilized peer review.

TIP

   For more information and steps on assigning peer reviews, head to the Canvas Community website at https://community.canvaslms.com and search "peer reviews."

10. **Select who you'd like the assignment to be assigned to in the Assign text-box, shown in Figure 10-10.**

   We recommend assigning it to "Everyone" unless you only want specific students to be able to submit the assignment.

11. **Create a due date for the assignment in the Due field.**

   You can also indicate a time frame when the assignment is available.

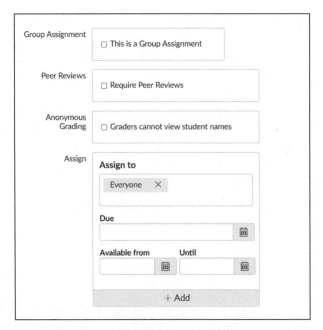

FIGURE 10-10:
The Assign text-
box where you
input a due date.

12. **Click the +Add button to add additional students to the assignment with different due and availability dates.**

This option works well if you have a student who needs a different due date, perhaps because they were sick and missed school.

TECHNICAL
STUFF

13. **(Optional) If you want to enable multiple reviewers to grade an assignment, such as in a higher education setting, check the Moderated Grading checkbox.**

This setting may be most useful in high school and higher education settings in which teaching assistants may be helping with the grading, or the teacher wants to have students review each other's work.

14. **If enabling moderated grading, check the Anonymous Grading checkbox if you want to hide student names from graders.**

15. **Finalize your assignment by selecting the Save button or the Save & Publish button if you are ready to have the assignment post to the course immediately.**

Once an assignment is saved and published, as shown in Figure 10-11, it appears in a number of places within Canvas. It appears in the Assignments window that appears when students click the Assignments link in the Course Navigation Menu, it appears on the Canvas Calendar, and it appears in students' to-do lists on their Dashboards. If the assignment is part of a module, it also appears within that module. This redundancy makes it tough for students to miss something assigned to them.

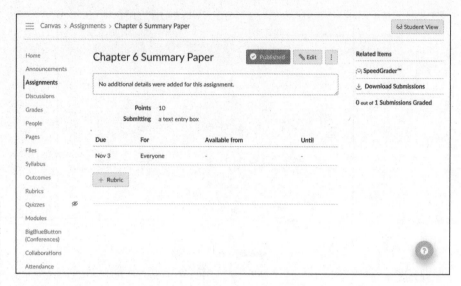

**TECHNICAL
STUFF**

If you see a Sync to SIS button when creating an assignment, please consult with your IT department. This is one of those elements that you need to consult with the IT and SIS (Student Information System) folks on.

Selecting submission types and entry options

When creating an assignment in Canvas LMS, you have several options for how you'd like that assignment submitted by students: No Submission, Online, On Paper, or via an External Tool. Table 10-2 lists the submission types and provides definitions of each.

Selecting Online in the Submission Type drop-down menu reveals a menu of even more options, as shown in Figure 10-12. Because we are tech geeks at heart and because we are Pandas who want to do things as efficiently as possible, the online submission options are right up our bamboo tree. We outline each option in the following sections.

Text Entry

The first online entry option — Text Entry — is probably our least favorite. It is effective for extremely short responses from students, but generally speaking, if students need to type more than a sentence or two, we recommend allowing them to use a Google Doc or a Microsoft Word document to enter their answers. This enables students to save their work, revisit it later, recover it later, and potentially collaborate with others.

TABLE 10-2   **Assignment Submission Types**

Submission Type	What It Means
No Submission	You aren't collecting any deliverables from students, such as for an assignment done in class and not collected for credit.
Online	You want students to submit the assignment through Canvas LMS using any of the default online submission options: Text Entry, Website URL, Media Recordings, Student Annotation, File Uploads.
On Paper	You want students to submit the assignment in class and not through Canvas LMS. There are a wide variety of applications here, but often you may find that it is easier to deliver instructions within Canvas because of tools like the Media Recorder and Immersive Reader, but you still want the actual deliverable to be on paper or in some other form.
External Tool	You are using an external tool such as the Google LTI, or any number of other LTIs, to submit an assignment and have an LTI enabled for your course. (We cover LTIs in more detail in Chapter 12.)

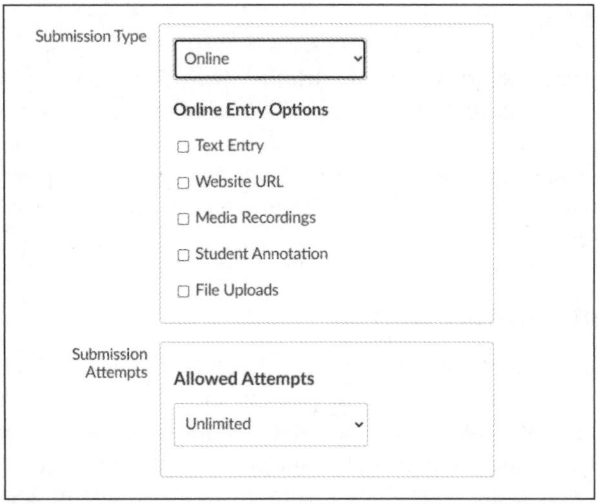

FIGURE 10-12:
Options for
online
submissions.

If you pose a question and set the submission type as Text Entry, it is a one-shot situation. We appreciate the ability to invest time, save work, and revisit work that comes with the other submission options. If you choose online submission with text entry, the assignment should be fairly quick in nature and something that doesn't require any work beyond that moment in time.

Website URL

The Website URL submission option is an easy way to have students submit many types of work because so much of what we do is web-based. What that means is that most of the things we create online have an associated URL, or a location on the Internet. So, students can provide links to their work using this option. More often though, this is a great option for a teacher to have students do online research and supply a particular website as a resource. For example, "During our chapter on isosceles triangles, we defined them and calculated angles. Provide the URL to an image of a real-world isosceles triangle."

Media Recordings

As you are probably aware by this point in the book, we are all about using the Media Recorder as a submission option. And with the Media Recordings option, a seemingly endless number of possibilities are available for teachers and students. With this option students can create audio or video recordings as a response to an assignment. They can create it from right within the assignment, or upload a previously recorded file.

TIP

We have also had great success with the Media Recordings option as a vehicle for students with language challenges. Whether a student struggles with verbal expression, has speech accommodations as part of a learning plan, or is an English-Language Learner (ELL), Media Recordings can provide those learners with a safe place to practice and improve on those verbal skills. They can gain confidence here.

Student Annotation

How many of you have ever thought, *I just want to make this PDF editable. How do I do that?* We have heard this for years in the education technology world. While the concept of a digital worksheet or editable PDF can be controversial, and we definitely have feelings on the subject, the Student Annotation option may be the next best thing. It enables you to provide any sort of document, PDF, slide deck, map, or literary passage that students can annotate and "mark up" from right within Canvas LMS and without additional tools. It is a beautiful thing!

File Uploads

File Uploads is another helpful submission option. You can ask students to upload a file as the submission for an assignment. You can also restrict file types to ensure that you get the type of content you want in the form you want it. In our experience with web-based Google and Microsoft environments, File Uploads is less necessary these days. However, the availability of multiple submission types provides great flexibility for teachers and students.

TIP

We have found success by enabling multiple online entry types for students for a given assignment. Allowing students to submit responses in multiple ways accomplishes a few things:

>> **It makes turning work in on time easier for students.** Sometimes students have issues that may inhibit them from turning in work in one submission type, but not another. So, we like providing options for the sake of logistics when possible. For example, if you want to nearly guarantee that regardless of what happens on students' devices or whether or not their Internet connection is stable or not, assign work that allows both a Website URL submission and a File Upload option. That way students are able to take two pathways to turn in their work. More flexibility, fewer excuses!

>> **Providing multiple submission options allows for some student choice and/or differentiation.** For example, maybe your desired outcome is for your chemistry students to properly describe the steps in a process of a chemical reaction. What is the desired outcome? The desired outcome is probably that the student can effectively and accurately communicate the steps of the chemical reaction. You may not actually care whether that is done in written form in a Google Doc, in a presentation using Google Slides, or in a video recording using the Media Recorder. In a case like this, we recommend considering allowing multiple options for students to submit evidence of what they know.

IMPORTING YOUR OWN COURSE CONTENT

As much as we love creating and building content for learners within Canvas LMS, we realize that there are other options that are equally effective, time-saving, and impactful for students. Does Marcus prefer to build content himself? Absolutely! Is it always the most timely approach? Of course not!

If you are crunched for time or need a little boost to your efficiency, importing and copying content from your other courses is the way to go. This enables you to repurpose content you've already created and quickly move it wherever you want it within another course. No need to reinvent the wheel every time! Things like announcements, assignments, and modules can easily be duplicated and added to your other courses. For example, do you have to make the same announcement to three of your eight courses? Simply build that announcement once and copy it to the other courses.

REMEMBER

Some assignment options aren't as frequently used but could be effective for your course and your students. Maybe using Peer Review is not really useful in your fourth grade class. Maybe there isn't much of a need for the Website URL entry option in your welding course. The great thing is that Canvas LMS provides a variety of options at your fingertips. If one type doesn't suit your course, several others just may. The more you become adept, the more you learn, and the more comfort you gain, the more creative you eventually become.

Launching Quizzes and Question Banks

The Quizzes and Question Banks features in Canvas enable you to assess student understanding of your course material. With the Canvas Quizzes feature, you can administer online quizzes and tests. And question banks — a repository of questions you can add to quizzes across your courses — can be a lifeblood of any assessment created.

Quizzes

The Quizzes feature in Canvas is where you can create assessments to measure student mastery of course content. Quizzes have become quite the conversation starter within Canvas LMS user circles as of late. Over the past few years, Canvas has slowly and methodically been redesigning the Quizzes feature and it now offers two quiz engines (as of this writing): Classic Quizzes and New Quizzes. New Quizzes is the newest quiz engine and features continue to be added to it. In this section, we take a look at creating a quiz with the New Quizzes quiz engine.

Are you ready to get your paws dirty and develop a quiz? Here's how:

1. **Navigate to your Course Card from the Dashboard and click it to open the course.**

2. **Click the Quizzes link in the Course Navigation Menu.**

   The Quizzes window opens. If you haven't created a quiz for this course yet, this window will be empty, as shown in Figure 10-13.

3. **Click the +Quiz button located in the top-right corner of the Quizzes window.**

4. **In the Choose a Quiz Engine dialog box, select the New Quizzes option, as shown in Figure 10-14.**

   An empty quiz window appears, ready for you to add content (see Figure 10-15).

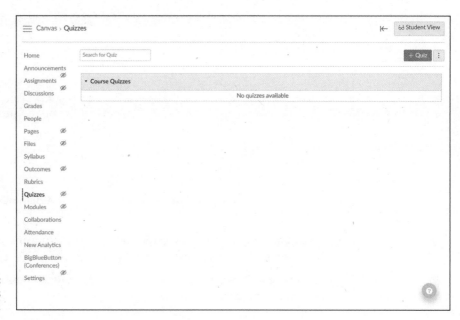

FIGURE 10-13:
An empty Quizzes window.

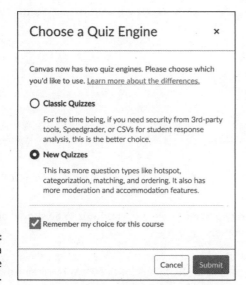

FIGURE 10-14:
The Choose a Quiz Engine dialog box.

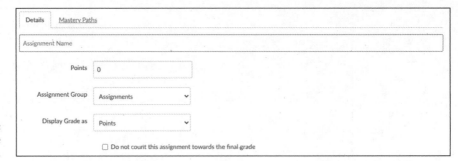

FIGURE 10-15:
Adding in the quiz details.

5. **Give the quiz a name, a set of points, and select the Assignment Group for this quiz.**

6. **Determine how you want the grade displayed (as points or percentages), and whether the results count toward a final grade.**

7. **Select who you'd like the assignment to be assigned to in the Assign text-box, shown in Figure 10-16.**

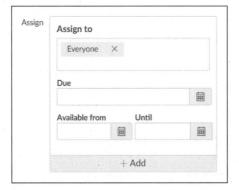

FIGURE 10-16:
Assign the quiz and set a due date.

8. **Select a due date and when you'd like your quiz to be shown or not shown in your course.**

At this time in your quiz-creation process, you can choose to save your quiz details and come back to it later to build in questions by clicking the Save button. You can choose the Save & Publish button, which returns you to the page where you opened the quiz. Or you can choose the Build button, which walks you through the steps to build out your quiz.

It's time to build, so seatbelts, everyone!

9. **Click the Build button.**

The Build window opens. Here you can edit the quiz title and description, view any item banks you've created, or preview the quiz as a student.

10. **To add content to your quiz, click the + (plus sign) button, as shown in Figure 10-17.**

The Insert Content window appears, as shown in Figure 10-18. The Canvas Quizzes feature offers 12 content additions or checks for understanding, so take your time and let the tool help you in accomplishing your goals. The following question types are available:

- Categorization
- Essay
- File Upload
- Fill in the Blank
- Formula
- Hot Spot
- Matching
- Multiple Answer
- Multiple Choice
- Numeric
- Ordering
- True or False

We have to admit, there are so many options and categories of quiz questions to use that it can be a bit overwhelming. For our example we are going to create a simple one-question quiz with a true or false answer.

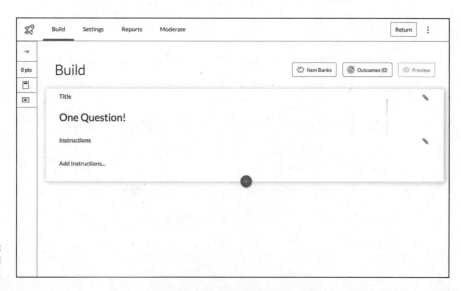

FIGURE 10-17:
The Build
window.

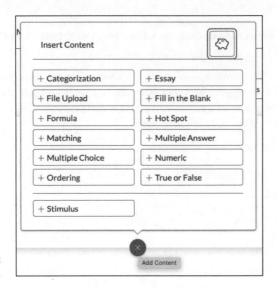

FIGURE 10-18:
Add Content.

11. **Select the True or False option from the Insert Content window.**

The Question Editor opens, as shown in Figure 10-19, where we enter the details of our question including the question stem, the answer, and how many points it is worth.

12. **When finished, click Done to save the question.**

Congratulations! You created your first quiz with a true or false question. Now you can dive in and create robust learning for your students.

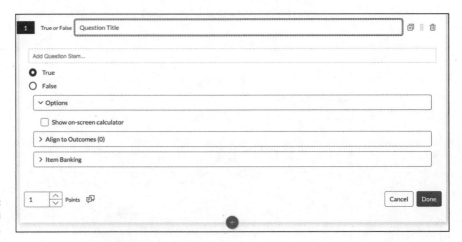

FIGURE 10-19:
The Question
Editor window.

Question banks

In Canvas, question banks (called "item banks" in the New Quizzes quiz engine) are places to house questions you can then add to quizzes across your courses. Marcus always looked at the Canvas Question Banks feature as the online version of the old filing cabinet he used to have that was full of past quizzes and tests. Whenever he was creating a quiz, he could dig into his filing cabinet and pull questions from there. He could edit them, adjust the language, adjust the questions and answers, and do basically whatever he wanted with them. He was starting with a basic question that he didn't have to create in his mind. The Question Banks feature in Canvas functions in a similar way. It can be a powerful time-saving tool in Canvas LMS because you don't need to reinvent the wheel every time you need to create a quiz.

WARNING

The following steps walk you through how to add question banks to your course using the Classic Quizzes quiz engine. Because the Quizzes feature is still evolving, these steps are a brief overview of how to create new questions and question banks to get you started. The best resource for the most current information on question banks and quizzes — and updated information on creating question banks using the New Quizzes quiz engine (which calls them "item banks") — is always the Canvas Community website at https://community.canvaslms.com.

Follow these steps to create a question bank for a course using the Classic Quizzes quiz engine:

1. **Navigate to your Course Card from the Dashboard and click it to open the course.**

2. **Select the Quizzes link from the Course Navigation Menu.**

3. **Click the Option menu ("three dots menu") next to the +Quiz button in the upper-right corner of the screen.**

4. **Select Manage Question Banks from the options available.**

   The Course Question Banks window appears. This is where you can add question banks to your liking.

5. **Click the +Add Question Bank button that appears in the upper-right corner and give your Course Question Bank a name.**

TIP

   This is yet another place where your naming conventions are vitally important. Please don't name your Question Bank "Quiz" or "Quiz Questions." You are going to need to be very specific and consistent in how you name question banks. Doing so can help keep your entire workflow smooth and efficient. Instead of naming a Question Bank "Quiz Questions," we recommend something more like "US History_Ch1."

6. **Once you've created and named a question bank, click the name of your newly created question bank to open it.**

You are now ready to begin adding and creating actual questions.

7. **Click the +Add a Question button.**

A template that looks and feels similar to the RCE appears in which you are able to build questions of all types. Here you are able to choose from a number of different question types, assign a point value to the question, write the question, and provide the correct answer(s).

8. **Compose your question and click the Update Question button when finished.**

Just like that, you've created your first question within a question bank.

That question can now be added to any upcoming quiz or test, and can even be moved or copied into another question bank. The flexibility we celebrate within Canvas is really apparent here.

The good news is that you now have a basic knowledge of how the Canvas Question Banks feature works using the Classic Quizzes quiz engine and how you can create questions that will eventually populate future quizzes. The not-so-good news, if you're feeling pessimistic, is that there is more learning to come as the platform continues to develop and improve. Always check out the latest news on the Canvas Community website. The learning never stops, Pandas! That's why we teach.

IN THIS CHAPTER

» **Discovering the ins and outs of using the Gradebook**

» **Creating a grading workflow with SpeedGrader**

» **Navigating and sorting with ease**

» **Understanding rubrics and outcomes**

» **Targeting feedback and communication on deliverables**

Chapter **11**

Grading Efficiency for Panda Naps

In this chapter, we talk about something we probably all value a great deal: time! Educators have so much to do and never seem to have enough time in which to do it all. However, we believe that your hard work goes hand in hand or shall we say, paw in paw, with working intelligently. You've heard it before: work smart, not hard. No educator exists who isn't working hard. So instead we like to say, work smart *and* hard! With few things as enjoyable as a good nap, one way to have time for this bliss is to learn the tricks of the trade for grading within Canvas LMS.

Yet again, you are an educator and you bring an abundance of skills to your use of Canvas LMS. One of your skills is the knowledge of best practices in grading and assessment of student work. What you may quickly realize when beginning to grade deliverables within Canvas LMS is that the grading looks and feels very intuitive. And, the built-in flexibility Canvas provides for grading allows you to be as simple or as intricate as you like.

In this chapter, you discover the ins and out of using the Canvas LMS Gradebook, and then you take a look at using Canvas SpeedGrader. When we talk of time savings and potentially blissful Panda naps, there is no better example within Canvas

LMS than SpeedGrader. You also explore SpeedGrader's feedback feature, which enables you to provide targeted feedback to students in a multitude of ways.

In addition, leveraging rubrics and outcomes within Canvas LMS can make everything you teach more consistent for learners, just as they do outside of the LMS. Rubrics help make expectations and assessments clear for everyone involved. And outcomes help students find mastery of the skills you teach. At the end of this chapter, you discover how to simplify the grading process by creating rubrics and outcomes.

Let's get started on the grading journey.

Navigating the Gradebook

So many things within the educational field have evolved over the years. Depending on your level of experience and "years in the game," you may immediately recall some of the old and antiquated grading methods and tools you have used. However, the concept behind the gradebook itself really hasn't changed much.

At its basic level, a gradebook is a spreadsheet. You've got your students listed vertically on the left side of the page and your assignments, tasks, quizzes, and so on, listed across the top and along the bottom of the page. Where those horizontal rows of student names intersect with the vertical columns of tasks to be graded is where you enter the grade for that student on that task. No matter what platform you use, this intuitive standard has remained mostly unchanged.

Canvas LMS capitalized on that comfort level we have with traditional gradebooks in the design of its Gradebook feature. Upon opening the Canvas LMS Gradebook for the first time, you see that it looks like most every gradebook you've ever used as an educator. Phew!

Opening the Gradebook and filtering your view

Let's start with some basics. To open the Gradebook in Canvas LMS, simply click on a course tile from the Dashboard to open a course. Then, click the Grades link in the Course Navigation Menu. Once in the Gradebook, you see a screen similar to what is shown in Figure 11-1. This is the main Gradebook window.

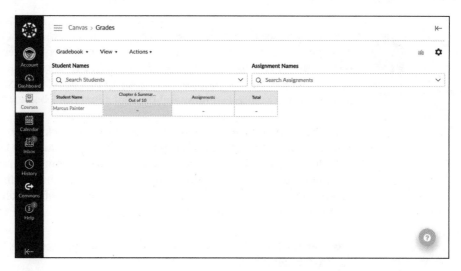

FIGURE 11-1:
The main
Gradebook
window.

As we state earlier, what you see here is similar to what you've probably seen in gradebooks for as long as you've been teaching. However, Canvas LMS takes the standard gradebook to another level. It includes sorting options that enable you to organize your gradebook, student data, and assignment data to best suit your needs.

The main Gradebook window enables you to see all students, assignments, and grades; however, with the Gradebook tab, located in the top-left corner of the Gradebook window, you are able to filter this view. When you click the Gradebook tab, a drop-down menu appears where you see the following filtering options (see Figure 11-2):

» **Individual Gradebook:** This option enables you to filter the gradebook to see only one student and one assignment at a time.

» **Gradebook History:** This option opens the Gradebook History page, which lists a history of all the Gradebook changes made in the course.

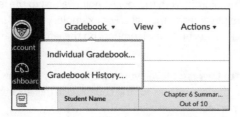

FIGURE 11-2:
The Gradebook's
filter options.

You may also see the Learning Mastery option in the Gradebook filtering options drop-down menu. As of this writing, the Learning Mastery Gradebook is an opt-in feature that you must enable from the Feature Previews section in the Course Settings screen. For our purposes and goals in this book, we focus our discussion on the main Gradebook window and the Individual Gradebook.

The next filtering options are found in the View tab. Clicking the View tab reveals a plethora of options at the tips of your panda paws. The Arrange By option, shown in Figure 11-3, enables you to arrange the vertical columns in a number of different ways. Some of these options are certainly more familiar and intuitive than others, but you have choices. You can choose from any of the following arrangements of your vertical columns within the Gradebook:

>> **Default Order:** This view is the assignment order you set in the Assignments page.

>> **Assignment Name – A-Z:** In this view, assignments are shown in alphabetical order left to right from A to Z. This arrangement may be helpful if you know the name of the assignment is "Aristophanes Quiz," for example, and you want to quickly see that assignment in the far-left column.

>> **Assignment Name – Z-A:** In this view, assignments are shown in reverse alphabetical order left to right from Z to A. So that assignment you called "Zebra Stripes Homework" appears in the farthest left column.

>> **Due Date – Oldest to Newest:** This view is likely the most conventional and familiar arrangement within the Gradebook. Similar to your old paper and pencil gradebook, the oldest assignments show up on the left side and progress to the newest assignments as you proceed to the right.

>> **Due Date – Newest to Oldest:** Want to see the most recent grades on the far left? This is the view for you. In this view, the newest assignments show up on the left side and get older as you proceed to the right. This arrangement allows you to do very little left-to-right scrolling in order to get to the most recent assignments in the Gradebook.

>> **Points – Lowest to Highest:** Arranging the Gradebook assignments in this manner moves the columns with the lowest point values to the left and those with the largest point values to the right. For example, you may see bell-ringer activities and quick "heat check" assignments on the left and exams and projects to the right.

>> **Points – Highest to Lowest:** Maybe you want to quickly see how a student has performed on the larger tasks for the course. Use this arrangement to get all those "big bopper" columns moved to the far left.

- » **Module – First to Last:** If you've fallen in love with modules like we have, you may gravitate to this arrangement. This view arranges your Gradebook in chronological order by module from left to right. Note that you must first have modules added to your course in order for this arrangement option to appear.

- » **Module – Last to First:** In this view, you see the most recent modules on the left, thereby eliminating a lot of scrolling to see the the latest grades from the most recent modules. Again, you must have modules set up in your course to see this option.

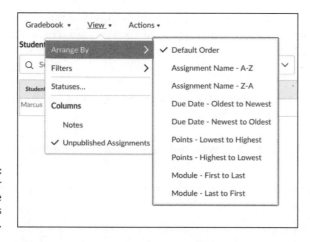

FIGURE 11-3:
Options for arranging the vertical columns in the Gradebook.

Now that you've seen the different ways you may choose to arrange the vertical columns in your Canvas Gradebook, let's now check out how to add filters to what you see in your Gradebook.

TIP

Gradebook Filters are just like filters you use regularly when online shopping or when finding the perfect way to make that Instagram moment really pop. Gradebook Filters simply cut down the content available for you to see within the Canvas Gradebook. In Chapter 10, you discover how to create assignment groups with names such as Homework, Classwork, Bell-Ringers, Quizzes, and so on. The Filter option in the View drop-down menu enables you to filter your gradebook by those groups.

Maybe you've noticed that a student does well on all the work that is done in class, but when the student has an assignment within the Homework assignment group, that student performs poorly. To view just the Homework assignment group, click View ⇨ Filter ⇨ Assignment Groups. With Assignment Groups selected, the All Assignment Groups drop-down menu appears in the upper-right corner of the

Gradebook window. Click this menu to filter your entire gradebook by the Homework assignment group or whichever group you wish to see.

The final filtering option in the View menu enables you to show or hide the Notes column and the Unpublished Assignments columns in the Gradebook. The notes column is a phenomenal way to literally keep notes on important information you'd like to remember about a student, such as student's preferred name. Students do *not* see these notes; they are only available for you, the instructor.

What do all these colors mean?

The Gradebook includes several icons and colors that may display in the assignment columns, assignment groups, and Total column. These icons and colors you see throughout the Gradebook are simply indicators to assist you with course grading.

As you can see in Figure 11-4, there are five statuses for anything entered for a grade in the Canvas Gradebook:

>> **Late:** This status means the task assigned was turned in, but after the due date.

>> **Missing:** This status means the task assigned was not turned in at all by the student.

>> **Resubmitted:** This status means the student has turned in a resubmission of a task. For example, if you allow students to submit corrections to homework and turn them in, you may see this status in the Gradebook.

>> **Dropped:** This status means a student's grade has been dropped based on a rule you established when you created the assignment. For example, if you create a rule to drop the lowest grade within an assignment group, this status would appear next to the grade that was dropped per that rule.

>> **Excused:** This means you have manually chosen to excuse a student from this task.

In the View tab you can set the color you want each of these statuses to be; just click View ⇨ Statuses and then click the pencil icon to set a new color.

In all cases concerning the status of a task within the Gradebook, you can click the cell in which the task's grade would go and then click the arrow icon to apply a status to it, provide a grade, and even provide text-based feedback.

FIGURE 11-4:
Assignment
statuses.

Viewing assignment details

Have you ever named an assignment or task in your gradebook and then basically forgotten what the assignment was all about? No? Just Marcus? Okay then. For Marcus and his fellow forgetful Pandas, viewing assignment details from within the Gradebook is as easy as one click. Simply click the column title to open the assignment summary window, as shown in Figure 11-5.

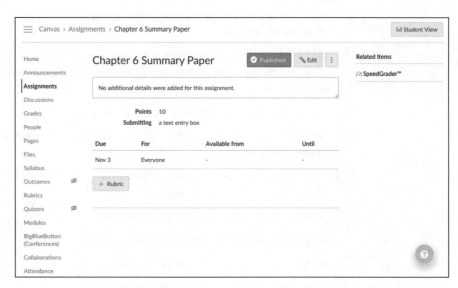

FIGURE 11-5:
Assignment
details.

This feature is also helpful for those of you who ignored our "It's vital to create consistent and predictable naming conventions for everything you do in Canvas LMS" rant. Maybe you are prone to naming tasks, assignments, and quizzes in much too vague a manner. Fast-forward to the end of the grading period, quarter, or semester and you have no recollection of what the heck that "Tuesday Homework" assignment was. Click "Tuesday Homework" in the assignment column to bring up the assignment details screen with everything you need to know to refresh your memory.

Messaging "Students Who"

We feel that one of the best features in all of Canvas LMS is the "Message Students Who" option in the Canvas Gradebook. This feature has been one of our favorites since the beginning. Basically, what this feature does is enable you to immediately message students who fit your selected criteria for a given assignment from right within the Canvas Gradebook. For example, maybe you want to remind students who have yet to turn in their prewriting/planning activity for an upcoming essay. You can simply go to the assignment in the Gradebook, select "Message Student Who" from the assignment's Options menu ("three dots menu") and whip off a message to remind them in no time. Here's how:

1. **Click on a course tile from the Dashboard to open a course.**

2. **Click the Grades link in the Course Navigation Menu to open the main Gradebook window.**

3. **Go to any assignment in your Gradebook and click the Options menu ("three dots menu") that appears to the right of the assignment name when you move your mouse over the assignment box.**

   The assignment's drop-down options menu appears.

4. **Select Message Students Who from the Options drop-down menu, as shown in Figure 11-6.**

   The Message Students Who dialog box opens for that assignment where you can choose from four options (see Figure 11-7):

   - Message students who haven't submitted yet

   - Message students who haven't been graded yet

   - Message students who scored less than

   - Message students who scored more than

5. **Select the group of students you want to target with your message.**

   Student names automatically populate based on the option you select, and you have the option to remove certain students if you'd like from the communication.

6. **Title your message in the Subject textbox.**

7. **Craft your communication in the Message field.**

8. **Click the Send Message button when you are ready to send the message.**

Students will not see who else is included on the message.

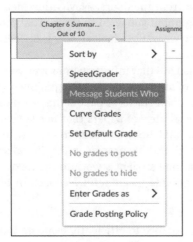

FIGURE 11-6:
Selecting
Message
Students Who
from the Options
drop-down menu.

FIGURE 11-7:
Message
Students Who
options.

The Low-Down on Canvas SpeedGrader

Entering and editing scores is a breeze in the Canvas LMS Gradebook. No longer do you have to use a pencil just in case you mess up. No longer do you have to worry about accidentally entering an entire course's worth of grades into the wrong rows. Canvas LMS has made entering and editing grades easy. Simply open a course, click the Grades link from the Course Navigation Menu, and then click the Options menu for the assignment you want to grade. That provides you with a number of options, but the one we want to look at now is SpeedGrader.

SpeedGrader is a tool in Canvas LMS that infinitely improves your efficiency when grading student work. In both of our experiences with grading papers before using an LMS, we would have stacks upon stacks of papers that we'd constantly shuffle and rearrange. We'd have special piles of papers that needed extra comments or attention, stacks of papers for students we needed to meet with, and on and on. Ultimately, SpeedGrader streamlines this process in the digital space. With minimal clicks, you can move from one student's work to the next, easily grade that work, mark that rubric, and provide meaningful feedback in text form or even using the Media Recorder.

SpeedGrader gives educators a chance to efficiently evaluate individual students and group assignments. When we say efficient — we mean fast! SpeedGrader was designed to allow you the benefit of time by creating a workflow that gets you back to doing what you do best . . . teaching. Let's take a closer look into SpeedGrader and what it has to offer.

To open SpeedGrader, follow these steps:

1. **Click on a course tile from the Dashboard to open a course.**

2. **Click the Grades link in the Course Navigation Menu to open the main Gradebook window.**

3. **To access SpeedGrader, go to any assignment in your Gradebook and click the Options menu.**

   The Options menu is the familiar "three dots menu" that appears to the right of the assignment name when you move your mouse over the assignment box.

   The assignment's drop-down options menu appears.

4. **Select SpeedGrader from the drop-down menu.**

   The SpeedGrader window appears, as shown in Figure 11-8.

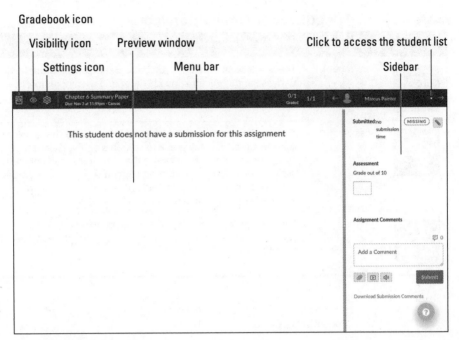

Gradebook icon

Visibility icon

Settings icon

Preview window

Menu bar

Click to access the student list

Sidebar

Chapter 6 Summary Paper
Due: Nov 3 at 11:59pm · Canvas

0/1
Graded

1/1

Marcus Painter

This student does not have a submission for this assignment

Submitted: no submission time

MISSING

Assessment
Grade out of 10

Assignment Comments

0

Add a Comment

Submit

Download Submission Comments

FIGURE 11-8:
The SpeedGrader window.

The SpeedGrader window is divided into several areas to help you view and grade student submissions. Let's take a closer look at those areas next.

The menu bar

So many tools, so little time! The SpeedGrader menu bar that appears at the top of the SpeedGrader window includes several tools to help you grade assignments. Table 11-1 lists the navigation icons available in the upper-left corner of the SpeedGrader menu bar.

You access the SpeedGrader Options menu by clicking the Settings icon from the menu bar selecting Options. In this menu, shown in Figure 11-9, you have multiple options to sort your students' assignments. Again, what is our focus in this chapter, Pandas? *Saving time!* You can sort students' work three different ways in the SpeedGrader Options menu:

>> By student name

>> The date they submitted the assignment

>> By submission status

TABLE 11-1   **SpeedGrader Navigation Icons**

Icon	Name	What It Does
	Gradebook	The Gradebook icon takes you back to the Canvas Gradebook. Often new Canvas Pandas get into SpeedGrader and then not know how to quickly return to the regular Gradebook. This is the easiest way.
	Visibility	The Visibility icon posts or hides the assignment. This is helpful when you want to either post the grade to students or if you want to hide the grade or assignment from students. Note that this option can only be used *after* an assignment has been graded with SpeedGrader. In the Gradebook, this option can be set so that grades are hidden before all grades are entered. This is especially useful to hide quiz grades and feedback.
	Settings	The Settings icon opens a drop-down menu where you can select options for sorting students, open a list of keyboard shortcuts, and open the SpeedGrader Guide for help.

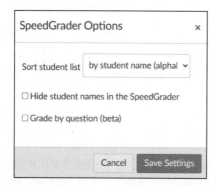

FIGURE 11-9: The SpeedGrader Options menu.

You also have the ability to hide student names in SpeedGrader. Just click the checkbox next to this option.

TIP

Why would you want to hide students' names in SpeedGrader? We urge you to experiment with this setting. As much as we all believe we are not in any way biased in our assessment of students, hiding student names within SpeedGrader could very well shine a light of clarity onto your own grading practices. As a high school English teacher, Marcus was probably guilty of judging a student's written response before reading it. C'mon folks, we are in the trust tree here, right? Now, he is optimistic that even being guilty of pre-judging a written response that he would adjust his assessment after reading. However, if you want to remove any potential bias or feelings, implement the "hide student names" option in SpeedGrader.

The middle section of the menu bar is chock-full of information from the title of the assignment, its due date, and how many of these students have been graded. You can also click the name of the "course" to take you back to the home page, or click directly on the assignment.

TIP

If you need a reminder of the assignment directions, simply click the assignment name from the menu bar at the top of the screen to open a summary of the assignment in a different window. Then as you're grading you can click back and forth to remind yourself of the directions. This is especially useful for Discussions if you want to scroll through the full discussion while grading.

Moving over to the right side of the menu bar in SpeedGrader, you can view the student list for the assignment. You can even quickly see the status of each student's submissions. By clicking the down arrow that appears on the right side of the student name (refer back to Figure 11-8), you can view the full list of students. SpeedGrader defaults to the first student in the course Gradebook, which is organized alphabetically by the students' last names. For students whose work you've already graded, a green checkmark appears next to the student's name. For students whose work you still need to grade, an orange circle appears.

The preview window

Once you've sorted the list of student work for a particular assignment and are ready for lightspeed in SpeedGrader, it's time to get down to the actual grading. When you select a student from the list, that student's work appears in the Speed-Grader preview window.

The preview window is flexible, dependent upon the type of submission you asked for in the original assignment. For example, the preview window can show you student work submitted as a Google Doc or Microsoft Word document, as a Google Slides or Microsoft PowerPoint file, as a PDF, or as any other file type you have requested for students to submit.

The sidebar

The sidebar is an important part of SpeedGrader that populates on the right side of the SpeedGrader window under the name of the student selected, as shown in Figure 11-10. Some of the information shown in the SpeedGrader sidebar includes:

>> Submission details, including the date and time the assignment was submitted

>> A link to download the submission file (if necessary)

>> Assessment grade

>> A button to view the rubric for grading (if available)

>> Assignment comments

Assessment
Grade out of 10

Assignment Comments

Add a Comment

Submit

Reassign Assignment

Download Submission Comments

For more about adding comments in SpeedGrader, see the next section, "Targeting Feedback with Laser-Focused Communication."

REMEMBER

One reminder regarding the sidebar in SpeedGrader: If you choose to provide text-based feedback in the sidebar, you need to click the blue Submit button. Doing so saves your feedback and makes it visible to the student.

TIP

Another helpful bit of information that appears in the sidebar is when a student viewed the assignment grade and feedback. Once a student views the assignment grade, a heading that reads "Student Viewed Document" with the date viewed appears here.

Targeting Feedback with Laser-Focused Communication

Of course, the Canvas Gradebook is a fully functioning and multifaceted online gradebook. However, we feel the most important grading tool available in Canvas and in SpeedGrader specifically — a feature that enhances our ability to assess student achievement — is the ability to provide feedback. Feedback is the key. And that is what sets SpeedGrader apart.

TIP

Students don't always care much about their grades. Now, most of you probably did because you became educators. However, sometimes the most transformative thing we can do for students is to provide them with concise, personal, timely, and specific feedback. In SpeedGrader, you are able to provide feedback in a number of different ways: via text, video, audio, or by attaching a file.

Let's start with the basic text-based comment. Located in the right sidebar of SpeedGrader when a student submission is selected, the Assignment Comments section is where you can enter a text-based comment (see Figure 11-11). Simply click inside the Add a Comment textbox, enter your comment, and click the Submit button. Once you've clicked submit, that comment is available for students to see.

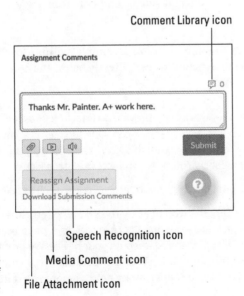

FIGURE 11-11: The Comments section of SpeedGrader.

Suppose you have really taken to this whole time-saving approach, but you also really and truly value, as we do, the importance of providing feedback to students. Well, there is a solution for that, too. May we present to you, the Comment Library.

TIP

When you click the Comment Library icon (it looks like a tiny dialog window; refer to Figure 11-11), the Manage Comment Library screen opens. Here you can select a comment that you commonly use with students to add to the Add a Comment textbox. This comment is added to your Comment Library and auto-generates in the comment textbox as you type the first few letters if you enable the "Show suggestions when typing" option. So within the Add a Comment textbox alone, you have several options for providing text-based feedback: manually entering in a comment, opening the Comment Library and selecting from a list of commonly used comments, or using an auto-generated comment if you have enabled this option.

However, that may not be the route you want to take. Maybe you want to ensure that nothing gets lost in translation and nothing you type here is misunderstood or misconstrued by a student or caregiver. In this case you may want to consider using the Media Comment option. This is our favorite option for feedback. Historically, we have seen that a teacher's spoken words, facial expressions, mannerisms, and voice are immeasurably impactful for students. Plus, we are talking about trying to save time. How many of you can probably talk through your thoughts more quickly than you can by typing them? With SpeedGrader, you have the option to record both audio and video comments from right within the Speed-Grader sidebar.

TIP

Leveraging the Media Comment option is simple within SpeedGrader. Within SpeedGrader, note the three icons located directly below the Add a Comment textbox (refer to Figure 11-11):

>> **File Attachment:** Click this icon to provide an attachment as feedback using the universally recognizable paper clip icon. One fun idea is to attach an image or GIF as feedback for students with this icon in addition to your text-based or media-recorded feedback. Your K-12 students may get a kick out of this.

>> **Speech Recognition:** Click this icon to record your speech to text.

>> **Media Comment:** Click this icon to easily record and insert either audio or audio/video content. You can record it here in real time, or you can upload a file you've already recorded and is saved on your device. We prefer simply clicking Start Recording and sharing your feedback with your student. It's also not a bad idea to jot down a couple talking points before you start recording.

We feel confident that with just a bit of practice, using the Media Comment option may prove to be one of your most valuable Panda skills for providing feedback.

Creating Rubrics and Outcomes

Grading student work is sometimes difficult, and it is almost always a time-consuming task. One strategy educators have taken to cut down on this time is to focus their efforts on simplifying the grading process through the use of rubrics. A rubric is a great tool for setting very clear and concise expectations for a particular task. A rubric explicitly states what elements earn what grade or point value so that teachers, students, and caregivers all have a shared vision of what earns an outstanding grade versus what would earn a poor grade.

Luckily for you, Canvas thought of this, too. You can build rubrics within Canvas and attach them to any deliverable item (assignments, discussions, and so on). On top of that, Canvas also enables you to add outcomes to those rubrics so that you can easily track skills and student mastery of the subject. Let's take a look at how they work.

Rubrics

We know *plenty* of educators who love a good rubric. Maybe you are one of those Pandas who loves creating and implementing rubrics. The value of a rubric is clear. Not only does it assist in establishing structured methods for assessing student work, but it also provides that clarity of expectations for students. Students often thrive and even enjoy rubrics because with a rubric, they can be process-oriented and more methodical in their approach to proving their knowledge or mastery. Ultimately, rubrics let students clearly know what is expected of them and how they can meet or exceed those expectations.

TIP

If you are an educator who has had issues with students or parents questioning students' grades, how they earned a grade, and so on, and you didn't use a rubric, now is the time to learn. Rubrics also eliminate a large amount of ambiguity in grading and assessment. Less ambiguity means less potential conflict, less confusion for students, and better overall communication from educator to caregivers.

In project-based classes, rubrics are invaluable as they, again, provide teachers, students, and groups a basic roadmap of expectations throughout a project. Not only can rubrics be tied to outcomes, but they can also provide you simple and manageable ways to grade using SpeedGrader.

Let's create a rubric now so that you can see the process.

REMEMBER

Your institution may have created domain-wide rubrics or you may have access to state standards that have been pre-loaded. Check with your institution to see if these are available for quick access. If not, you are free to create your own rubrics within Canvas exactly the same way you would in a non-digital setting.

To create a rubric for one of your Canvas courses, follow these steps:

1. **Navigate to your Course Card from the Dashboard and click it to open the course.**

2. **Click the Rubrics link in the Course Navigation Menu.**

   The Rubrics window opens, as shown in Figure 11-12.

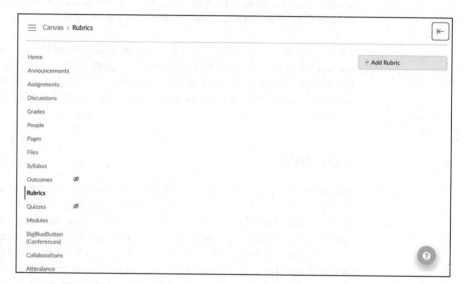

FIGURE 11-12:
The course
Rubrics window.

3. **Click the +Add Rubric button located in the upper-right corner of the Rubrics window.**

   The rubric template opens, as shown in Figure 11-13.

4. **Add a title for the rubric in the Title field.**

5. **Enter a criterion description by clicking the pencil icon in the Criteria column and entering a description in the Edit Criterion textbox that appears.**

   You can add a short description and a long description in this textbox.

6. **Click Update Criterion when finished.**

7. **Click the Range checkbox if you want to create a point range instead of using the default rating, which is an individual point value.**

   When Range is enabled, the first rating in the Ratings column (Full Marks) shows the total point value as a range, as shown in Figure 11-14.

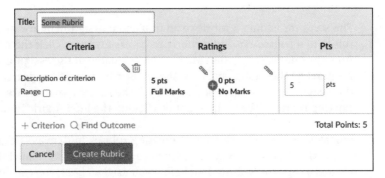

FIGURE 11-13:
An empty rubric
template.

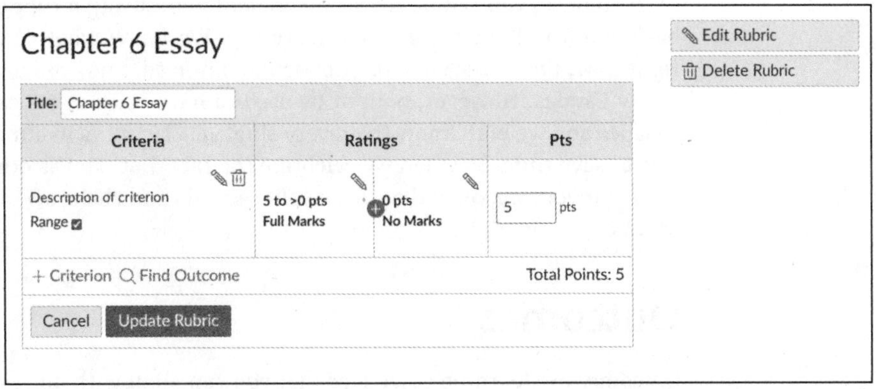

FIGURE 11-14:
Selecting a point
range for the
rubric.

8. **To add another rating for a ranged criterion, click the + (plus sign) that appears in the Ratings column.**

The Edit Rating textbox appears where you can add an additional rating for the rubric. Click the Update Rating button when finished.

9. **To edit the total points for the rubric, enter the number of points in the Points column.**

10. **Add an outcome to the rubric by clicking the Find Outcome link.**

Creating outcomes to attach to a rubric are discussed in the next section.

11. **When you are finished making changes to the rubric, click the Create Rubric button to finalize your rubric.**

The new rubric appears in the Rubrics window. You can also edit or delete rubrics from this screen as needed.

TIP

The steps for adding a rubric to an individual assignment are similar to adding a rubric to a course. To add a rubric to an assignment, click the Assignments link from the Course Navigation Menu, click the name of the assignment to which you want to add the rubric, and click the +Rubric button that appears at the bottom of the assignment summary screen to open the rubric template. You can also add an existing rubric to the assignment by clicking the Find Rubric link.

Probably our favorite part about creating rubrics in Canvas is that they are fully interactive. The same way you may have created a rubric, added score boxes, and printed a copy for each student before you used an LMS, you can do the exact same thing within Canvas. And you know what's even better? With a few simple clicks of the mouse, you can be assessing student work using a rubric, all the while the basic math is done for you automatically. We know what you may be thinking right now, *Guys, I can do basic arithmetic in my head.* And, you are absolutely right, lovely Pandas. However, both of us used to have roles as educational technology coaches and we both know that every single click counts in our ever-present pursuit to save time. So when we celebrate the fact that Canvas does the basic arithmetic for you, we know that those split seconds and clicks add up to save you tons of time.

Outcomes

Outcomes are learning objectives that you can align with an assignment rubric to track student mastery within a course. Including outcomes not only helps you define mastery, but also it enables you to track skills. So often in education, students and educators are asked to track and show mastery, and rightly so. However, many of us often feel ill-equipped to accomplish all this data-tracking. Once again, Canvas LMS has you covered. The Outcomes feature within Canvas LMS enables you to efficiently track and assess student progress and mastery of skills.

The process of creating outcomes is going to be different for each person reading this book. Some educators love the fact that they can track mastery, while others do it because it is part of the job. Marcus isn't much of a data tracker, unless it relates to Fantasy Football, but he does recognize the value. The truth is that many of us did not get enough data analysis education in our undergraduate careers. Marcus recalls little to no data dive coursework. So if you are a teacher and you're asked to track data for students, interpret data, and then act upon that data in the most efficient and impactful ways to lead to student achievement, how do you even know where to start or how to begin?

Canvas Outcomes can at least help you be more methodical about how you approach student learning. The more you utilize outcomes, the more you are able to fine-tune them and improve.

Here's how to create outcomes for a course rubric:

1. **Navigate to your Course Card from the Dashboard and click it to open the course.**

2. **Click the Outcomes link in the Course Navigation Menu.**

   The Outcomes window appears where you are provided with a blank slate of outcomes, as shown in Figure 11-15.

TIP

   If your district has pushed outcomes and rubrics throughout the district, these appear here. For our example, we are going to create our own.

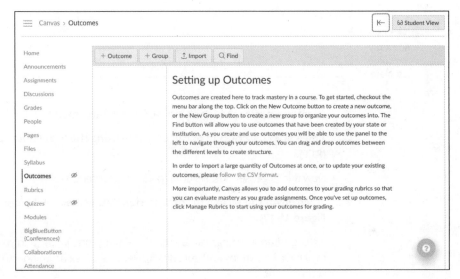

FIGURE 11-15:
The Outcomes
window.

3. **Click the +Outcome button located in the top menu bar of the Outcomes window.**

   An empty outcome template appears, as shown in Figure 11-16.

4. **Name the outcome.**

TIP

   This is the name that appears in the Learning Mastery Gradebook. If you choose, you can allow students to see the outcomes you create in the Gradebook. However, because you may have a large number of outcomes and mastery objectives, it may be nice to create a friendly name for your student view. Basically a "friendly name" is one that is easily understood by your students. For example, maybe the outcome is that you want students to show mastery of Standard 7.2.8. You can easily edit the outcome so that it is something more memorable and clear for students.

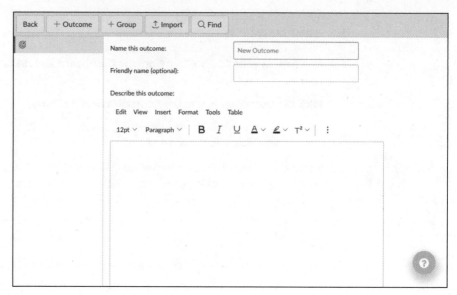

FIGURE 11-16:
An empty
outcome
template.

5. **Create an optional friendly name for the outcome.**

6. **Add a brief description of the outcome using the Rich Content Editor (RCE).**

   Now things get serious. It's time to add your criterion ratings.

7. **Scroll down the screen to the Criterion Ratings section below the RCE (see Figure 11-17).**

   Adding criterion ratings can be tricky and time-consuming (and your district may have limitations and guidelines). Here we break down how to create a simple rating.

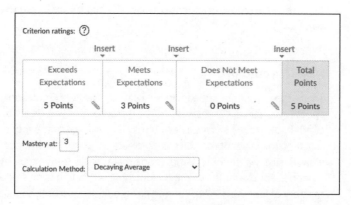

FIGURE 11-17:
The Criterion
Ratings section.

8. Click the pencil icon within each criterion to edit the criterion rating.

You can change the names and adjust the point values of the criteria here.

9. Click the OK button to save the changes you make (if any) to each criterion.

10. Click the Insert link that appears between each criterion to add additional ratings, if needed.

11. Enter the mastery point value in the Mastery at textbox.

Here you are indicating the points that must be earned for mastery of the criterion.

12. Select the calculation method for the outcome in the Calculation Method drop-down menu.

You have four options: Decaying Average, n Number of Times, Most Recent Score, and Highest Score. Refer to Table 11-2 for definitions of these options.

13. When you are finished adding criterion ratings, click the Save button to save your outcome.

When finalized, you should be able to view your created outcome in the Outcomes screen, as shown in Figure 11-18.

TABLE 11-2   **Outcome Calculation Methods**

Option	What It Means
Decaying Average	The average of all assessment items is factored, while the most recent submission is weighted at a higher percentage.
n Number of Times	Students must meet or exceed mastery on a set amount of aligned items if this option is selected. Scores that do not meet mastery are not included in the calculation.
Most Recent Score	The score for the most recent assessment item is selected.
Highest Score	The highest score for all assessment items is selected.

REMEMBER

Part of the impact of outcomes is when you do allow students to see that they have, in fact, accomplished the goal that they have been working toward. This is truly a thought shift for both students and teachers. Though many, if not most students, probably think they have mastered a skill if they do well on one assessment, quiz, or assignment, the reality is that we likely need more data points to confidently prove that mastery. Outcomes that are visible to students help with student agency and ownership of their own learning.

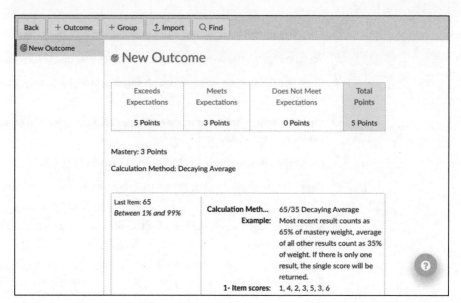

FIGURE 11-18:
The finished
outcome.

4

Collaborating with Your Panda Pals

Discover what LTIs are in Canvas and how implementing third-party apps can provide further engagement in your courses.

Tour Canvas Studio, ePortfolios, and MasteryConnect and discover how these third-party tools can benefit you and your students.

Become familiar with Canvas Commons and discover how to search and share content with other educators.

Connect with fellow Canvas users on Twitter, Facebook, Instagram, and via the #CanvasFam hashtag.

Find out how to become a Canvas Advocate and help share your knowledge of Canvas with fellow educators around the world.

» Using Canvas Studio to create videos and interactions

» Showcasing learning with ePortfolios

» Extending learning through project-based and skills-based pedagogy

Chapter **12**

Running Wild: How to Own Student Ownership

Have you ever wondered about whether any of the add-on Canvas integrations would benefit you and your students? Now is your chance to find out. In this chapter, you discover how external applications known as Canvas *LTIs* can add helpful and engaging functionality to your Canvas LMS courses. We showcase three tools that we feel can have a significant impact on student engagement and thus, student learning: Canvas Studio, Canvas ePortfolios, and MasteryConnect. We provide a high-level overview of how using these tools can have a positive effect in your classroom, whether you teach in a K–12 setting or in a university-level organic chemistry class. You also explore ways Canvas LMS can help extend learning by supporting project-based learning and skills-based learning techniques.

REMEMBER

Before we dive in, a caveat: Some of the Canvas LMS software integrations we showcase here may be available to you as part of your Canvas domain, and others may not. Because of this, we take a high-arching approach to introducing you to ways LTIs and integrations can help you on your journey with Canvas. Please keep in mind that your access and experience may vary, depending upon what your district's or institution's access is to some of these tools. Often we find that we are a couple of the luckiest guys around because we get to talk about awesome Canvas tools, share our excitement for them, and then help educators gain access or even obtain the funding needed to add these platforms.

Impactful Integrations

We've taken the guesswork out of where to begin when looking at adding external tools to your Canvas courses. In the following sections, we introduce several Canvas integrations that have not only helped us create engaging courses and professional development opportunities for our students and teachers, but many of these tools have also become "go to" recommendations when we speak and present to educators about Canvas LMS at conferences nationwide.

Once again, Canvas LMS is flexible and can be modified to fit your needs. The following tools are just a few additional ways you can tap into new and interesting approaches to digital learning within Canvas LMS.

Canvas LTIs

We know that most of you have found yourselves building and creating tons of content for your students using free and paid educational technology tools. Whether you have built hundreds of Google Slides or PowerPoint presentations, interactive virtual reality experiences, digital manipulatives, or interactive videos using any of the dozen or so platforms out there, you've likely invested a great amount of time, care, and energy. Not only did you put a lot of effort into building out learning experiences in other tools, but you may have even shed a few tears in the process! Both of us have found ourselves using our *teacher voice* directed toward our computers on more than one occasion as we struggled through some of those lovely, inexplicable tech obstacles.

TECHNICAL STUFF

With Canvas LMS, you have the ability to bring some of those dependable, "go to" tools with you into the Canvas ecosystem through partnerships called Learning Tools Interoperability (LTI) integrations — known casually as *LTIs* — and other third-party applications. LTIs can work in a number of different ways that are not only easy to add to your Canvas environment, but are also integral toward furthering learner engagement in your courses.

Marcus likes to compare LTIs to being the *power-ups* for Canvas. Searching the App Center on Canvas results in a myriad of options from popular platforms like YouTube to textbook publishers' digital content. All of these LTIs can assist you in delivering high-quality content directly to students.

TIP

The best part about external apps is that they allow you, as an instructor, to take full control over adding and implementing them into your courses. There is a robust variety of LTIs available within Canvas LMS. Some you can enable on your own, while others require a bit of help from your district's or institution's IT department. Some LTIs allow for a full experience inside Canvas, while others even add gradebook functionality and assignment syncs.

To access the Canvas App Center, open a course and select the Settings link from the Course Navigation Menu. Click the Apps tab that appears at the top of the screen to open the Apps window, as shown in Figure 12-1.

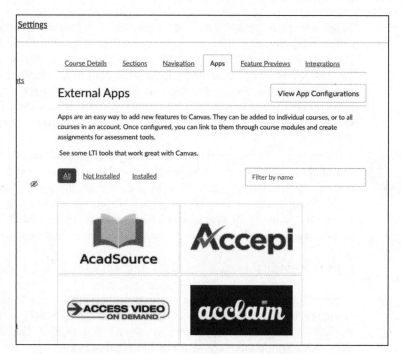

FIGURE 12-1:
The Canvas App
Center.

Canvas Studio

As a career and technical education (CTE) instructor, Eddie spent years in the classroom searching for an engaging platform that would facilitate teaching with video that would compel students to create and elicit buy-in and excitement from fellow teachers. No other platform caught his eye quite like Canvas Studio. He even created what Marcus affectionately calls a *fanboy video* about Canvas Studio a few years ago. That video has nearly 20,000 views on YouTube at publication of this book. If you ask any kid from the age of about 5 to 15, they will tell you that with that number of views, he is considered a famous YouTuber! (If you're curious, you can check out Eddie's video at www.youtube.com/watch?v=AqcZrcOLhfE.)

Canvas Studio is a simple and intuitive video communication tool that enables educators to record themselves presenting a virtual lesson, add YouTube video content, embed notes and reminders into the video, and create quiz opportunities through prompts, without students ever leaving Canvas LMS. We have said it about a million times over the course of our careers: *Canvas Studio is a game-changer for both teachers and students using Canvas LMS.*

REMEMBER

Best practice, especially for young learners, is to try to keep students within Canvas LMS as much as possible. This means that hyperlinks that either cover up the Canvas LMS tab or open a new tab may cause issues for learners and anyone helping those young learners at home. "Keep 'em in Canvas!"

As an add-on to your district's or institution's instance of Canvas LMS, Canvas Studio offers multiple avenues for learning, the best of which is student creation. We all know our learners love creating and watching videos on their mobile devices. Spend any time walking around the mall or at a local ball game and you see that our littles are glued to their devices. The rise of Snapchat, TikTok, and so many other instant communication social media apps has not only changed the way our learners are consuming content, but also how they are creating it.

TIP

As educators, we have the opportunity to continue to foster and develop those creative skills in a safe space. By creating opportunities for students to curate content within assignments, you give learners a chance to share their voices in limitless ways. Creativity comes when we truly allow students a safe and supportive outlet. We believe that some of the best learning happens when we provide the tools, the time, and the *wiggle room* for students to find their creativity and show what they know.

Let's take a walk through some of the basics of Canvas Studio.

If your district or institution is currently subscribed to the Canvas Studio platform, the Studio option is available in the Global Navigation Menu that appears on the left side of your Canvas screen, as shown in Figure 12-2. Clicking Studio opens the Canvas Studio interface, as shown in Figure 12-3.

FIGURE 12-2:
Canvas Studio in the Global Navigation Menu.

Canvas Studio

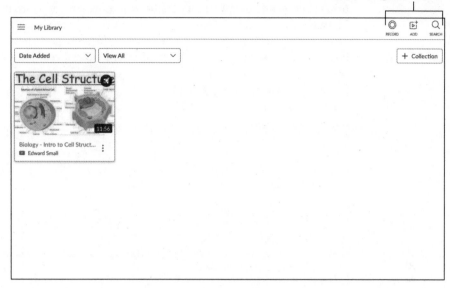

FIGURE 12-3:
The Canvas
Studio interface.

By default, Studio opens to the My Library page, which shows all of your uploaded and recorded content. You can view any media that was shared with you by clicking the Navigation Menu icon (the three horizontal lines or "hamburger menu") to bring up the Shared with Me link shown in Figure 12-4.

FIGURE 12-4:
View shared
content by
clicking the
Shared with
Me link.

The Studio Navigation toolbar is found in the top-right corner of the Studio interface. The tools here enable you to record media, add media, or search your media inside your Canvas Studio platform.

Uploading media is easy. Media you've saved on your computer, such as the videos you've kept that are your go-tos, are simple to import into Canvas Studio by selecting the Add button in the Studio Navigation toolbar. Clicking the Add button brings up the Add to My Library dialog box, as shown in Figure 12-5. Here you can browse for files already save to your computer or you can add video directly from an external source such as YouTube or Vimeo. Simply paste the URL into the text-box and select Add Video. You can even record video directly into Canvas Studio by utilizing the Record button.

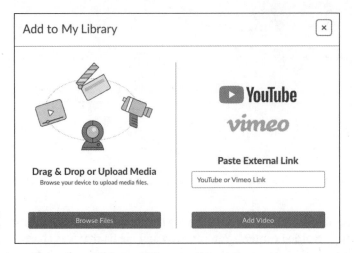

Canvas ePortfolios

An *electronic portfolio,* or ePortfolio, is a collection of electronic projects, submissions, or other coursework or work products that can be shared digitally. Canvas ePortfolios provides a singular place within Canvas LMS for students to showcase their learning and experiences. Imagine a place where students can display their projects and completed coursework and then share that content with friends, coworkers, family members, or even future employers.

Canvas ePortfolios has a number of potential applications across learning modalities. Students can use ePortfolios to create educational journals or even demonstrate mastery by providing multiple examples or artifacts of their learning. Multiple industries recognize some of these online portfolio platforms as a way to generate a pipeline of employees for their businesses. So when we talk about solutions within Canvas LMS that further student learning and even push that learning into the next professional phase of a student's career, ePortfolios is a powerful option.

TIP

Linked to a student's user profile and not to a specific course, ePortfolios can provide students with a powerful cache of content that they can leverage in their favor after graduation.

Students access ePortfolios in their Account settings, and creating new ePortfolios involves only a few steps:

1. **Select Account from the Global Navigation Menu to open your account settings screen, as shown in Figure 12-6.**

2. **Click the ePortfolios link.**

   The ePortfolios screen opens, as shown in Figure 12-7.

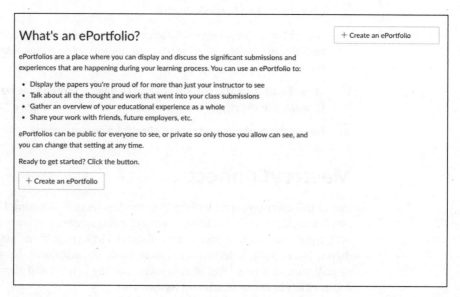

3. **To create a new ePortfolio, select the +Create an ePortfolio button.**

   The Make an ePortfolio screen appears, as shown in Figure 12-8.

4. **Name your ePortfolio and select the option to make it public.**

   ePortfolios can be public so that everyone can see them, or set to private so only those you allow can see them.

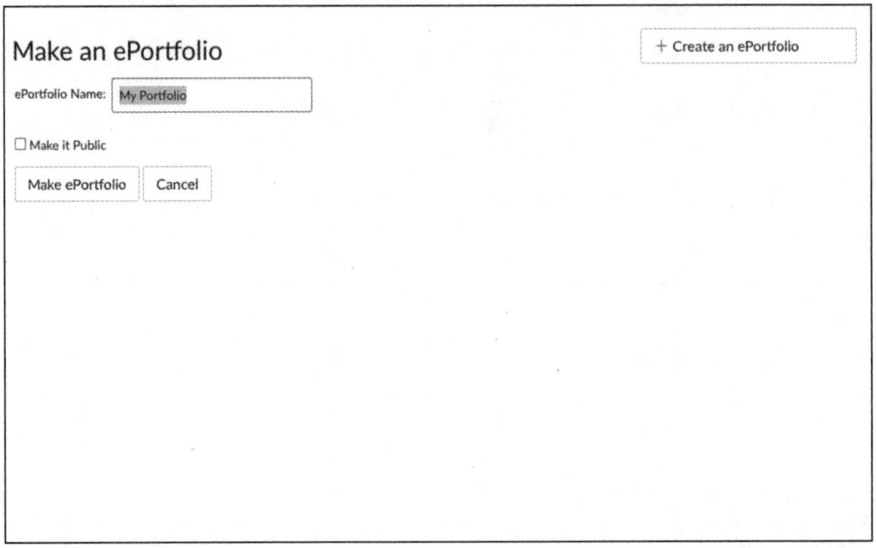

FIGURE 12-8:
Add a name for your ePortfolio in this screen.

5. **Click the Make ePortfolio button.**

   The Welcome to Your ePortfolio screen appears, as shown in Figure 12-9. It is here where Canvas makes the next few steps to creating your ePortfolio simple.

6. **Click the Getting Started Wizard link to open a screen that walks you through the ePortfolio creation process, as shown in Figure 12-10.**

7. **Follow the prompts and create ePortfolio awesomeness.**

MasteryConnect

One of the most powerful tools within the Instructure Learning Platform is MasteryConnect. Not only is MasteryConnect a formative assessment platform in its own right, but its integration into Canvas LMS truly takes assessment, data-driven instruction, interventions, data analysis, standards-based grading, and remediation to a new level of efficiency, putting it head and shoulders above the competition in terms of student assessment.

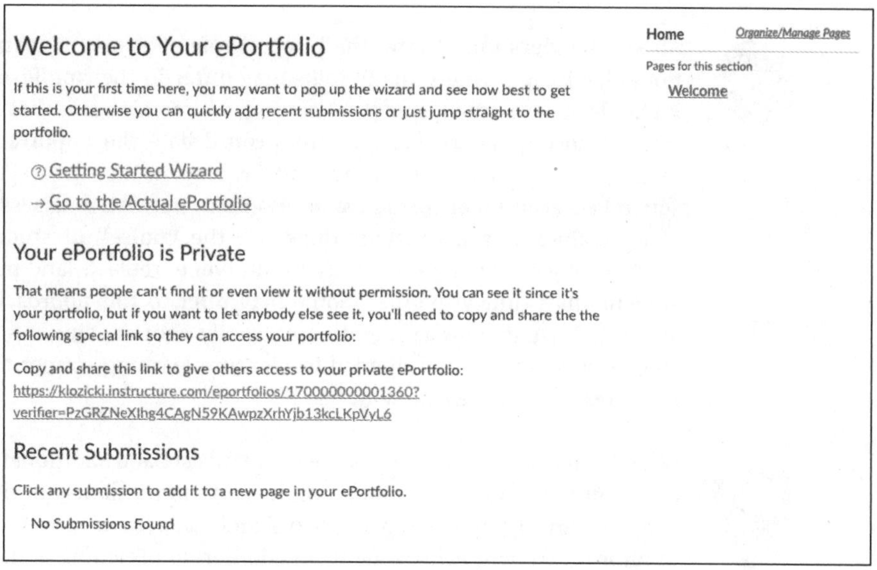

Welcome to Your ePortfolio

If this is your first time here, you may want to pop up the wizard and see how best to get started. Otherwise you can quickly add recent submissions or just jump straight to the portfolio.

⑦ Getting Started Wizard

→ Go to the Actual ePortfolio

Your ePortfolio is Private

That means people can't find it or even view it without permission. You can see it since it's your portfolio, but if you want to let anybody else see it, you'll need to copy and share the the the following special link so they can access your portfolio:

Copy and share this link to give others access to your private ePortfolio:
https://klozicki.instructure.com/eportfolios/170000000001360?
verifier=PzGRZNeXIhg4CAgN59KAwpzXrhYjb13kcLKpVyL6

Recent Submissions

Click any submission to add it to a new page in your ePortfolio.

No Submissions Found

Home   *Organize/Manage Pages*

Pages for this section
Welcome

FIGURE 12-9:
The ePortfolio welcome page.

Getting Started

ⓘ **Introduction**
▤ **Portfolio Sections**
▤ **Section Pages**
+ **Adding Submissions**
⚙ **ePortfolio Settings**
→ **Let's Do It**

ePortfolios are a place to demonstrate your work. They are made of sections and pages. The list of sections are along the left side of the window (show me). Each section can have multiple pages, shown on the right side of the window (show me).

FIGURE 12-10:
The Getting Started Wizard.

Marcus spent two years as the corporation test coordinator (CTC) for a district in Indiana. He also worked closely with the CTC in another district. As a CTC, he was solely responsible for all state testing and worked closely with the curriculum director to ensure that the district-wide assessment plan was aligned to what students would see on the state summative tests. During these years, Marcus learned a great deal about assessment, data, and how to leverage data toward improved student achievement. One of the biggest obstacles connected to assessment is the data itself. Many educators, including ourselves, only truly learned how to properly interpret data while teaching. In other words, we have been learning "on the fly" — basically building the plane while it's in the air.

While working as a CTC, Marcus was also responsible for the implementation of two different assessment platforms that were different from the two he had used as a high school English teacher. Unfortunately, MasteryConnect was not used in the districts in which he worked. In both cases, and in both districts, there was a harsh realization that the decision to purchase assessment platforms was necessary for the districts, but they hadn't chosen the best option for their teachers or students.

FIGURE 12-9: The ePortfolio welcome page.

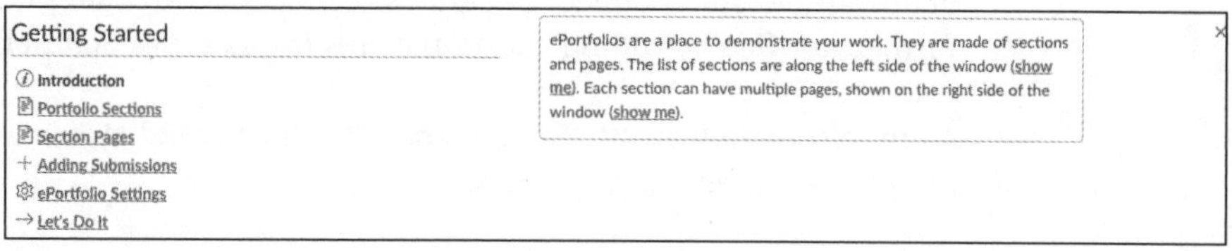

FIGURE 12-10: The Getting Started Wizard.

Marcus spent two years as the corporation test coordinator (CTC) for a district in Indiana. He also worked closely with the CTC in another district. As a CTC, he was solely responsible for all state testing and worked closely with the curriculum director to ensure that the district-wide assessment plan was aligned to what students would see on the state summative tests. During these years, Marcus learned a great deal about assessment, data, and how to leverage data toward improved student achievement. One of the biggest obstacles connected to assessment is the data itself. Many educators, including ourselves, only truly learned how to properly interpret data while teaching. In other words, we have been learning "on the fly" — basically building the plane while it's in the air.

While working as a CTC, Marcus was also responsible for the implementation of two different assessment platforms that were different from the two he had used as a high school English teacher. Unfortunately, MasteryConnect was not used in the districts in which he worked. In both cases, and in both districts, there was a harsh realization that the decision to purchase assessment platforms was necessary for the districts, but they hadn't chosen the best option for their teachers or students.

CHAPTER 12 Running Wild: How to Own Student Ownership   215

TECHNICAL STUFF

All stakeholders understand the integral role of assessment in the K-12 educational landscape. Where many folks may differ in their philosophies on the best methods of assessment in a K-12 setting, we can all agree that formative assessment is absolutely crucial. Educators can debate the importance of benchmark testing and summative assessment all day long. At Instructure, the focus has been squarely placed upon formative assessment. Formative assessment is really all about maintaining a constant finger on the "pulse" of student learning with teachers always having the ability to intervene, reteach, and provide feedback to students in a timely manner. Some may refer to this approach as *assessment as learning*. Formative assessments are usually shorter, single-standard or multi-standards assessments intended to measure learning, rather than measure how much test endurance a student has.

TIP

With its ability to align to any state standards set and additional standard sets like Common Core, MasteryConnect implementation in a school district is probably one of the most immediately impactful and measurable moves a district can make to improve student achievement. In addition to providing a platform for assessment, building questions that align to standards and mimic standardized test platforms, MasteryConnect integrates seamlessly into Canvas LMS. It also can be further fortified by adding question banks from Certica Solutions.

More information about MasteryConnect can be found at www.instructure.com/product/k-12/masteryconnect.

Extending Learning Beyond the Ordinary

Eddie comes from a career and technical education background where he spent a great deal of time learning about and implementing project-based learning (PBL) strategies. On the other hand, Marcus, without knowing it at the time, was prone to a more project-oriented approach to teaching. When he learned more about PBL, he realized that he had been dipping his toe into that world for years without knowing it. Overall, our experiences have always been focused on placing a great value on the process toward a greater goal or accomplishment with learning, rather than a one-and-done approach. Canvas LMS enables teachers and students to extend learning in a number of different ways, including via project-based learning and skills-based learning. Let's take a look at both.

Project-based learning

Project-based learning, or PBL for short, refers to a learning modality that is heavily focused on producing an outcome rather than delivering curriculum and giving assessments. Students are typically given parameters that might include a rubric that allows them to produce a project based on deadlines. The exposure to PBL has led us both to believe that Canvas is a perfect fit for this modality and something you might consider when building out your course structure.

TIP

Another term Eddie likes to use for PBL is *product*-based learning, as usually an end result of the students' learning is to present some sort of product. And that product could be a presentation or a tangible object used as evidence for learning. In Eddie's experience, PBL is truly a gift that allows all learners to showcase their skills at varying levels.

Because of this, Canvas LMS works hand in hand with educators in developing modules and rubrics that can be delivered with outcomes to create a timeline of learning that is easy to follow and can be managed and modified.

One of Marcus's favorite experiences with PBL and Canvas LMS comes from when he was lucky enough to teach a multimedia class a few years ago. The class was designed to provide high school students with the ability to create and deliver school announcements on video each day. Held during second period, the class was made up of about 6 to 8 students per semester. The students would produce a 10- to 20-minute news show each day that would be shown schoolwide during homeroom, which was right after lunch. Students would deliver the school announcements, but in addition to that each day, they would build out what were called "special features" for the week. Students would brainstorm, develop, write copy, and record audio and video "special features" throughout the week that would generally be part of upcoming episodes. Because of the amount of planning and advanced work and preparation required, Canvas was used as the main communication tool, and everything Marcus did in the class was run through the Canvas course. You can imagine how important Canvas was for Marcus in keeping the teenagers focused on planning and time management.

Skills-based learning

Like PBL, where the end focus is on projects, skills-based learning lends itself to applying specific skills and strengths to any learning. What we love most about using Canvas LMS is the ability to break down learning in a number of ways that can enhance individual skills in ways traditional learning has struggled with. For example, think of how assignments can deliver multiple submission points. Maybe you'd like your students to work on written communication skills. Set your assignment submissions to only allow text-based or document files to be uploaded. Are your students working to improve verbal communication? Allow students to submit their assignments with such tools as Canvas Studio or the Media Recorder.

CREATING COMFORTABLE WIGGLE ROOM

As we mention in this chapter, we love providing students with the support, safety, and wiggle room to be creative in their learning experiences. All of the avenues we discuss in this chapter provide options for students to create or to show their mastery of a skill in multiple ways. Isn't that what learning is all about?

Canvas LMS has that flexibility — or wiggle room — built in. You can build multi-step, project-based experiences using modules to guide and pace the project or learning. You can add LTIs to enhance the learning experience for students. You can embed media like audio, video, and photos into any announcement, assignment, quiz, or discussion. Even those popular and widely used platforms like Google and the Microsoft apps play very well within Canvas LMS.

The list of creative opportunities within Canvas LMS is really only limited by you and your comfort level. And that's another reason why you may be reading this book — you want to get more comfortable with Canvas LMS. With that comfort often comes a more open-minded willingness to let your learners use the wiggle room you provide for them to do cool things!

Your work with skills-based learning may include self-paced modules based on selection of skills for self-paced work. As an educator, you can also offer a scalable, flexible module that can not only be marketable for students' skills, but also allow you to further their skills-based learning.

Chapter **13**

Collaborating with Fellow Pandas

One of the great aspects of Canvas LMS is that there are so many passionate Canvas Pandas out there in the world. These Pandas work hard to create, provide, and share help with the world of Canvas users. Chances are good that if there is something you need for your course, it likely already exists in Canvas Commons. Canvas Commons is where you can go to find pre-built Canvas courses, modules, templates, quizzes, and more.

Everyone in your school district does not have to become an expert in Canvas LMS course design. We believe that when it is possible, we should share our skill sets with others. Iron sharpens iron. So when you may need help with course content, course design, or alignment of courses to state standards, once again, we have you covered.

In this chapter, you discover how to search for content in Canvas Commons and how to share your own content for fellow Pandas in the Canvas Community to use. You also look at how using Blueprint courses is a truly powerful way to provide consistent learning experiences for your students.

Finding Inspiration in Canvas Commons

As a Panda Cub learning to find your way around the jungle of Canvas LMS, one of the best resources available to you is Canvas Commons. Think of Canvas Commons as a giant Canvas marketplace! Canvas Commons offers a cache of resources made publicly available to all Canvas LMS users. By uploading content to Canvas Commons, users are giving fellow Pandas full permission to use that content as they see fit. These resources range from pre-built Blueprint courses, template courses, modules, quizzes, pages, and more.

REMEMBER

Canvas Commons must be enabled by your district administrator(s).

If Commons is enabled for your district, you will find the Canvas Commons icon in your left-side Global Navigation Menu, as shown in Figure 13-1. When clicked, the main Canvas Commons window opens, as shown in Figure 13-2. Here you find an intuitive search screen where you can search for content by title, name, institution, or tag. You can also sort your results by clicking the drop-down menu to the right of the search textbox. You can sort by Most Relevant, Latest, Most favorited, and Most Downloaded content.

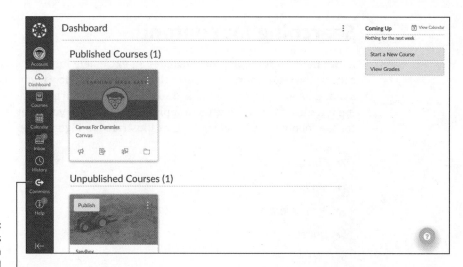

Canvas Commons icon

FIGURE 13-1:
The Canvas
Commons icon in
the Global
Navigation Menu.

Canvas Commons icon

Total number of entries to date

Enter search terms here   Sorting options   Filter button

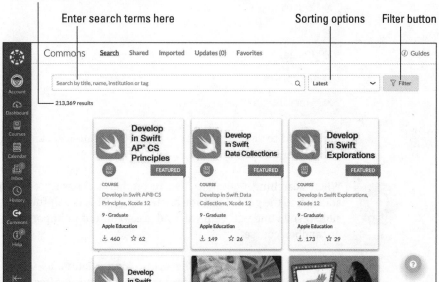

FIGURE 13-2:
The main Canvas
Commons
window.

TIP

When he worked as an instructional coach, Canvas Commons was always the first place Eddie would start with new educators who were looking for examples or content to insert into their courses right away. It offers thousands of content pieces and hundreds of courses to choose from. Whether you are a third grade educator looking for a math quiz or a tenth grade computer science teacher hoping to jump start your course with new content, you're likely to find what you need in Canvas Commons.

Searching for content

As we note earlier, Commons includes an extremely intuitive search engine. You can use the search box at the top of the Commons window if you know what you're looking for already, or you can add search filters to find exactly what you are looking for. Click the Filter button to apply search filters to your search. You can search for the following types of content, as illustrated in Figure 13-3:

» Courses

» Modules

» Assignments

» Quizzes

» Discussions

» Pages

» Documents

» Videos

» Audio

» Images

» Templates

» Open Textbooks

In addition to searching by type of content, you also can search that content by grade level.

TIP

When searching Commons, we recommend choosing adjacent grade levels in addition to the grade level you are teaching. This is helpful in getting the best possible results and will help you find great content to import into your own courses or sandbox course.

Let's look at an example. The main Canvas Commons window notes there are 213,369 possible content entries (as of this writing). After typing "Algebra" in the search box, the results automatically update from the hundreds of thousands down to just those that have something to do with algebra, as shown in Figure 13-4. Again, you can sort these results and filter them even further. Notice that each item in the results list includes an icon showing what type of content it is. Examples include Module, Course, Quiz, Page, and Assignment.

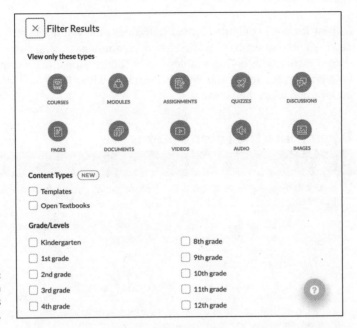

FIGURE 13-3:
Filter view in
Canvas
Commons.

FIGURE 13-4:
Searching
"Algebra" in
Canvas
Commons.

Vetting content

A question you may be asking yourself at this point may be with all of these options, how do you vet content in the Canvas Commons? It can be confusing with an open platform to choose from a seemingly limitless option deck of courses, quizzes, templates, and documents, but ultimately that decision lies in what can be best for your students. Canvas LMS does give you a few clues in how to drill down additional content. Eddie always recommends using the Filter option discussed earlier. This option enables you to filter the results for things such as content type, grade level, and who it is shared with. Table 13-1 outlines the filter options and what they mean.

TABLE 13-1   **Digging into the Filter Options**

Filter By	What It Means
Approved Resources	If your Canvas Administrator has enabled this option, you can filter only approved resources.
Type	You can search for these specific types: Courses, Modules, Assignments, Quizzes, Discussions, Pages, Documents, Images, Videos, or Audio.
Content Type	You can filter by Template or Open Textbook.
Grade/Level	You can filter by any level, K-12, Undergraduate, or Graduate.
"Shared with. . ."	Kona Jones, Director of Teaching and Learning at Richland Community College in Decatur, Illinois, provides a great application of this filter: *As a Canvas Admin at my school, I can create "groups" that my faculty can then see when they share resources and then also use to filter for resources from things shared to that group (in other words, "Shared with"). For example, my Biology faculty use this option to share resources between each other.*

Another clue as to the usefulness of a particular piece of content is provided on the Content Card, as shown in Figure 13-5. The Content Card displays under your search results with information that gives clues into what type of resource it is: the title, the grade level, and the author of the content. The Downloads and Favorite icons are key markers as to how many other educators have liked or even downloaded the specific piece of content. This bit of information gives you, the educator, a great marker in what content seems to be the "most popular."

Once you have found the content you want, simply click the tile for that content. This displays a preview of the content and allows you to investigate the content *before* importing it into one of your courses (see Figure 13-6). In addition to the ability to preview the content itself, you can also click the Details tab to see a quick summary of the content, author information, grade-level appropriateness, and tags (see Figure 13-7).

FIGURE 13-5:
The Content Card in Commons.

PAGE

Welcome to Algebra Class
Home Page Template Design

6 - 12 Grades

Kathryn Dixon

⤓ 946 ☆ 97

— Favorite icon

— Downloads icon

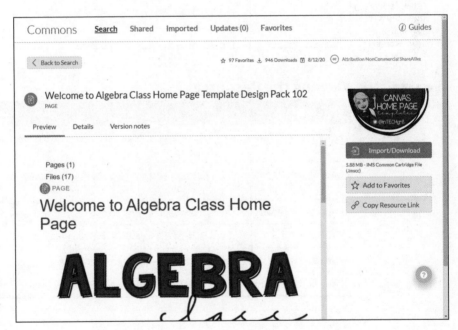

FIGURE 13-6:
The Commons Course Preview screen.

Table 13-2 lists the elements shown on a course's Preview screen.

When Marcus first discovered Canvas Commons and began investigating it, things were different in Canvas-land. This is one of those "OG" moments that we like to talk about with Canvas. An "OG" moment is when an OG (original gangsta) of Canvas LMS talks about "the old days." It's basically the same as when your parents talked about walking to school, uphill, in a blizzard, with a broken leg, while fighting zombies. Anyway, we digress.

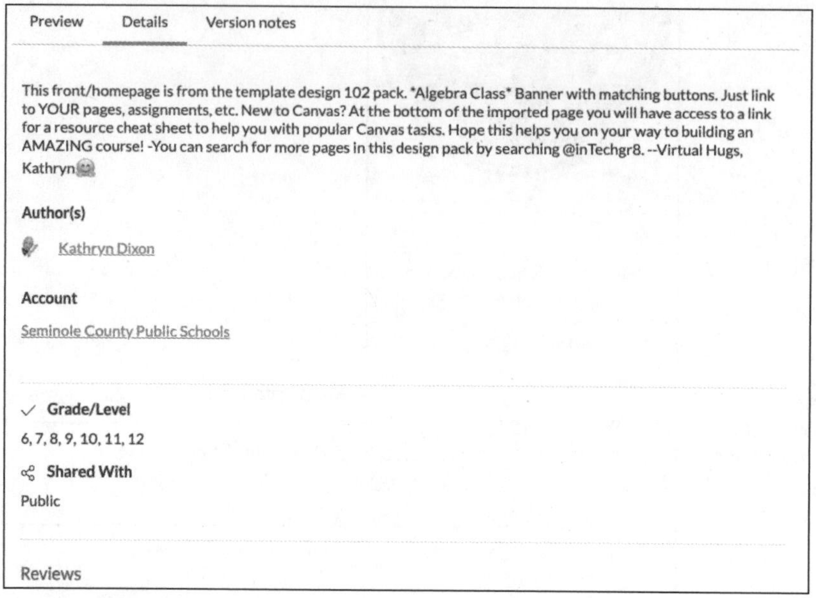

This front/homepage is from the template design 102 pack. *Algebra Class* Banner with matching buttons. Just link to YOUR pages, assignments, etc. New to Canvas? At the bottom of the imported page you will have access to a link for a resource cheat sheet to help you with popular Canvas tasks. Hope this helps you on your way to building an AMAZING course! -You can search for more pages in this design pack by searching @inTechgr8. --Virtual Hugs, Kathryn😊

Author(s)

Kathryn Dixon

Account

Seminole County Public Schools

✓ **Grade/Level**

6, 7, 8, 9, 10, 11, 12

∝ **Shared With**

Public

Reviews

FIGURE 13-7:
The Commons Course Details screen.

TABLE 13-2

Viewing the Resource

Element	Definition
Favorites and Downloads	The number of times a resource has been liked or downloaded
Date of Last Update	Date of when content was last updated by the author
Import/Download	Download or import the resource
Size/Type	Size of the resource and type of content
Add to Favorites	Add the resource to your favorites
Copy Resource Link	Copy the resource link to the clipboard

There once was a time when in order for you to even see the content from Commons, you had to actually download it first. So for a few years in the early days, teachers would have tons of sandbox courses full of random content from Commons that they may or may not have used or even liked. As you can imagine, that made for a messy situation. Luckily for you, as Canvas always does, it listened and created a solution. Now, you Pandas have it so easy. You just click the Commons icon, search for the exact content you want, preview it, pick and choose what you want to import, and then import it to whatever course you desire. It's almost *too* easy. Canvas LMS has cut down the bamboo for you.

TIP

If you have never visited Canvas Commons, please take time to do so soon. If you are an educator who would like to work "smarter not harder," Commons is a great starting point for you to build a course and populate it with quality content. The content is always growing and developing, so if you love online shopping, this is the geekiest online shopping with the biggest reward: improving our teaching practices in Canvas LMS.

Sharing Content in Canvas Commons

Canvas Commons is an amazing resource for all Canvas users in K–12 through higher education. Not only can you "go shopping" in Canvas Commons, but you can also upload your own content there to share with the world. We believe that the sharing nature of Canvas Commons is a big reason why the Canvas LMS user community is so strong. Basically, we educators like to share ideas, content, strategies, and general knowledge with each other because we are all better at this education thing if we are working together.

Maybe you've worked really hard designing some awesome buttons for your courses. Share them in Canvas Commons! Maybe you've developed a state standards–aligned chemistry course that you're really proud of. Share it in Canvas Commons! Or, maybe you built a professional development course on Social-Emotional Learning for the teachers in your district and you want that content to be available for others to use and learn from. Share it in Canvas Commons! You get the idea.

So you've created the content and your course looks fresh. You are not only proud of your accomplishments but you've also been asked to share that course with the masses on Canvas Commons. Here's how to get this done quickly and efficiently.

To upload and share content on Canvas Commons, follow these steps:

1. **Go to your Dashboard and click the tile of the course you'd like to add to Canvas Commons.**

   Clicking the course tile in the Dashboard brings up your course home page, as shown in Figure 13-8.

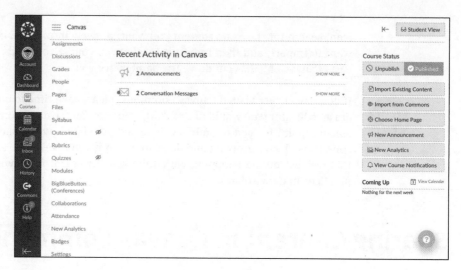

FIGURE 13-8:
The course home
page.

2. Click the Settings link in the Course Navigation Menu.

The Course Details screen opens, as shown in Figure 13-9. Note the Share to Commons button at the top of the right sidebar.

3. Click the Share to Commons button.

The Commons screen opens where you are presented with a number of Sharing Options from who can access or use the resource to what content license you'd like to attach. These options may look different depending on what your IT department has made available.

FIGURE 13-9:
The Course
Details screen.

4. Fill in the information about your content including the Content Type, License, Title, and Description.

If you are sharing your content publicly, you'll see the question, "Want this resource reviewed by the Commons community?" under the Tags heading. Selecting this option enables you to actively request user reviews. While any Canvas user can review content in Commons, this option prioritizes content from users who actively want to receive the feedback.

5. Use the sliders to select the appropriate grade level in the Grade/Level section, as shown in Figure 13-10.

6. Click Share when you are ready to post your content.

It may take anywhere from 30 minutes to 24 hours for your content to appear in Canvas Commons.

WARNING

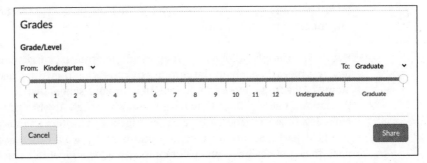

FIGURE 13-10:
Select the appropriate grade level.

TIP

If your IT department sets it up, your district may have its own section within Canvas Commons. This would be a place where only educators within your district could share content and where only educators within your district could access that content. We have seen this option used in so many amazing ways. For example, we strive to provide consistent learning experiences for all of our students. You have likely had hundreds of grade-level or department-level meetings concerning just this goal. Now, what if your team could work together to create a page, a module, or even an entire Canvas LMS course and simply drop that right into your district or university's Canvas Commons section? Now, everyone who needs that exact content can easily find and import it into their own Canvas instance and be ready to go.

Another helpful way to use Canvas Commons to share resources is to create common formative assessments in Canvas LMS and drop them into your district's section in Commons. That way, if you're a ninth grade language arts teacher, you can go to your district's section in Commons and get this month's formative assessment quickly and easily. Think of this approach to Canvas content like a shared Google Drive folder. It becomes a place to store and share all your grade-level and content-area resources that are Canvas LMS dependent or must be delivered to students using Canvas LMS.

Leveraging the Power of Blueprint Courses

Blueprint courses are a truly powerful way to provide consistent learning experiences for students. *Blueprint courses* are courses that would be created and designed by teachers and administrators ahead of time and pushed to teachers at the beginning of a school year or term.

Here's an example: Suppose a group of administrators, curriculum directors, and teachers meet throughout the summer to build what they think a state standards–aligned Algebra 1 course should look like for your school district. They include all the content needed. Once they have the mother of all Algebra 1 courses built, they make it a Blueprint course that all the Algebra 1 teachers use for the school year. The IT department and/or Canvas administrators would then use their magic to push that pre-designed blueprint course to all the Algebra I teachers in the district. Therefore, all the Algebra I courses would be somewhat consistent in design and feel at the beginning of the year.

REMEMBER

Blueprint courses are not an option that teachers can enable or disable. They are generally part of a larger curriculum and instruction plan.

We hope the idea behind Blueprint courses is exciting to teachers in the potential impact they can have on learning, but the truth is Blueprint courses are an element within Canvas LMS that requires all team members to design and implement. We first heard about Blueprint courses from a guest we had on one of our earliest podcasts who told us all about how his school district in Indiana was leveraging Blueprint courses to ensure that each student, regardless of teacher or building, was ultimately seeing a very similar Canvas course.

For example, building one course as the foundational starting point for all Spanish 1 courses for the district provides each teacher with the course design and content they need to hit the ground running each school year. Some may say that this is just "canned curriculum." Do we have consistent content that covers the district standards, a design that works for all learners, and learning experiences that our curriculum team and teachers agree upon? If the answer to these questions is yes, then we are all starting at the same point.

The great thing about utilizing Blueprint courses within a school district or university is that once teachers or professors start the year with the same content as everyone else teaching that course, they can edit the content as they wish throughout the year and the original Blueprint course remains unaffected. And similarly, through what we call *Canvas Magic,* a curriculum director, department leader, or teacher leader can make a change to the Blueprint course once and push that change to all the teachers using that Blueprint.

We realize that you just read through some pretty high-level computer geek talk. If you are a classroom teacher, hopefully you see the power of Blueprint courses. If you are a person within your district or institution who has a hand in course content, curriculum design, state accreditation, curriculum mapping, and so on, we are betting that you are setting up a meeting with your team right now to begin the work of building Blueprint courses for your district.

website

Chapter **14**

Joining the Canvas User Family

In this chapter, we let you in on one of the most alluring, inspiring, and fun elements of the Canvas LMS — the Canvas user family, also known as the #CanvasFam. We start with an introduction to the powerful Canvas Community website where you can get almost any question about Canvas LMS answered by fellow Pandas. You then discover a little bit about one of our favorite programs, the Canvas Advocates Program, which can launch you into an elite group of users, connect you with amazing people, and inspire you to leverage Canvas LMS toward outstanding learning experiences.

We also fill you in on some of the amazing people who make up what we call the #CanvasFam. For us the #CanvasFam has been invaluable. Not only for the way the users interact and collaborate across most social media platforms, but also for their willingness to drop everything and *help*. Whether you are a "search and find" kind of educator, or someone who enjoys connecting with fellow Pandas and growing your professional learning network, this chapter is for you.

Exploring the Canvas Community Website

The Canvas Community website (`https://community.canvaslms.com`) is your go-to site for all things Canvas. With millions of members and hundreds of thousands of posts, the Canvas Community website, shown in Figure 14-1, contains an absolute wealth of knowledge and networking opportunities for Pandas worldwide.

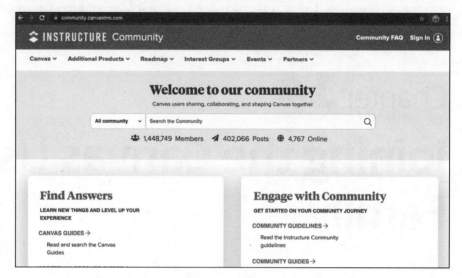

FIGURE 14-1:
The Canvas Community website.

First things first. Go ahead and log in to the community to check it out for yourself. Click the Sign In button in the top-right corner and enter the credentials (username and password) you use for your school's Canvas LMS account. Most Panda cubs only have one instance of Canvas to keep track of; however, some Pandas may have a number of different Canvas LMS instances. If that's the case for you, you'll see a screen like the one shown in Figure 14-2 asking you to choose which Canvas account you want to use to log in to the community.

When you log in to the Canvas Community website for the first time, you must complete your profile to register with the community, as shown in Figure 14-3. Your profile is a great place to not only share your interests, but also to tell the community about yourself. You are welcome to provide as much or as little information as you'd like, but be warned: Users love to learn more about you. The more we know about you, the better we can help. And now, as officially part of the #CanvasFam, we are basically family at this point.

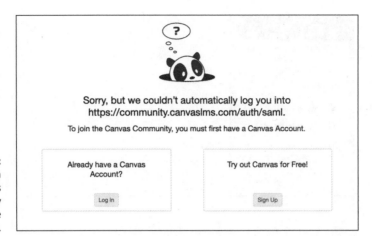

FIGURE 14-2:
The login screen
for the Canvas
Community
website (multiple
instances).

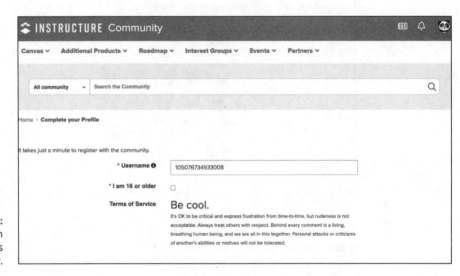

FIGURE 14-3:
Registering with
the Canvas
community.

Once you've logged in to the Canvas Community, we recommend clicking on your avatar, which looks like a head and shoulders silhouette in the upper-right corner of the screen. When you click on your avatar, a drop-down menu appears, as shown in Figure 14-4. Choose My settings to edit your profile and select a unique avatar. The head and shoulders silhouette is nice, but not very interesting when you can choose from one of several different panda avatars (see Figure 14-5). In addition to a panda avatar, you can also upload your own image.

TIP

The avatars to choose from are also a fun way to express yourself. Choosing a unique avatar is a fantastic way to dip your toes into building a virtual you to interact with your fellow Pandas.

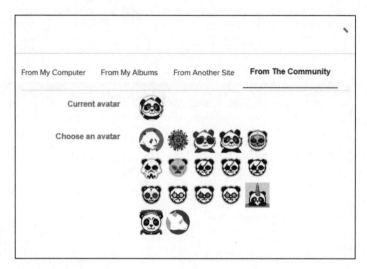

FIGURE 14-4:
The drop-down
menu where you
can customize
your Canvas
Community
experience.

FIGURE 14-5:
Which panda do
you want to be?

Within this same drop-down menu, you can truly customize your Canvas Community experience by adjusting My settings, My subscriptions, My feed, and My Groups. You also have a convenient FAQ option here.

Once you are registered, the easiest way to dive right in and learn something new about Canvas LMS is to click the search bar at the top of the Canvas Community page and type in a question. Soon you are greeted with a number of questions and responses by community members just like you who are willing to help. We've always said that we aren't the first people ever to struggle with a specific educational technology (edtech) tool, and we won't be the last. This fact becomes apparent the moment you load up your first query in the Canvas Community website. Thousands of educators, district leaders, and technology coordinators are here, all collaborating, troubleshooting, and sharing innovative ideas. Those solutions are at your fingertips just by being a part of the Canvas Community, and it's why we love being a part of it.

Now, it's time to snoop around in the Canvas Community. The following sections describe the contents of each tab of the Canvas Community website and how each feature interacts to connect you to content.

The Canvas tab

The first tab along the top of the Canvas Community website is the Canvas tab. Clicking this tab takes you to featured content like recent videos, upcoming live sessions and conferences, and blog posts. As you scroll down the page, you can choose to view resources for your Canvas role and begin to drill down the content on the site to the type of content you are looking for (see Figure 14-6). For most of the Pandas reading this lovely bit of literature, you'll likely visit the Admin, Designer, and Instructor sections most often. However, never forget that you can get a lot of additional insight on the user experience from a Parent or Student perspective, too.

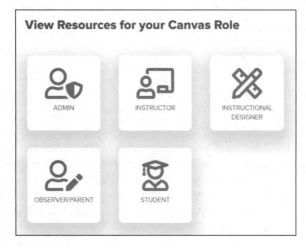

FIGURE 14-6:
Choose a role to view more tailored content.

TIP

If you choose to "mouse-over" or hover your mouse pointer over the Canvas tab, a menu appears providing you with the same content in list form, as well as content provided in nine languages.

Choosing the Question Forum link from the Additional Resources section of the Canvas tab menu takes you to a feed of content, reminiscent of what you may see on your favorite social media platform. Here you are able to ask a question and view unanswered topics as well, as shown in Figure 14-7. The "Unanswered Topics" section has been helpful to us in two ways. First, if we have a question and it is listed in the "Unanswered Topics" sidebar, then we know we're not losing our minds and others have the same question. Second, it can also be a place where you can share your Panda Powers. You may see something here and think to yourself, *Self, I think I know how to help resolve this question.* And like every bad influence in your life, we say to you, "If it feels good, do it!"

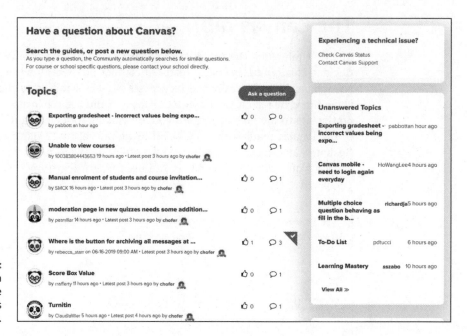

FIGURE 14-7:
The Question
Forum in the
Canvas
Community.

TIP

Also within the Additional Resources section of the Canvas tab menu is a Training link. Click this link to see an absolutely lush forest of *free* training opportunities. You can also select "Browse All Training Offerings" to view all of the free and paid options available. This is an absolutely amazing resource for district leaders, curriculum directors, and instructional coaches as you plan and design professional development opportunities for your staff.

The Additional Products tab

Next up is the Additional Products tab. Click this tab to view product categories such as Certify, Encase, MasteryConnect, Navigate Item Banks, Portfolium, Canvas Studio, and Videri. As on the Canvas tab, as you scroll down the page, you see content broken down by product and then resources by type. Again, if you mouseover or hover over the Additional Products tab, the same content appears in list form for quick access. The Guides section of the Additional Products tab menu is broken down into all of the different entities that live within Canvas LMS.

The Roadmap tab

If you are interested in being that person at your school or university who is always "in the know," then the Roadmap tab is your Panda Paradise. Later in this chapter we hook you up with even more great ways to get hooked into the Canvas Cool Kids Club, but for now, let's stay here and look at the Roadmap tab.

TIP

One of the greatest qualities of Instructure and Canvas LMS is the openness in communication and sharing of ideas among users. If you click the Roadmap tab and then Idea Conversations (see Figure 14-8), you find that this area is dedicated to ideas users share to improve Canvas LMS. When you are logged in to the Canvas Community website, you can suggest an idea of your own, and you can upvote ideas you like. Quite often, these ideas find their way into Canvas LMS.

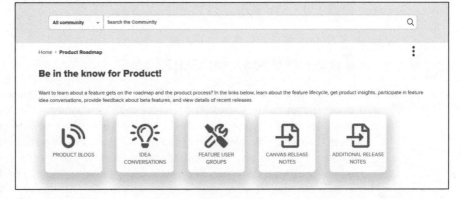

FIGURE 14-8:
The Roadmap tab keeps you in the know of the latest Canvas updates.

The next area for Pandas to investigate to be "in the know" is in the Release Notes section. Hover your mouse over the Roadmap tab and then select any of the products or platforms you're interested in to read the latest release notes. In our experience in the K-12 environment, most of the time the only person reading or knowing about the release notes were your technical directors, chief technical officers, and the mega-geeks, like us. Those folks would read these, and teachers may get an email or a short professional development course or nothing at all concerning the latest and greatest changes to the platform. This is on the Internet, folks! It is not 007 Super-Secret Stuff. Be the Power Panda in your hallway; regularly check in to this area of the Canvas Community website to stay "in the know."

Another informative section of the Roadmap tab is the Known Issues section. Believe it or not, every digital platform you use in your classroom or learning environment has a public page like this that alerts you to the known issues that are currently being worked on. On the right side of the Known Issues page is the Canvas Status Page link. This page provides a real-time update on whether there may be an outage that could affect your teaching or learning that day.

TIP

It is worth your time to bookmark the Canvas Status Page so that you can quickly check for any disruptions in service.

Keeping a close eye on both the Known Issues section and the Canvas Status Page can be your secret weapon for making a lot of Panda Pals in your building or district. We have been teachers, technology coaches, and administrators in the K-12 setting, and we know how valuable it is for us to be able to convey important information like this to teachers in a timely manner. If we have a known issue or an interruption in service, anyone can share that information out to fellow teachers and staff members. It doesn't have to just be the "tech geeks." There have been many instances where we were able to see an outage, email our staff, and save everyone a bunch of headaches for that period of time. With that being said, Canvas has what is called an "uptime" of about 99%, so you won't need to worry much about Canvas being "down." You've got a better chance of being struck by lightning while skateboarding in Amsterdam than you do of seeing a significant or long-term Canvas LMS outage.

The Interest Groups tab

The Interest Groups tab — or what we like to call the "Group Hug tab" — is another spot on the Canvas Community website where you can locate your Panda Pals. We are the types of people who just love meeting new people and learning from them. We both come from the K-12 environment, specifically secondary education and career and technical education, but we can learn something new and awesome from a Pre-K teacher just as easily as we can from a professor in higher education. Therefore, to start your Panda journey with Canvas LMS, the Interest Groups tab is an efficient way to connect with the exact content, user groups, and languages that can help you immediately. Once you've dipped your Panda paw into Interest Groups, you may realize that there is so much awesomeness happening out there that you'll want nothing more than to be a part of it all. Marcus refers to this as "geek FOMO (Fear Of Missing Out)." Check out Figure 14-9 for a listing of just some of the Interest Groups available from this tab.

The Events tab

It's a Panda Party and you're invited! The Events tab is a quick place to check in on the latest live events and conferences. Not only can you catch up on past events, but also the Events tab is where you can get details on upcoming live events, free webinars, and most important, InstructureCon. Yep, we have an annual conference dedicated to all things Instructure, including the great Canvas LMS.

Becoming a Canvas Certified Educator

One of the best actions you can take to proceed from these early stages of learning about Canvas LMS to becoming a true Power Panda, is to take the leap into becoming a Canvas Certified Educator (CCE). This program includes people from around the world who use Canvas as teachers, coaches, and administrators. This group of Power Pandas showcases the work of other users in their districts and generally spreads the Canvas LMS love to all who want to learn more.

The Canvas Certified Educator Program is similar to other edtech certification programs in which educators take a series of online courses that are designed to teach best practices for using Canvas in the classroom. Participants register, learn, hone their skills within the platform, and ultimately take an assessment to prove their knowledge.

As a Canvas Certified Educator, you are able to

>> Network with fellow Canvas users on a global scale.

>> Continue to hone your skills in creating engaging course content within Canvas.

>> Use technology to better align to state standards and desired learning outcomes.

>> Learn more about the bonds between pedagogy and instructional design.

At this point you may be thinking, *I ain't got time for all that!* But before you skip the rest of this section, hear us out. The benefits of becoming a Canvas Certified Educator are truly amazing and extremely beneficial to your teaching. For example, the Canvas Certified Educator Program is divided into the following four core areas to bolster student learning:

>> **Core 1 — Foundational Frameworks:** Looks at the impact of technology on student learning

>> **Core 2 — Engagement Strategies:** Looks at strategies to foster engagement and motivate students

>> **Core 3 — Personalized Learning:** Looks at creating opportunities for student choice within the learning environment

>> **Core 4 — Transformational Practices:** Looks at taking your knowledge of Canvas to a deeper level to enhance learning

TIP

Check out www.instructure.com/canvas/canvas-certification for more information on how to register for the Canvas Certified Educator Program. Also, scholarships for teachers are sometimes available. Watch social media posts from Instructure and Canvas LMS for these opportunities.

Connecting with Fellow Pandas

The Canvas Certified Educator Program is one way to continue to improve your Panda Powers. However, another powerful way to connect with other Pandas is — you guessed it — social media.

Twitter

You may have noticed us referring to the #CanvasFam hashtag throughout this book. #CanvasFam is the Twitter hashtag you can use to easily search for content related to Canvas LMS on Twitter. Of course, it's helpful to also follow other Canvas-related Twitter accounts including @CanvasLMS, @Instructure, and @canvascasters. Now, we aren't here to teach you how to use social media, but we *can* tell you how we upped our own Twitter game to make sure we were following all the right people.

To discover new people to follow, we suggest following @CanvasLMS and @canvascasters, and then looking at who those accounts follow. Scroll through the list and start following some of those people. You can also search the #CanvasFam hashtag and begin following fellow Pandas that are actively using that hashtag.

Twitter also provides the opportunity to connect and mutually discuss and/or troubleshoot issues that you see happening in your Canvas course or with other users at your school or university. Not a day goes by that someone isn't posing a question and getting nearly immediate feedback and help from fellow Pandas on Twitter. Honestly, it's kinda amazing. This generosity of knowledge has always impressed us about the Canvas community of users. It really is unlike anything either of us has experienced in education. If you have a question or a challenge, or simply need advice or guidance on how to improve your Canvas LMS use, you now have both the Canvas Community website *and* Twitter to see you through.

Facebook and Instagram

Okay, so you don't use Twitter. That's fine, though we really believe you're missing out on some impactful content there. Do you use Facebook or Instagram? Both platforms have Canvas LMS users actively facilitating learning and innovative ideas, as well.

If you are familiar with Facebook, you know that it has Groups, and there are a number of groups focused on online learning and specifically, the use of Canvas LMS that you can join. Simply visit the Groups section on Facebook and search for "Canvas LMS." There are a number of groups from the Canvas For Littles group to more specialized groups.

The most popular Facebook Canvas user groups are:

>> Canvas for Elementary (Over 113K members)

>> Canvas for Secondary (Over 25K members)

>> Teachers Using Canvas (Over 75K members)

>> Canvas LMS Users Group (Over 1.5K members)

Now, we didn't forget about Instagram. If you're into mixing your cute puppy videos, your dancing grandpa videos, and your Canvas learning, then Instagram is the place for you. The truth is, there are fewer resources on Instagram than on Facebook and Twitter, but it is another option.

INTRODUCING OUR #CANVASFAM

Back in 2019, your authors — yours truly — had an idea to start a podcast about Canvas LMS (we tell you that story a bit later in this chapter), and the first things we wanted to do in order to get our podcast up and running was discover the people using Canvas LMS, learn from them, and share their expertise with potential listeners. That is ultimately where the #CanvasFam Twitter hashtag came from. We did some investigating and dug deep into the Twitter archives to find that although we may have been "early adopters" of the #CanvasFam hashtag, our good friend and fellow Panda Amanda Ketay and others were using it well before we were.

We have probably said this thousands of times over the past few years, but what makes us so passionate about Canvas LMS is not the platform; it's the people who use it. The beautifully dedicated, passionate, loving, helpful, creative, and diverse family of users who share so much in common while also being an amazingly diverse group. It is absolutely inspiring. Though we certainly could dedicate chapter after chapter to the #CanvasFam, here we simply list some folks to follow on social media who have helped us along the way and who are flat-out and simply put, outstanding human beings:

- Beth Crook @bethcrook: The Inspirational Panda!
- Brad Moser @bmos: The Rad Panda!
- Carrie Gardner @Cbgardner16: The Canvas For Elementary Panda!
- Cat Flippen @CatFlippen: The Solution Seeking Panda!
- Chris Giles @ohcanadatweet: The Power-User Panda!
- Don Lourcey @dlourcey: "The Don" Panda!
- Dr. David Timbs @davidjtimbs: The Running Panda!
- Dr. Megan Tolin @mltolin: The First Ever Guest Panda!
- Greg Bagby @Gregbagby: The Positive Vibes Panda!
- Hildi Pardo @Hildi_Pardo: The Perfect Panda!
- Jim Wolf @wjameswolf: Our Panda Brother!
- Jonathan Yoder @EdTechYoder: The Comedy Panda!
- Katie Fielding @KatieF: The Smarty-Pants Panda!
- Kona Jones @KonaRJones: The Canvas Queen!
- Lindsey Hallett @BV_Hallett: The Canvas For Elementary Panda!
- Rosie Santiago @Rosielivenlearn: The Powerhouse Panda!
- Sky King @skyvking: The Most Loving Panda!
- Suzel Molina @SuzelMolina: The Powerhouse Panda!

The Canvascasters Podcast

"It all started in an Airbnb . . . ." We jokingly start the story of how we started our podcast with that line because we know it sounds super-awkward and weird. However, that is in fact where we recorded our very first attempt at the podcast (see Figure 14-10). Though we both live in Indiana, we live about two hours' driving distance away from each other. That isn't far by any stretch of the imagination, but it is just far enough to be inconvenient. So after a few weeks of talking through whether doing a podcast was a good idea, we decided that it was time to meet up, put our heads down, turn our mics up, and make something.

FIGURE 14-10: Eddie at the Airbnb recording our first podcast attempt.

We knew from our conversations about Canvas that we may have an interesting mix of perspectives between us: Eddie was somewhat new to Canvas LMS, while Marcus was a veteran Canvas LMS user. We also already felt good about our working relationship because we had collaborated on a number of projects already throughout the state of Indiana. So we felt good about our working relationship, and we were friends who talked nearly every day.

We set up our extremely modest equipment at the kitchen table, popped the tops off a couple of beers, and decided to give it a shot. It was fun, we thought it sounded good, and though it was a bit rough around the edges, we thought we may just be on to something.

We soon began to realize that this podcasting thing wasn't going to be as easy as just chatting on a mic and recording it. We quickly developed and fine-tuned our working habits and processes for the podcast. Eddie is the technical guy. He's an expert in audio/video production and was even a radio DJ for a while. He handles the audio levels, mic settings, and editing to create the final product you hear. He has an amazing ear and hears things that most people wouldn't detect. And beyond that, he has the expertise to fix it. Marcus is the one more focused on the content, the writing, the messaging, and the delivery. He does the bulk of the guest contact, episode planning, and social media activity.

We also realized that we needed to have a process to plan each episode's questions and breaks, and to establish the vision or flow of the episode. And we realized that we had to share that vision with the guests ahead of time. Some guests like to wing it, while others almost script their responses beforehand. Either way, we figured that being prepared was key to the entire process and that having a roadmap was much better than flying by the seats of our pants. So when you listen to the podcast and think that we are just chatting it up, realize that we are, in fact, on or at least near our roadmap and the skill is in knowing how to "stay close" to the established path of conversation.

For us, the podcast was a way to connect our stories to users across the community. Through our work with Canvas, we realized that so many Canvas users in our network are not only extremely passionate about Canvas, but also their stories connect to a larger audience. The truth is that our podcast is fundamentally based in what we believe quality teaching can and should look like. We try to connect amazing educators and allow them to *share their shine* with our listeners. We generally tell folks that we are simply the conduit between great teachers and other great teachers. We simply facilitate the conversations that may not have happened otherwise.

In those early days, and truly ever since, we have been extremely lucky to welcome some of the real power users and Jedi Masters of the Canvas universe as guests. When we started the podcast, we joked with each other that it would be cool to be able to do this as our actual job. Here we are, a few years later, and this silly little podcast has completely changed our lives. We recommend checking it out by subscribing on your favorite podcast player from `https://anchor.fm/canvascasters` (see Figure 14-11).

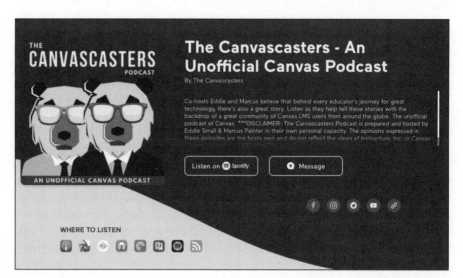

5

The Part of Tens

Discover interesting Canvas facts and figures and why the Canvas mascot is a panda.

Explore various Canvas add-ons you may want to add to your repertoire of Canvas tools including the Google and Flipgrid LTIs, the Redirect Tool, ClassCraft, and Impact.

Tour the Canvas mobile apps and discover how they can help foster greater engagement, help keep parents up to date, and help keep students on task.

» Checking out Canvas's scope in the United States and worldwide

» Discovering why Canvas is the number one choice for higher ed

» Learning why the Canvas mascot is a panda

Chapter **15**

Ten Canvas Facts and Figures

f you are new to the Canvas LMS ecosystem, welcome! Canvas is an exciting place, filled with equally exciting facts and figures. In this chapter, you discover some interesting nuggets of knowledge about Canvas LMS.

The Canvas Community Is Huge

The Canvas Community is an online forum where active Canvas LMS users share ideas on how to use Canvas (see Figure 15-1). It provides a wealth of information, such as product user guides, roadmaps of upcoming additions to all the Instructure products, and upvoting of ideas that users like you think would improve Canvas. It should be your first stop on your journey to mastering the LMS.

Currently the Canvas Community has 1,413,783 members and holds over 395,905 posts at the time of this writing. That means not only is this group a massive force in creating guides and troubleshooting issues, it also becomes an ocean of resources for you as an educator or administrator.

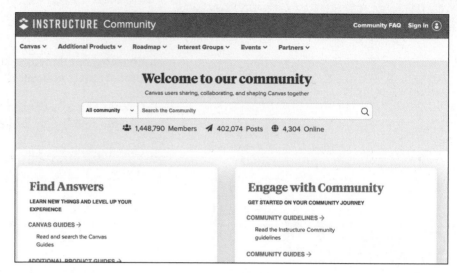

FIGURE 15-1:
Canvas
Community
home page.

Be sure to bookmark the Canvas Community website at `https://community.canvaslms.com`.

Whether you seek something new or are looking for a solution to an issue, you are bound to find the answers here. Not only are solutions to Canvas questions available, you'll also find many Canvas users who love to dig into and resolve the complex issues you may be running into.

Canvas Is Updated Frequently

Let's be realistic here. When it comes to technology, we all know that innovation and creativity drive new ideas. As much as we may like the comfort of things staying the same, the truth of the matter is that pushing to continue to improve is the best example we can set for learners. As teachers, we all do this. We create, iterate, recreate, and self-reflect all in the name of being the best we can be for our students.

Canvas is no different. Canvas continues to update and add features that are most impactful for all users. A core focus of Instructure and specifically, Canvas LMS, is to always look to improve. That improvement can come in many different forms, but one is simply maintaining a collectively open mind and open ears to what users need.

TIP

If you haven't taken a look at the Product Roadmap yet, we recommend giving it a quick review. Through the feedback features in Canvas, the product engineers compile a list of most requested features and create an outline for development for the future.

This part of Canvas is one of the many things that sets Instructure apart from so many other education technology companies, in our opinion. You can truly watch an idea enter the Canvas Community, watch it gain traction and attention from other users who think it would be helpful, watch upvotes increase over time, and eventually see that idea become an actual addition to the platform. Now, there are a number of factors that have to go into this process, but this is basically like a suggestion box on steroids and we love that it exists.

TIP

The Product Roadmap is public and can be viewed by selecting the Roadmap tab on the Canvas Community home page (`https://community.canvaslms.com`), as shown in Figure 15-2. There you also find links to product release notes and a blog site. It's always fun to see that some of your favorite features may be just around the corner. You can also bookmark the page directly at `https://community.canvaslms.com/t5/Product-Roadmap/ct-p/roadmap`.

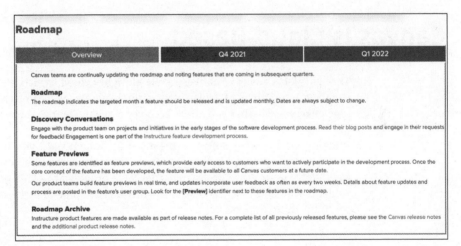

FIGURE 15-2:
The current Canvas Roadmap.

Canvas Uptime Is 99.99%

Canvas has always prided itself as being the learning management system that "just works." That has always been our experience, and its claim of "99.99% uptime" has proven to be one of the most impressive facts about the platform.

We have all been there before. We design a lesson using our latest, favorite educational technology tool, app, or website. We have gotten through all the logistics of getting students to the critical point of actually being able to do something awesome, only to discover that the amazing app or website is down. Being the forward-thinking educators that you are, you do some digging to discover that sure enough, there is an outage. Now what? Well, again, because you're educators and this sort of course correction is part of your DNA, you do just that. That doesn't mean you aren't frustrated or even saddened, but you seek solutions and move on. With 99.99% uptime with Canvas, though, you can sleep easy with the confidence that whatever awesomeness you create for learning within the platform will be ready to rock and roll when your students flood into the classroom.

REMEMBER

Uptime is paramount when it comes to technology in the classroom. As we have both experienced through the years, when there are issues with educational technology tools, that means learning is hindered. Learning never stops in the classroom of a dedicated educator like you. However, we can absolutely relate to the frustrations that technology downtime creates for you and your students. The commitment that Canvas has to keeping the product running with virtually no stoppages in service is impressive.

Canvas Is Cloud-Based

That is right, Canvas LMS lives in the almighty cloud, which means not only do you have access to all of your stuff at school, but also you can have the exact same type of access whether you are at home or traveling across the world.

Utilizing cloud-based software means that not only do you have on-demand access to the system, but your students have on-demand access to learning as well. We've even heard of districts that have provided the LMS on flash drives to students who don't have access to the Internet at home to make sure learning can continue. Quite impressive!

Canvas Is Brought to You by Instructure

Canvas LMS was built and created by a lesser known parent company called Instructure (www.instructure.com). Just because the brand name isn't familiar doesn't mean it hasn't been innovating in the educational space for years. Canvas LMS is the software that started it all. The Instructure website is shown in Figure 15-3.

Instructure is now also home to other great products such as MasteryConnect, Portfolium, Certica, Impact (formerly Eesysoft), and many more. Each product is designed to make the experience of educators and users better in every way.

Canvas Has Been Adopted in 13 States

While there are school districts in all 50 U.S. states that use Canvas, as of this writing, state education leaders in 13 states have adopted Canvas LMS as a state-wide solution for all of their school districts. Alaska, Iowa, Nebraska, Nevada, New Hampshire, New Mexico, North Carolina, South Carolina, Texas, Utah, Vermont, Virginia, and Wyoming have all adopted Canvas LMS statewide due to its collaborative interface, which allows for a centralized place for hybrid, remote, and even in-person learning to take place. That list is likely to continue to grow as the demand for multiple learning pathways increases. Instructure continues to work with state departments of education and state service centers to create new partnerships to better serve learning.

We love the fact that state departments of education and state-sponsored educational service centers consistently look to Instructure products for help in their endeavors to streamline, become more efficient, and ultimately provide the absolute best service and support to users within their states.

Canvas Is Worldwide

Not only is Canvas LMS a great tool used in the United States, but it also is known worldwide and has seen increased adoption and implementation overseas. Multiple schools in Latin America, Europe, and the Asia-Pacific enjoy Canvas in the same great ways we do here in North America.

You can even pull in Canvas content and courses from across the world through Canvas Commons. Because Canvas is cloud-based and because it has users around the world, there is a community of people out there ready, willing, and able to collaborate and share. Within Canvas Commons, you can often see that content you may be looking at has come from somewhere outside North America. How amazing is that?

Canvas Is the Number One Choice in Higher Ed

Canvas LMS originally was built with higher education in mind, which is why it is beloved by over 4,000 higher education institutions worldwide. Canvas's ability to take learning beyond the walls of a classroom, lab, or lecture hall meant that colleges and universities could expand offerings to their students and, better yet, enroll more students.

We believe that the fact that so many higher education institutions of learning have embraced Canvas creates a great opportunity in the K–12 space as well. Isn't it refreshing to know that your students who choose to go to college will have the opportunity to learn on a platform they are already familiar with? Students who are exposed to a robust LMS system early on will have a leg up on those who never used the platform before.

Canvas Offers Three Mobile Apps

Canvas LMS offers three mobile apps designed for the teacher, parent, and student in mind. Available for both iOS and Android devices, you can find them by searching the Apple App Store or Google Play for:

>> **Canvas Teacher:** The app designed for those teaching using Canvas

>> **Canvas Student:** The app designed for students enrolled in Canvas courses

>> **Canvas Parent:** The app designed for parents or guardians of students enrolled in Canvas courses

By differentiating the mobile platforms, each segment or audience can find exactly what it needs easily.

TIP

As educators, we find it helpful to download the parent and student versions of the app to see how things are displayed across both versions. It is very helpful as an educator to see exactly what your content looks like on tablet or mobile device.

Marcus did all of his "work" in Canvas from his computer. However, he downloaded the Canvas Teacher app on his phone. How many wasted minutes do you have in a typical day or week waiting to pick up the kids from school, from practice, and so on? Marcus found that instead of waiting for 5 to 10 minutes in the parking lot for his gym to open in the morning, he could grade a couple of student assignments in that time. It may not sound like much, but he found that those "dead moments" in a day could be more effectively used because he had the Canvas Teacher mobile app on his smartphone.

Canvas Loves Pandas

We've spent a lot of time talking about pandas in this book. So much so that you may be wondering what in the world is going on.

Depending on who you talk to, a number of rumors exist for the birth of an "unofficial" mascot for the company. Rumor has it, a former employee and higher-level employee used to love pandas and added the animal throughout his offices. As the legend grows so does the panda lore throughout the halls of Instructure.

Chapter **16**

Ten Favorite Canvas Add-Ons

Sometimes the power of Canvas LMS gets an additional boost with add-ons that further enhance teaching and learning. We recommend the ten items listed in this chapter to really up your level of Canvas geekdom. Now, full disclosure, some of the add-ons do come with additional costs. However, we denote those that have additional expense involved in the descriptions that follow.

Canvas Studio

Canvas Studio (`www.instructure.com/product/higher-education/canvas-studio`) is an all-in-one video creation, screencasting, and video quiz-creation tool. It is an add-on provided by Canvas at an additional per-user fee. We've said it before and we'll say it again: We feel Canvas Studio is — by far — the number one Canvas LMS add-on. No other tool allows you the same level of video engagement packed into the platform as Canvas Studio.

Imagine no longer having a folder on your web browser called "YouTube Videos." With Canvas Studio, you can put everything into one place that can be easily accessible. Did we mention video quizzes? With Canvas Studio you can create quizzes directly within the videos you include in your courses.

We know how beneficial multimedia content is for learning. We know how often something as simple as a quick video can make learning more memorable and engaging for students. And, we also know that sometimes you have to create quick checks or quizzes based on that audio/video content to ensure your students are capturing the pertinent information and seeing the learning outcomes you have in mind. With Canvas Studio, you can simply drop in a video from YouTube, Vimeo, or almost any other video-sharing site, including video you may create yourself, and build simple quiz questions directly into those videos. That means learners can watch the video on their devices, and when it's time for a quiz question, the video pauses and a question pops up on the screen for them to answer.

There are similar tools out there in the wilderness of education technology (edtech), but none have the level of simple functionality streamlined directly into Canvas, nor do any have nearly the power of Canvas Studio. To see Canvas Studio in action, check out Figure 16-1.

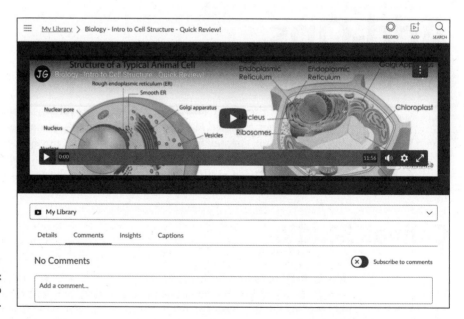

FIGURE 16-1:
Canvas Studio in action.

MasteryConnect

MasteryConnect (www.masteryconnect.com/canvaslms) is a digital assessment management system (AMS) that provides tools for teachers to track student progress and mastery of content. Districts all over the world use MasteryConnect. It can be used as a stand-alone assessment platform, or integrated with your Canvas LMS instance at an additional cost.

The folks at Instructure have worked diligently to create an extremely powerful direct integration of MasteryConnect into Canvas LMS. That seamless integration has truly been a game-changer for districts looking to truly use assessment data to drive instruction.

Do you have department meetings where you are expected to discuss data and adjust teaching and learning outcomes based on that data? Do you ever look at that data, student success on state standards, and all those graphs and think, *I honestly don't know what any of this really means anymore; I'm a bit overwhelmed.*? If so, you're not alone. MasteryConnect's true power is in its ability to assist school districts in building consistent assessments and assessment experiences for students; in providing truly actionable data that is clear, concise, and easy to act upon; and in its ability to empower teachers, learners, and caregivers.

Google Assignments LTI

Though we wrote this book hoping that all Canvas LMS users would find something to gain from having read it, the truth is that the most likely Pandas to read this book are those of you who are new to the Canvas jungle. Maybe your district recently adopted Canvas and you're in your first year of using Canvas. Maybe your district is getting ready to adopt Canvas and as a typical educator, you are planning ahead for that. It is also likely that many of you have had a good deal of experience working with Google Docs, Sheets, Slides, and so on over the past few years. And maybe, as was the case for Marcus, your district up until recently used a far lesser platform as a substitution for a true learning management system and you've grown accustomed to the look and feel of working within that "classroom."

Well, regardless of how you got here, Canvas LMS and Google have collaborated on an LTI (Learning Tools Interoperability) integration that basically allows for a more "Google-y" feel for students to submit Google-based assignments within Canvas. What does that mean for you and your students? It means that all of your current Google Docs and Assignments can integrate directly into Canvas without the need for you to hunt for share links or feel like you have to rebuild content you've already created in a Google tool, into a Canvas tool.

The Google Assignments LTI continues to evolve and improve and should provide a seamless transition into using Canvas for your assignments. For more on the Google Assignments LTI, check out the Canvas Community at `https://community.canvaslms.com/t5/The-Product-Blog/New-Meet-Google-Assignments-LTI/ba-p/388622`.

Flipgrid LTI

Another great video response tool is Flipgrid. Flipgrid is a free video discussion tool that has become such a fun and engaging platform for students of all ages to use. It enables threaded video discussions in your Canvas course. The LTI integration is so slick and smooth it allows you to be able to use Flipgrid directly inside the Canvas platform (see Figure 16-2).

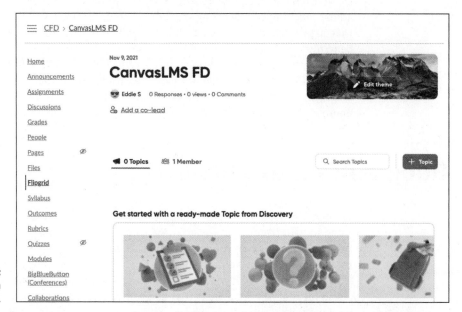

Students can work on Flipgrid assignments directly in Canvas without the need to sign out of Canvas or have separate logins. Because the Flipgrid LTI is seamlessly built into your Canvas instance, it makes it easy for students to create content and share their voices without additional time wasted by the need to log in to different platforms. This is a win-win for all involved.

At the start of the COVID-19 pandemic in early 2020, Marcus was teaching an eighth grade elective technology course. The principal's exact words were, "Just do awesome stuff with kids and technology." As a lover of Canvas and a lover of all tech tools, this was all the permission he needed to take the opportunity to do "all the things" while leveraging Canvas LMS.

The class started normally, pre-pandemic, so he was lucky to have the opportunity to lay the groundwork for students. However, it wasn't long until schools were closing and people began getting sick. Flipgrid became an absolute necessity for his class that semester to keep the conversations going. The more they used Flipgrid, students grew more and more comfortable with speaking into the webcam. They improved fluency. They learned the writing process even while speaking because they quickly learned that they needed to prepare themselves before hitting the Record button. But most important, Flipgrid's easy integration into Canvas made it possible for students in his class to talk to him and to their classmates in a safe place when times were tough.

Visit `https://info.flipgrid.com` to learn more about Flipgrid and refer to `https://community.canvaslms.com/t5/Canvas-Admin-Blog/Using-FlipGrid-in-Canvas/ba-p/274626` for information on how to get started with Flipgrid within Canvas LMS.

Redirect Tool

The Redirect Tool is a hidden gem. The Canvas LMS Redirect Tool (`https://canvas.instructure.com/courses/1014370/pages/navigation-redirect-tool`) is an app that enables you to add an external link to any webpage or website to the Course Navigation Menu. Think of the Redirect Tool as a way to build navigational features into your course that aren't already available. It is simple to use and we have seen great success from educators who use it to simplify navigation for students.

For example, if you need your students to access an external link to a digital ebook, or you'd like them to access a special club page you've built, you can add a link to that content or page with the Redirect Tool directly to the Course Navigation Menu. With this tool, you reduce the number of clicks for your students in order for them to find and access the content they need.

Here's how to add the Redirect Tool to a Canvas course:

1. Go to your Dashboard and click the tile of the course you'd like to add the Redirect Tool.

2. Click the Settings link in the Course Navigation Menu.

3. Click the Apps tab that appears at the top of the Course Details screen.

4. In the Filter by Name search box, type Redirect.

5. Click the Redirect app tile.

6. Click the +Add App button, as shown in Figure 16-3.

    The Add App dialog box appears, as shown in Figure 16-4.

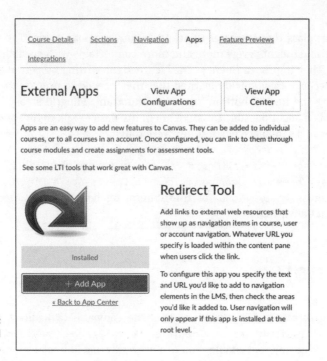

Course Details   Sections   Navigation   **Apps**   Feature Previews

Integrations

External Apps

| View App Configurations | View App Center |

Apps are an easy way to add new features to Canvas. They can be added to individual courses, or to all courses in an account. Once configured, you can link to them through course modules and create assignments for assessment tools.

See some LTI tools that work great with Canvas.

Redirect Tool

Add links to external web resources that show up as navigation items in course, user or account navigation. Whatever URL you specify is loaded within the content pane when users click the link.

Installed

+ Add App

« Back to App Center

To configure this app you specify the text and URL you'd like to add to navigation elements in the LMS, then check the areas you'd like it added to. User navigation will only appear if this app is installed at the root level.

FIGURE 16-3:
The Redirect Tool
in Canvas.

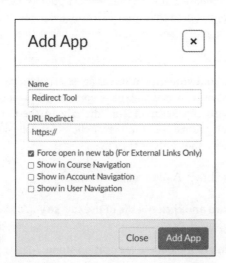

Add App   ☒

Name

Redirect Tool

URL Redirect

https://

☑ Force open in new tab (For External Links Only)
☐ Show in Course Navigation
☐ Show in Account Navigation
☐ Show in User Navigation

Close   Add App

FIGURE 16-4:
The Add App
dialog box.

7. In the Add App dialog box, enter a name for the link.

What do you want this link to be called in the Course Navigation Menu? Do you often send your students to a specific website? Maybe you want to send your third graders to the school's lunch menu so that they can decide what they want for lunch each day.

In our example, we're typing "Lunch Menu" in the Name Field.

8. Copy and paste the URL of whatever site or page you want the redirect link to go.

In our example, we're pasting the URL for the school lunch menu.

9. Check the appropriate boxes based on your preferred functionality.

We always check the box next to *Force open in new tab (For External Links Only)* because we prefer to always have students' Canvas tab available. We don't want to cover that up, but students clicking on links could replace this tab. Instead, we want links to open in a new tab.

10. Click the Add App button when you are finished making your selections.

The external link appears in your Course Navigation Menu.

YouTube

If you love to embed links to YouTube videos into your Canvas course assignments, announcements, and/or pages, adding the YouTube app to your course is an invaluable step toward keeping learners within the Canvas platform. With the YouTube app you can embed a YouTube video directly into the Rich Content Editor (RCE). *What does that even mean?* you may ask.

Again, keeping students within the learning platform is essential. Instead of providing students with a hyperlink to click that opens a new tab for the YouTube video you want them to watch, with the app you are able to have the video play directly inside Canvas. Less clicks for learners, less navigating and renavigating in order to learn.

Here's how to add the YouTube app to a Canvas course:

1. Go to your Dashboard and click the tile of the course you'd like to add the YouTube app.

2. Click the Settings link in the Course Navigation Menu.

3. Click the Apps tab that appears at the top of the Course Details screen.

4. **In the Filter by Name search box, type** YouTube.

5. **Click the YouTube app tile, as shown in Figure 16-5.**

6. **Click the +Add App button.**

   The Add App dialog box appears. You can rename the app if you choose, though YouTube is fairly well-known, so renaming it probably wouldn't make much sense.

7. **Enter a Channel Name if you choose.**

8. **Click the Add App button.**

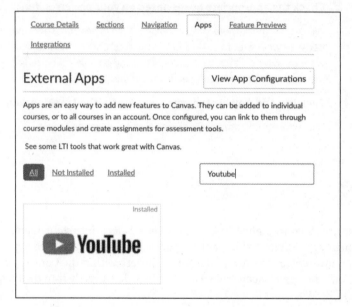

FIGURE 16-5:
The YouTube LTI.

Now when you create content using the RCE, you can click the External Tools icon and choose YouTube. That enables you to embed the YouTube video into anything within Canvas that uses the RCE! You can adjust the size of the video viewer as well.

InSpace

When Eddie saw InSpace for the first time, he immediately became obsessed. Not many tools are able to replicate in-class communication and collaboration, but InSpace comes as close as it gets. A virtual conferencing platform, InSpace (https://inspace.chat) provides a close replication of the in-classroom experience. The ability for educators to build communities with flexibility is so important in today's hybrid and remote learning environments. By adding special audio and allowing your students to work within groups, InSpace is able to deliver a smooth and clean user interface. Check out InSpace in action in Figure 16-6.

FIGURE 16-6:
The InSpace app
in action.

ClassCraft

Want to find a cool way to get started with gamification of your classroom? Take a quick peek at ClassCraft (`www.classcraft.com`), the online program that enables your students to create avatars and defeat enemies as they build on their learning. ClassCraft provides tools to increase student engagement, foster communication, and meet students where they are in a gamified, virtual environment.

We have seen ClassCraft used in a number of ways over the past few years. We once attended an edtech conference where we got to compete throughout the day using ClassCraft. Because we don't really classify ourselves as being particularly "adult," we found that day to be a blast! All the educators who attended agreed that ClassCraft was a really engaging way to gamify our own professional learning, and we could easily see how it would be fun for our students as well.

However, don't be fooled by the word *gamification* and think that it is just for younger learners. We have seen examples of ClassCraft used in higher education all the way down to elementary grades. Learning can — and should be — fun and engaging for all learners.

ClassCraft integrates with Canvas via LTI, just as the Google Apps and Flipgrid LTIs.

ePortfolios

ePortfolios are invaluable in a skills-based learning environment. With ePortfolios in Canvas (Portfolium), students are able to showcase their work, skills, and accomplishments within their Canvas profile, eliminating the need to print dozens of pages of coursework, resumes, and examples of learning and carry them around in bulky three-ring binders.

ePortfolios enables students to present their learning in an innovative way that can be shared virtually with potential college recruiters and employers. Imagine your students sharing their work virtually and showing their skills directly to hiring opportunities. As skills-based learning and the platform continue to grow, so do the possibilities of our students.

Check out the Canvas Community for more on ePortfolios: https://community. canvaslms.com/t5/Portfolium-Articles/What-are-Portfolium-ePortfolios/ta-p/257992.

Impact by Instructure

Formerly known as EesySoft, Impact (www.instructure.com/product/higher-education/impact) is a tool offered by Canvas LMS's parent company, Instructure. Impact is a tool that provides Pre-K through higher education institutions with immediate feedback on edtech integrations, real-time and targeted support, and customized messaging.

Have you ever visited a website and had tutorials or instructions magically pop up to guide you through what to do? Marcus has seen this when adding a new app to his smartphone or tablet. It acts as sort of a "click-by-click" tutorial to guide you through how to get started using the site or app. That is just one element of what Impact can do within Canvas. Imagine having the ability to create a tour of your Canvas course for students and caregivers that they can click through to learn how your course is designed, where to go, and what to click.

TIP

Impact is also able to recognize things like a missing assignment or an upcoming assignment in Canvas. It can, for example, prompt students who have not yet turned in a particular assignment to do so. It is basically providing that reminder based upon its recognition that there is not yet a turn-in from those students.

Even more powerful is that Impact can also assist your favorite IT geeks with basic support and troubleshooting. Impact can recognize an issue and help a teacher or student fix the problem, thus cutting down the number of tech requests that go to the IT department each day. Our minds were blown when we first saw Impact and its capabilities. There are so many ways Impact can — you guessed it — *impact* users within Canvas.

Chapter **17**

Ten Productive Ways to Use the Canvas Mobile App

The Canvas LMS mobile app is the mobile version of Canvas that enables you to access your Canvas LMS account from anywhere on a smartphone or mobile device. It comes in three flavors: Canvas Teacher, Canvas Student, and Canvas Parent. The apps are available for both iOS (iPhone and iPad) and Android devices and may be downloaded from the iOS App Store and Google Play.

Canvas Teacher is essentially a paired and user-friendly version of Canvas LMS in your pocket. A list of all your courses is shown on the Courses screen, while you can access your to-do list and manage messaging with students through the Canvas Inbox.

Canvas Student enables students to see their Dashboards, access their calendars, check off their to-do lists, and manage notifications. Students can also communicate directly with their teachers with the Inbox feature.

Canvas Parent is just that — the parent version of the app. It enables parents and caregivers to view course events and alerts such as upcoming assignments and grades. Parents are also able to communicate with their child's teachers through the app.

In this final chapter of the book, we outline ten productive ways to get the most out of the Canvas mobile apps.

Shift Your Mindset

Remember Chapter 2? Mindset shifts play an important role in our development as educators, as students, and as parents. While not necessarily a way to *use* the mobile app, this tip offers advice about how you think about the mobile app in general and how your students may be using it. This "aha" moment came for Eddie early in his teaching career when he finally made the connection between what mobile learning was taking place and how it impacted his students.

One morning as students began to file into class, Eddie was asked by one of his seniors if he could print off his term paper for the English class he had coming up. Eddie always was being asked to print things because he had an industrial printer/copier in his room due to the work the audio and production students did each day. As Eddie granted him access, the student said, "I'm not sure how I'll get it to print on here, though. It's on my phone."

In that very moment Eddie had a visceral reaction. "Your phone? You typed your entire term paper — all 18 pages — on your phone?!" The student explained to Eddie that it was easier to get his paper done during the moments he had free time if he did it on his phone, whether that was between practices or going to basketball games. Using his phone just became an extension of his laptop or notebook. It was comfortable for him and in turn, it made him more successful.

From that moment forward Eddie knew mobile would be the only way most of these students would access their Canvas content. And six years later, if you poll any of your device-carrying students, he's sure you will find the vast majority are using their phones for school in ways you could have never imagined.

Set a Profile Pic

It may seem silly, but adding a profile picture from your mobile device may be one of the easiest things you can do in the mobile app. We are huge believers in the need to personalize your Canvas course, and bringing in that relationship-building piece is as simple as snapping a selfie.

To set a profile picture through the mobile app, simply open the app and tap the hamburger menu (the three horizontal lines that appear at the top-left corner; some people also call these the "pancakes"). By simply tapping your profile picture from the drop-down menu that appears, you have the ability to take a photo or choose one from your camera roll.

Say cheese!

Help Students Set Up Notifications

Getting students to respond to any communication has plagued educators since the beginning of time. With notifications in the Canvas LMS mobile apps, we can meet students where they are.

Every day students access their mobile devices. They likely look at those devices hundreds of times throughout the day. Therefore, you are more likely to get pertinent information to your students by not balking at the use of mobile devices, but instead helping them set up their Canvas notifications correctly.

TIP

Every district or institution has its own expectations concerning mobile device use within the classroom. In Marcus's last few years in the classroom, he decided that rather than fight what he felt was a losing battle against smartphones, he decided to embrace them — kinda. For example, at the start of the school year in his senior English class, he dedicated time to walking his students through the steps to download the Canvas Student app to their phones and set up notifications. What he found is that students were more communicative and more successful when they had access to their course, assignments, and announcements through the app on their phones. This approach may not be for everyone, but for his students, it was powerful.

Take Attendance

Did you know that the Canvas mobile app has a built-in attendance tool? This surprises most Canvas users because attendance is largely a Student Information System (SIS)–built application that requires a separate login with separate credentials, but the mobile app version was developed as a way to take attendance in a pinch. Note that the attendance tool must first be enabled by your administrator before you can use it for a course.

TIP

To learn more about this hidden gem, check out the Teacher Guides on the Canvas Community website at https://community.canvaslms.com/t5/Canvas-Mobile-Users/gh-p/mobile.

Keep Calendar Events Up to Date

We can't tell you how many times we access our calendar each day. Too many to count. As such, the Canvas LMS Calendar can be a tool that becomes top of mind with your students and their caregivers.

By accessing the Calendar Events page in the Canvas Parent version of the mobile app, parents are able to take ownership in their student's learning. As a parent of a student now using Canvas, Marcus has grown very appreciative for the teachers who are active in Canvas and keep things up to date. As a parent, simply knowing that his daughter's teachers are making the deliberate effort to enable caregivers to be active in their children's learning is crucial. We all know that some caregivers are more involved than others, but we feel this is a really easy way to keep the lines of communication open.

As educators, you likely get communication from caregivers asking questions that could easily have been answered if they just talked to their children and asked them. By keeping the calendar updated in Canvas, caregivers can access and check in whenever is convenient for them (and do not have to ask their children, who may not remember the minimum day schedule, for example). That ease is what makes Canvas so empowering to students, educators, and caregivers alike.

Add Audio and Video Comments

We spend a number of pages in this book talking about how feedback can create a successful learning environment and build community in your virtual space. The Canvas mobile app takes that idea to the next level by enabling you to add text, audio, and video comments directly to students in your courses.

TIP

To access this feature, open your course on the mobile app and navigate to the Assignments page. Open an assignment to see a list of submissions. Select a student submission to open it and then tap inside the "Comment" section. You are next presented with a screen that enables you to "Record Audio/Record Video."

It's that simple to provide direct and engaging feedback to your students. It's a must-use feature that sets your course apart.

Send Messages

If there is anything we can do to encourage relationship building and community in our classroom, it is to increase communication whenever possible. The mobile app provides multiple places for students and caregivers to send messages to educators. It also allows educators to communicate with students quickly and conveniently, even if they are away from their computers.

Again, the power of the mobile apps are in the fact that they are everywhere your students and caregivers are. Sending messages through Canvas allows for those lines of communication to stay open and to be more readily available and accessible for everyone. Caregivers are more likely to reach out to you if it is easy to do so. And what is easier than sending a message through an app on your smartphone?

TIP

Earlier in the book we mention some ways that using Canvas Inbox can help with building and maintaining rapport with students in your courses. Most likely, your communication through Canvas is limited to sending reminders and updates about the coursework. However, never forget the power of a quick note of encouragement to individual students or to entire classes. Never devalue a short check-in with students. How amazingly happy would a student be if that student got a notification on their phone from a teacher who noticed that, for example, they seemed to be having a rough day? How empowered would a student feel just to get a reminder from a teacher that they were seen and cared for? These things happen when we leverage the power of communication in Canvas LMS.

Access Student View

Designing course content that is also friendly for mobile devices is key to any successful course. Just as you likely check the Student View a few times when you are working on a course on your computer to be sure everything looks good, you can do the same within the Canvas Teacher mobile app. We call it "double-checking your design." You can access the Student View directly from the mobile app to see how your course content looks on the "small screen."

Add Files Directly to Your Course

The mobile app is so versatile that it enables you to add files directly into your course from your smartphone. Forget to upload an important file students need to complete an assignment and you are nowhere near your computer? Use the mobile app. You can even record audio or use the camera to take photos or film video directly and upload the content to your course.

We have heard of and seen so many great examples of this in practice. Following are two of our favorite examples.

A high school art teacher gives students an assignment to locate and upload images of objects out in the real world that convey concepts that students have learned in class. That art teacher sees a great example while taking a walk after dinner. The teacher snaps a picture and uses the mobile app to share it with the class in real time.

What about the geometry teacher who is teaching acute and obtuse angles? The students are asked to upload images of these types of angles throughout the school building as an assignment. Why not provide an example as the teacher? Boom!

Join the Canvas Mobile Users Hub

You have surely noticed throughout this book that we provide a number of links to the Canvas Community website. The great thing about using these Canvas Community links is that they direct you to the absolute best vetted content available to support your use of Canvas.

The same is true for the mobile apps. While not necessarily a productive way to *use* the app, we feel a productive move to keep your mobile app prowess up to speed is to join the Mobile Users Hub on the Canvas Community website (`https://community.canvaslms.com/t5/Canvas-Mobile-Users/gh-p/mobile`).

Not only is this one of the best places for information on using the mobile apps, but also you can find mobile app resources and connect with other mobile users. It includes guides by app type and platform (Android and iOS). It also includes a user forum for help and a blog dedicated to all things mobile.

Index

A

Accessibility Checker, 64–67

Account section (Navigation bar), 37–42

Add a New Section dialog box, 58

Add App dialog box, 264, 265

Add Assignment Group dialog box, 166

Add Content drop-down menu, 143

Add Item icon (modules), 142

Add Module, 139, 140

Add to My Library dialog box, 212

Add Video (Canvas Studio), 212

Additional Products tab (Canvas Community), 238

Additional Resources section (Canvas Community), 237, 238

add-ons

  Canvas Studio, 209–212, 238, 259–260

  ClassCraft, 267–268

  ePortfolios, 42, 212–214, 215, 268

  Flipgrid LTI, 60, 262–263

  Google Assignments LTI, 261

  Impact, 268–269

  InSpace, 266–267

  MasteryConnect, 214–216, 238, 260–261

  Redirect Tool, 263–265

  YouTube, 60, 265–266

Address Book, 92, 96, 140

administrators, use of Canvas LMS by, 9–10

Adobe Spark, creating images on, 54

Agenda view (Calendar), 111

All Assignment Groups drop-down menu, 185–186

Allow Threaded Replies (Discussion options), 163

Alt Text, 78, 79

AMS (assessment management system), 260

Announcements

  adding attachment to, 126

  adding audio and video content to, 131

  creating Easter eggs in, 130

  creation of, 124–131

  as element within Canvas LMS, 70, 71

  with embedded media file, 84

  letting students hear your voice in, 132–133

  practicing RCE's capabilities with, 83–85

  scheduling of, 129–130

  sending one to multiple classes, 127–129

  targeting specific groups with, 130–131

  timing and scope of, 129

  as tool of Canvas LMS, 16

  varying the type of, 130

App Center, 208–209

Approved Integrations section, 39

apps (toolbar) (RCE), 74

Apps tab, 58, 59–60, 209

Archive (conversations), 93, 94

archiving messages, 98

assessment management system (AMS), 260

assessments

  as element of instructional design, 28

  MasteryConnect, 214–216, 238, 260–261

Assign text box, 168, 169

Assignment Comments section, 195

Assignment Group drop-down menu, 167

assignment groups, creation of, 165–166

Assignment tab (Edit Event dialog box), 114

Assignments icon, 146

Assignments window, 165, 169

V

W

Y

About the Authors

Marcus Painter is the senior manager for leadership development at Instructure. Before starting at Instructure, Marcus spent 20 years in public education as a middle and high school English teacher, a media specialist, a technology integration specialist, a corporation test coordinator, a coordinator of digital learning, and a district administrator.

Born and raised in Indianapolis, Indiana, Marcus attended Warren Central High School and earned his degree from Purdue University. During his years in education, he became more and more interested in the profound impact educational technology has on student outcomes. That passion led him to an opportunity to collaborate with outstanding educators in Indiana on writing STEM curriculum for the Indiana Migrant Education Program. This opportunity meshed two of his passions — curriculum and technology — and the rest is history. This experience truly served as a launching pad for his professional career. From that point, Marcus was blessed with many opportunities to present sessions and keynotes throughout the state of Indiana. In 2020, Marcus had the honor of being chosen as a NextGen Emerging EdTech Leader through the Consortium for School Networking (COSN) and EdScoop.

Marcus is married to his wife, Carrie, and they have a 12-year-old daughter named Nola. They reside in West Lafayette, Indiana. In his personal time, he enjoys playing Fantasy Football, partaking in any and all physical endeavors but specifically triathlon sports, and collecting Funko Pops.

Eddie Small is the senior manager for advocacy at Instructure. In this role he serves to tell stories about the success of LMS usage across the nation. Eddie is also a former career and technical education (CTE) innovation coach for Central Nine Career Center in Greenwood, Indiana. Eddie has had direct involvement with students as an instructor for 11 years in education, including eight years at his alma mater directing a broadcasting program. In 2010, Eddie created WRLN 91.9 FM on the campus of Rushville Consolidated High School, and continued to use his knowledge and experience with audio production to foster state champions and runners-up in multiple audio production categories.

Eddie has been recognized as a Google Certified Trainer, a Google for Education Certified Innovator, and a G Suite for Education Administrator. In 2019, alongside his cohost Marcus Painter, he created The Canvascasters, an unofficial Canvas LMS podcast. You can follow him on Twitter at @smallindiana. He has a beautiful wife, Beth, who teaches third grade and a daughter, both of whom keep his focus on the future of our students.

Dedications

I truly can't believe that my life has taken me down a path where I would ever have had the chance to write a book! This book only happened because of the support, love, and understanding I received from my family, specifically, my wife, Carrie, and my daughter, Nola. The hours of work Eddie and I have dedicated to this book have been hours taken away from our families. Without that love and support, I know that I could have never done this work. The fact that my family has been loving and supportive is one thing, but their excitement about this project has seen me through some of the tougher moments over the past year or so of work.

I'm also extremely lucky to have been blessed with a friend like Eddie Small. Our ability to create, iterate, critique, and collaborate on this book and in our work at Instructure has been an awesome experience.

Beyond that though, what better way to show my daughter that anything is possible? Nola, I'm not special. I'm just a regular guy who works hard. When blessings come your way, you take them and work passionately to earn them. Never say "no" to an opportunity. Always be willing to bet on yourself. — **Marcus Painter**

I truly believe that I couldn't have done any of this without my wife, Beth, and my daughter, Charlotte. The hours spent away from them while writing this book can't be quantified in "thank yous." I'll never be able to repay the grace and understanding they had while we crossed the finish line.

To my wife: Your voice can be heard throughout the pages of this book. So many times when I found myself writing words on pages I was echoing so much of what I have learned from you. You have been and will continue to be my true north.

To Charlotte: You make me want to be a better dad each day. The future is so bright for you. Your kindness and enthusiasm for life is what drives me in life, in education, and in being a father. — **Eddie Small**

Authors' Acknowledgments

There are so many people we want to acknowledge without whose help, guidance, trust, and support, this book could never have been written. We want to begin, well, at the beginning. We already told the story of how our little idea for a podcast forever changed our lives. What we didn't tell you was that there were two very important people we spoke to who basically made all of this possible.

Becky Frost and Mark Boothe

We had done two to three episodes and the whole time we joked that it was only a matter of time before Instructure shut it down. We took the "act now and ask for forgiveness later" approach. We thought that day had arrived when we got an email to The Canvascasters Gmail address from Becky Frost and Mark Boothe. These two, who both worked for Instructure at the time, wanted to get on a Zoom call and "discuss the podcast." Well, we were convinced that this was the end. Our expectations were absolutely set that we were getting a cease and desist from Instructure. However, it was quite the opposite. They had listened to the podcast and loved it! They wanted to help us and we have stayed friends ever since. The truth is that they saw value in us way before we did. They saw the potential before we realized it. Both Becky and Mark took us under their wings, helped us, taught us, and believed in what we were doing. We can never thank you enough. #Oreos

The #CanvasFam

We don't have enough pages left to acknowledge all of the #CanvasFam. We came into the Canvas World guns a-blazin'. We wanted to do all of the things, talk to all of the people, and learn from all of the true gurus of Canvas. The worldwide collection of Canvas users we affectionately refer to as the #CanvasFam embraced us, invited us in, and have supported our podcast and this book like blood relatives would. We are eternally grateful to each and every one of you for contributing to learning worldwide, for caring about this craft we call teaching, and for always endeavoring to improve the world, one learner at a time.

Our Guests

Where do we even begin? Dr. Megan Tolin is, by far, the most daring guest we've ever had on the podcast because she agreed to be our very first guest! Thank you, Megan. You immediately brought credibility to what we were trying to do because of your amazing experience in education and your gleaming reputation within the world of online and blended learning.

The moment we realized that we may be on to something with the podcast was when Paul Towers reached out to us and wanted to talk Canvas. Paul Towers from Wolverhampton, England! We just about lost our minds that anyone was listening to us, much less from across the pond! What an honor and what an amazingly insightful human being Paul is.

Our Queen of Canvas, Kona Jones, has been on the podcast a number of times and, as the kids say, they are all bangers! In other words, every time we talk to Kona, the episode is gold. She is so great. We have truly looked to her for guidance and advice, and she was the Technical Editor of this fine piece of literature you're reading right now!

As a couple of boneheads from Indiana, we know that we can always reach out to our Hoosier friends, and we did just that when we asked Kyle Beimfohr to be on the podcast. He is an amazing leader and educator in Indiana and a truly genuine person. We also hit up Kevin Self, Stevie Frank, and a couple of outstanding teachers from our own schools while dipping into the bucket of outstanding Indiana educators.

As we began to gain traction and folks at Instructure began to listen, we were able to get access to some of the amazing people who work for Instructure. We were ecstatic to have Renee Carney and Scott Dennis on the show as the brains behind the amazing Canvas Community website. We got to chat with Jenn Mitchell and Ryan Lufkin, who were amazing to talk with and learn from, and we are lucky enough to now work with. And, when we got the honor of interviewing Melissa Loble, the Chief Customer Experience Officer of Instructure, we just about lost our minds with excitement!

We have met amazing folks from all over the world. Monica Burns, Khaled Al-ankar, Van Bardell, Ryne Jungling, Travis Thurston, Rosie Santiago, Stephen Taylor, Jonathan Yoder, Dr. Ellen Bloomfield, Snehal Bhakta, Tisha Richmond, Michael Alendy, Katie Fielding, Brad Moser, Chris Giles, Don Lourcey, Lindsey Hallett, Carrie Gardner, Greg Bagby, Jim Wolf, Cat Flippen, Suzy Lolley, and Dr. Betinna Love have all been guests on the podcast.

We have also met one of the most amazingly kind, powerful, and thoughtful humans in the world. Her name is Beth Crook. We can't dig into the history, but we can say that her experience, her power, and her love of education has consistently acted as fuel for us. Beth, you are an inspiration and a symbol of strength. Thank you for allowing us into your life.

To say that we are immensely grateful to all of you is an understatement. To say that our lives have been absolutely changed for the better by meeting you, learning from you, and having the honor to share your expertise with other educators using Canvas is a fact. We can call you folks guests, collaborators, influential educators, great teachers, lovers of learning, and the like, but most of all, we call you friends.

Publisher's Acknowledgments

Executive Editor: Steven Hayes

Senior Managing Editor: Kristie Pyles

Project Manager and Development Editor: Katharine Dvorak

Technical Editor: Kona Jones

Production Editor: Tamilmani Varadharaj

Cover Image: © monkeybusinessimages/ Getty Images

Take dummies with you everywhere you go!

Whether you are excited about e-books, want more from the web, must have your mobile apps, or are swept up in social media, dummies makes everything easier.

Find us online!

dummies.com

dummies
A Wiley Brand

PERSONAL ENRICHMENT

Staying Sharp

9781119187790
USA $26.00
CAN $31.99
UK £19.99

Facebook

9781119179030
USA $21.99
CAN $25.99
UK £16.99

Guitar

9781119293354
USA $24.99
CAN $29.99
UK £17.99

Investing

9781119293347
USA $22.99
CAN $27.99
UK £16.99

Beekeeping

9781119310068
USA $22.99
CAN $27.99
UK £16.99

Digital Photography

9781119235606
USA $24.99
CAN $29.99
UK £17.99

Meditation

9781119251163
USA $24.99
CAN $29.99
UK £17.99

Pregnancy

9781119235491
USA $26.99
CAN $31.99
UK £19.99

Samsung Galaxy S7

9781119279952
USA $24.99
CAN $29.99
UK £17.99

iPhone

9781119283133
USA $24.99
CAN $29.99
UK £17.99

Crocheting

9781119287117
USA $24.99
CAN $29.99
UK £16.99

Nutrition

9781119130246
USA $22.99
CAN $27.99
UK £16.99

PROFESSIONAL DEVELOPMENT

Windows 10

9781119311041
USA $24.99
CAN $29.99
UK £17.99

AutoCAD

9781119255796
USA $39.99
CAN $47.99
UK £27.99

Excel 2016

9781119293439
USA $26.99
CAN $31.99
UK £19.99

QuickBooks 2017

9781119281467
USA $26.99
CAN $31.99
UK £19.99

macOS Sierra

9781119280651
USA $29.99
CAN $35.99
UK £21.99

LinkedIn

9781119251132
USA $24.99
CAN $29.99
UK £17.99

Windows 10

9781119310563
USA $34.00
CAN $41.99
UK £24.99

SharePoint 2016

9781119181705
USA $29.99
CAN $35.99
UK £21.99

Fundamental Analysis

9781119263593
USA $26.99
CAN $31.99
UK £19.99

Networking

9781119257769
USA $29.99
CAN $35.99
UK £21.99

Office 2016

9781119293477
USA $26.99
CAN $31.99
UK £19.99

Office 365

9781119265313
USA $24.99
CAN $29.99
UK £17.99

Salesforce.com

9781119239314
USA $29.99
CAN $35.99
UK £21.99

Coding

9781119293323
USA $29.99
CAN $35.99
UK £21.99

dummies.com

dummies
A Wiley Brand